THE LAUGH & CRY MOVIE GUIDE™

Using Movies to Help Yourself through Life's Changes

CATHIE GLENN STURDEVANT

For information about seminars and lectures using movies to manage personal and organizational change, contact:

Cathie Glenn Sturdevant
LightSpheres Publishing and Consulting
P.O. Box 884
Larkspur, CA 94977
Tel: 415.925.1540
Fax: 415.461.7845
e-mail: sales@laughcry.com
web: www.laughcry.com

Design: Stuart L. Silberman
Editor: Janelle Gates

Library of Congress Cataloging-in-Publication Data
Sturdevant, Cathie Glenn

The Laugh & Cry Movie Guide™: Using Movies to Help Yourself through Life's Changes / Cathie Glenn Sturdevant.—1st ed.

Includes bibliographical references and index.
ISBN 0-9652964-2-3
1. Life Change Events—Psychological Aspects. 2. Film Reference.
I. Title.
158.94

Second Printing, 1998

Dedication

To all the storytellers who give us a laugh, a cry, and a lesson.

Contents

List of Illustrations

FOREWORD

How Movies Can Help You

The movie mogul Samuel Goldwyn once said "Anyone who would go to a psychiatrist ought to have his head examined." I'm sure he would have been surprised to see his beloved medium being used as a tool for emotional well being.

When working with people in psychotherapy, doctors seek to help their patients deal with feelings, memories, and reactions to difficult or problematic experiences. We do this through a multitude of techniques, including the discussion of dreams, thoughts, and relationships; shifts of behavior; family involvement; and the use of mood altering medication.

In this book, Cathie Glenn Sturdevant highlights a technique of change that is low cost, readily available, and familiar to everyone. Where going to a therapist can be an expensive, sometimes embarrassing, and often foreign experience, going to the movies is as American as *Gone with the Wind.*

As president of the American Association for Therapeutic Humor, I am charged with spreading the word about the physical and mental health benefits of humor and laughter. In this book, Ms. Sturdevant acknowledges the value of humor and then goes further by identifying the stages of emotional release and "feeling good." She eloquently describes the importance of these experiences in what she calls "life changes." Then, she offers a unique guide to movies categorized by life challenges, which enables the reader to find movies that are similar to or help with his or her own situation.

As a therapist, I have occasionally "prescribed" films designed to expose my patients to certain messages of life. The distance of watching, combined with the effect of seeing things on the screen, often has a profound positive impact. Whether seeing how others handle a situation, seeing oneself in a character portrayed, or just enjoying a two-hour vacation from one's troubles, movies are a powerful self-help and therapeutic tool.

I encourage all who read this book to do as you do when you watch movies. Immerse yourself in the content, suspend your disbelief, and allow the information to enrich your life. As George Santayana said, "There is little that we can do between birth and death save enjoy the interval." Movies are an easily accessible way to do just that.

I think Sam Goldwyn would love the idea.

Ed Dunkelblau, Ph.D.
President, American Association
for Therapeutic Humor

PREFACE

Why Laughter Is the Best Medicine

Norman Cousins found that watching Marx Brothers movies gave him a few of hours of pain relief as he was recovering from a life-threatening illness. He was so convinced about the therapeutic benefits of laughter that he funded my team's research effort in 1983 to scientifically validate the benefits of humor and laughing. And the discoveries are impressive.

We have documented that laughter activates the immune system. Our research results have proven that the physiological response produced by laughter is the opposite of what is seen in classical stress, supporting the conclusion that mirthful laughter is a eustress state—a state that produces healthy or positive emotions.

Our findings indicate that, after experiencing mirthful laughter, there is a general decrease in stress hormones and an increase in activity within the immune system, including:

- an increase in activated T cells (T lymphocytes). There are many T cells that await activation. Laughter appears to tell the immune system to "turn it up a notch."
- an increase in the antibody IgA (immunoglobulin A), which fights upper respiratory tract insults and infections.
- an increase in gamma interferon, which tells various components of the immune system to "turn on."

- an increase in Natural Killer Cell activity, cells which kill virally infected cells and tumor cells.
- an increase in IgG, the immunoglobulin produced in the greatest quantity in the body, as well as an increase in Complement 3, which helps antibodies to pierce dysfunctional or infected cells. The increase in both substances was only present while subjects watched a humorous video; moreover, subjects continued to show increased levels the next day, revealing a lingering effect.

Laughter decreases "bad" stress. In our research, the study group exposed to mirthful humor decreased their "stress" hormones, which constrict blood vessels and suppress immune activity. For example, levels of epinephrine were lower in the group both during anticipation of humor and after exposure to humor. Epinephrine levels remained down throughout the experiment. In addition, dopamine levels (as measured by dopac) were also decreased. Dopamine is involved in the "fight or flight response" and is associated with elevated blood pressure.

As a medical scientist, it is gratifying and fulfilling to continue to discover objective scientific data to support beliefs that many have held intuitively for centuries. This book serves as an innovative guide to finding movies that stimulate not only your sense of humor but also your immune system. "He who laughs, lasts."

Dr. Lee Berk
Assistant Professor
Pathology, Laboratory Medicine, Preventive Medicine,
Health Promotion and Education
Loma Linda University
Schools of Medicine and Public Health

Introduction

This book was written to help you move through your life's changes with a sense of fun, adventure, and elegance. We fear change because we envision it as cataclysmic. The true nature of transition is a gradual, reiterative process of release and integration focused by desire. Together, we will explore how to use movie viewing as a versatile tool for managing our life's changes. This can be helpful in many ways: boosting your self-esteem, releasing inappropriate emotions from your past, experiencing the full cycle of the emotional tides of a transition, identifying the stage of your life change, suggesting actions to move you forward, inspiring you to stretch and accomplish your dreams, designing happier outcomes, and relaxing and enjoying the rhythms of the journey of your life.

> *Learning is being able to see the relationship between things.*
>
> **JEAN RENOIR**

This book has come into being as one of the fruits of my dreams and my own frustrating, drawn-out, emotionally messy midlife work transition. As a lifelong movie buff, I used movies as soothing emotional grease to help me through my rusty, squeaking cycle shift. I viewed inspiring tales to renew my faith in my ability to realize my dreams.

In my mid-40s, I was operating a successful marketing consulting firm. After completing a large, exhausting project, there was one week before the next project. I simply could not force myself to solicit new business, the way consulting practices are fueled. My work seemed to have lost all heart and meaning. I literally did not know what to do next. I could not go back. I could not continue. Instead, I laid down for that week on my couch and watched several videos a day that made me laugh and/or cry. The emotional release was refreshing. My spirits lifted for the moment, and I was able to muddle on.

Six years, and many movies later, I realized my work life was based on my family's idea of success, not my own. Releasing my attachment to what others thought about my career freed up a tremendous amount of energy. Now I consult, coach, and write about transitions and managing change for individuals and organizations.

In reading this book, you may want to focus on a challenge facing you right now in your life. Based on my personal experience and that of my clients, movie viewing can be used in many ways.

- Movies are an inexpensive, accessible tool to help you feel better about where you are right now in your transition.
- Movies that make you laugh stimulate your immune system so you gain a sense of well being. Movies that make you cry can be used as a tool for stimulating emotional catharsis.
- Movies can offer you the actual experience of riding the complete cycle of the emotional stages of change from beginning to end. This can help you identify which stage you are in right now and indicate steps to move you forward.

- Movies can provide inspiration and motivation for continuing to work toward achieving your dreams and goals.
- Movies can supply a blueprint for creating a happier ending to your own transition.
- Movies are a fun and enjoyable foundation for managing lifelong growth as an adventure.

Life's changes are all about learning, and the only way to learn is through experience. Movies offer a powerful mechanism for gaining a firsthand understanding of the shifting tides of emotions. Being honest about your feelings can provide clarity about where you are on your emotional path and serve as a guidepost for taking actions that move you forward on a path of least resistance without pain and struggle.

Movie Selection Criteria

This process is designed to work with any movie that inspires you and makes you feel better after viewing it. To supplement your favorites, I offer a select list of movies chosen for their emotional truth, emotional release effect, and ability to uplift you through repeated viewing (see page 72). I am not a critic, but I am a fan. Personally, I have seen all these movies at least twice, and a few more than 50 times!

Check the list and see if your all-time favorite movies are there. It's okay if they're not. This is a very brief guide, of top movies for a given life change. Plot summaries are given on page 139. Use any movie that holds emotional power for you. Of course, there are other good titles you may want to critique on your own. Once you have the hang of it, it's easy and fun to apply the process to any movie—try it.

Movies are intended to be keys that unlock our creativity, provide a respite from the relentless small mind chatter, and move us into a place where our ingenuity can thrive.

This is an opportunity to escape from the narrow confines of intellectual, technical, and critical evaluation. In fact, traditional movie criticism has its limits, as evidenced by the panning of crowd-pleasing movies like *Sister Act, Flashdance,* and *Dirty Dancing*. You are the only judge here. If it works for you, that's all that counts. Think of this list of films like a movie-buff friend's word-of-mouth recommendations.

The Rating System

Movies are rated three ways in this guide with their related symbols:

Feel Better/Uplift	Inspiring, activating immune system
Laughing Release	Belly-laughers
Crying Release	3+ tissues required

The Feel Better/Uplift rating provides a sense of inspiration and motivation that lingers days and weeks later. The Laughing and Crying Release movies evoke that response no matter how many times you see it. This may be an issue of differing emotional responses. For example, I found the ending of *The Piano* to be life-affirming because a mute woman finally finds her voice, but my action-movie-fan friend felt it was the most sickeningly violent movie he had seen in a long time.

Lastly, I am an empath. What I see and hear on screen, I experience in my body. If violence is part of the context of the story, like war, you may want to do as I do and close your eyes and cover your ears at the theater or fast forward through the violent scenes at home.

Life's Changes Cross-Index System

This book provides a movie reference system that cross-indexes movies on five major areas of life transition:

Work & Prosperity

Relationships

- Lovers & Mates
- Family
- Friends & Colleagues
- Professional
- Love of Self

Finding Love

Transitions

- Birth to Age 27
- Age 28 to 54
- Age 55 to 81
- Relationship Transitions
- Work Transitions

Overcoming Obstacles

This indexing system offers you two advantages over traditional movie and video guides. First, you can locate movies with stories that are similar to your life transition experience. Second, you can select films that may change how you feel after watching them. You may want to take a minute to review the Life's Changes Cross-Index starting on page 119 for a better sense of how it might serve your situation at this time.

Scope of the Book

The purpose of this book is to show you how to use your favorite movies to understand the emotional aspects of your life's changes and how to relax and enjoy your personal growth as an adventure. This process involves several levels, which this book will guide you through.

First, we will examine the four steps to feeling better about your current life change because it is difficult to make plans or take action when you are in an emotional depression. You will learn how to select the best movies for your challenge, how to prepare the best viewing conditions, and how to relax and enjoy the show. When you are feeling better, you can perform after-viewing exercises that will help you lighten up and start enjoying your journey in the spirit of a good adventure film.

Then we will remove the mystery from the process of change and begin to view it as a deliberate act of release and integration focused by will. You will learn a way to remove the pain and struggle from your life's changes. You will see how to identify the best way to accomplish your goals with the least amount of effort, in the minimum amount of time, by using all your intelligences.

Next, we will review the five stages of emotional change, which I call The Moving Picture of Change. A quiz will help you identify which of the five stages you are in now. Knowing where you are now in your transition can clarify your situation and point to actions that can move you forward into the next stage. You will gain an experiential understanding of the full cycle of emotional change, from beginning to end, in movie-viewing exercises.

To clarify the emotional twists and turns, a detailed account of each emotional step of the five stages is laid out in a scene-by-scene description of the sexy baseball comedy *Bull Durham*.

Then, we will go through exercises to help you with specific life transition challenges and trouble spots. You can use movies to improve your past, find your true support group, transform your tragic first act into a feel-good third act, create new ways to accomplish your goals, stop resisting your lesson, build your self-esteem, and transform the obstacles to achieving your desires.

Finally, we will present a new picture of the life-long, progressive learning dramas that occur in long-term cycles, based on my synthesis of modern psychology, movie screenwriting, and ancient spiritual wisdom. The first cycle, from birth to the late 20s, is devoted to developing and testing the range of your talents and abilities. The second cycle, from the late 20s to the mid-50s, is focused on maximizing the power of your interests. The third cycle, from the mid-50s to the early 80s, is spent reaping the rewards of your talents by applying them in unique ways with wisdom. Based on your age, you will identify where you are now in these cycles and the appropriate focus of your actions.

It is my sincere wish that this book will help you feel better about yourself, release old emotions, understand the complete cycle of emotional change, feel inspired to create a happier ending to your transition, achieve your dreams and goals, have fun, and enjoy the adventure of your life's changes.

I would love to hear about your experiences with this approach to managing your life's changes and welcome your suggestions for future editions of this book. Feel free to e-mail me or use the form at the end of this book to forward your comments. Also be sure to visit our web site **www.laughcry.com** for updated movie listings and customized movie lists based on your own life situation.

CHAPTER 1

Four Steps to Feeling Better about Your Life's Changes

How to Create Your Own Feel-Good Transition

Films have the power to change how you feel about yourself and your life's changes. When you watch a movie, you release emotions: You laugh, you cry, you chuckle, you groan, you cheer, you hoot.

> *The secret source of humor itself is not joy but sorrow.*
>
> **MARK TWAIN**

This book shows you how to use your favorite movies to move through a life change. You will learn how to use movie viewing as:

- a self-healing tool to feel better about yourself and your transition
- a tool for emotional release and catharsis and immune system activation
- an experiential understanding of the complete cycle of the emotional tides of change and where you are now
- an inspiration for achieving your dreams and goals
- a blueprint for creating happier endings for your own life changes
- a fun and enjoyable foundation for managing life-long growth as an adventure

To get you started, the guide on page 71 rates movies on their ability to make you feel better; that is, Feel

Better/Uplift, Laughing Release, or Crying Release. The movies are cross-indexed by Life Changes and challenges shown here. Check the categories to see which ones best fit your own current life changes. Plot summaries, director, and cast information are provided on page 139.

After-View Feeling

These icons tell you how you'll feel when you've finished watching the film.

Feel Better

Laughing Release

Crying Release

Violent Content

Work & Prosperity

Loving Your Work
Realizing Dreams
Balancing Work & Family
Collaborating w/Colleagues
Destructuring Workplace

Relationships

Lovers & Mates
Lovers
Married Couples
Two-Career Couples
Divorced Couples

Family
Parent/Child
Working Parents
Single Parent
Multi-Generation Family
Siblings
Elder Care

Friends & Colleagues
Friends
Colleagues & Co-Workers

Professional
Teacher/Student
Boss/Employee
Leader/Follower

Love of Self
Self-Esteem
Breaking Old Patterns

Finding Love

Teen Years
College Years
20s
Age 28 to 54
Age 55 to 81
Over 81
Radical Age Difference
Same Sex

Transitions

Birth to 27
Pre-Teen Years
Teen Years
College Years
20s

Age 28 to 54
20s to 30s Passage
Mid-Life Crisis 30s & 40s

Age 55 to 81
Mid-50s Passage
60s & 70s
After Retirement

Relationship Transitions
Courting
Living Together/Moving In
Marrying
Divorcing
Moving Out/Separating
Losing Mate
Becoming Parent

Work Transitions
Landing First Job
Achieving Career Goals
Changing Careers
Losing Job
Surviving Downsizing
Retiring

Overcoming Obstacles

Sexual Prejudice
Racial Prejudice
Class Prejudice
Age Prejudice
Physical Abilities
Mental Abilities
Cultural Abilities
Loss
Entrapment
Creative Expression
War
Adventure

When we are in emotional slumps, it seems impossible to move forward. To gain a clearer perspective, we can let go of beliefs and feelings from the past through laughter or tears. In *Career Crash*, a 1994 sociological study of 400 laid-off baby boomers, Barry Glassner found that the first step in finding a new job is to release feelings about the last one.

When we were children, we allowed ourselves the freedom to laugh and cry. Perhaps that's why personal changes seem easier for the young. Movies can be used to improve our mood with a laughing release. Even if your personal situation doesn't seem amusing, try viewing a movie that gives you a laughing release. Or view a movie that intensifies a dark mood for cathartic release—get out the tissue box and indulge yourself in a crying movie.

One purpose of storytelling is to illustrate the emotional rhythm of personal change. Every time we see a movie, we obtain new insight into the details of the main character's quest. We learn how they prepare for their quest in the first act. We note how they try out different possibilities and overcome obstacles in the middle of their journeys. Vicariously, we experience the ebb and flow of their drama. In the process, we become more realistic about what to expect in our lives. In the end, we may be inspired to rewrite ourselves happier endings.

Step 1: Selecting the Best Movies for Your Life's Change

First, decide how you want to feel after viewing a movie. Select one of your favorite movies or choose one from this book. Review the films listed on page 71 and select several rated with the After-View Feeling you desire.

Next, refer to the Life's Changes Cross-Index columns: Work and Prosperity, Relationships, Finding Love, Transitions, and Overcoming Obstacles. Choose a movie with one of the following stories:

- a life transition theme similar to your current personal change
- a tale about a decisive time in your life that you now want to reevaluate, such as career choices you made in high school
- an account about an era or time in your family's past that you wish to review from a new perspective

Step 2: Preparing the Best Viewing Conditions

Watching movies at home actually offers some benefits over theater viewing. You can pause a video to reflect on a scene, even take notes about what you're feeling and how it relates to your situation. Or you can rewind and play impactful scenes again. Plus, you can enhance the smell, taste, and touch of the movie experience in your own home. Before viewing your video, get ready to indulge yourself in some movie-theater food, like popcorn, or your favorite childhood comfort food. Have something available to touch that reminds you of the time you are reconnecting with. Consider such things as a stuffed toy, a baseball mitt, a blanket, a pair of cozy slippers or pajamas. Then, prepare a comfortable place to sit or recline.

Step 3: **Relax and Enjoy the Drama**

Think of viewing a film as emotional grazing. It is like dipping into your past and having the opportunity to realign your beliefs and attitudes with your current life goals. This is an easy, painless way to learn about the rhythm of the search for wholeness—the optimism of preparation, the conflicted feelings, the fear of moving forward, the frustration and reluctance of letting go, the satisfaction of setting achievable goals, and the commitment to a new life.

Wait until you are relaxed and ready to have fun with the next step in your transition before proceeding to Step 4.

Step 4: **After-Viewing Exercises to Create Your Own Feel-Good Ending**

Here are some questions to ask yourself after viewing a movie. You may want to record your thoughts, feelings, and insights during and after viewing a film and compare how they change with each additional viewing.

- Did you find this film enjoyable? If so, why? If not, why not?
- How is the drama similar to your own life change? How is it different?
- What is the opening image that summarizes the main character's quest? What would the opening picture of your life change look like?
- What are you questing after—learning to trust yourself, learning to love and be loved, learning to express your own power with balance? What would you change if you focused on the positive aspects of what you desire? What would change if you restated your search for wholeness positively?

- What did you learn from the film about overcoming the obstacles you face?
- What approaches does the film offer about breaking through life's barriers?
- What physical things did the main character have to give up? What material goods are you willing to release now?
- What changes in emotions and feelings did the main character have to undergo during the film? What worries and anxieties can you begin to set free now?
- What beliefs did the main character change in the process of pursuing his or her desires? What beliefs can you transform now?
- About 75% through the movie, how did the main character restate his or her quest as a goal that could be achieved? How can you redefine your quest as a specific puzzle you have the skills to solve right now?
- In the final scenes of the movie, what did the main character accomplish that was much better than his or her original goal? How can you enrich and enhance your desires into something even better? What is the best possible outcome to your quest right now? Name three other outcomes that would surpass your original goal.
- Most people pursue their desires by moving from the negative to the positive. For example, if you were feeling powerless or unloved at the start of your life transition, visualize yourself as powerful and loved in the end. What does your new ending look like?

CHAPTER 2

Taking the Mystery and Pain Out of Your Life's Changes

Why Change Is Mysterious: Our Amnesia

The best movies transport us beyond time. We hitch a ride on the emotional roller coaster of the main character's quest. Along the way, we have fun, feel the thrills, laugh, and perhaps cry. In the end, we feel better. Our spirits and our immune systems are revitalized. We may have let go of a few of our own pent-up frustrations. Best of all, we may be lifted up to the point where we can embrace our own journey with renewed enthusiasm.

The very thought of change may conjure up disastrous pictures of precipitous shifts that threaten our safety and security. The 1990s are often considered a disconcerting time. Major institutions are destructuring—corporations, religions, schools, and governments. The new forms of organization have not arrived yet. The media frets about the loss of old forms and mourns the collapse, increasing the gnawing uncertainty. Change remains mysterious because there are no solutions to be found examining the minutia of the immediate chaos. The answers lie in seeing the bigger picture. Contrary to our worst fears, change is not cataclysmic. As John Briggs shows in his book *Turbulent Mirror: An Illustrated Guide to Chaos Theory* (1989), change is a gradual, reiterative process of altering

> *Drama is life with the dull parts cut out.*
>
> **ALFRED HITCHCOCK**

tiny fractions of the whole until, over time, a new pattern emerges. In the same way, we alter our beliefs and attitudes in very small, incremental ways over time. We grow by keeping the 95% that works for us in the moment and releasing the 5% that does not. As we learn, we resculpt ourselves with every 5% discharge. Yet we have little memory of how far we have progressed, lulled as we are by the amnesia-like nature of everyday life.

We go through life's changes similar to characters suffering from that convenient storytelling device, amnesia. We forget who we were and how we felt before we changed, making it difficult to see how our accumulated knowledge and feelings have transformed us into different people.

Watching movies about people undergoing changes similar to our own is a simple, playful way to observe this cumulative learning process and our blindness to personal transformation. For a few hours, we can escape the burden of our own troubles.

The 120-minute screenplay provides a template for ordering and understanding the emotions of life's changes. A powerful story offers a condensed step-by-step map of the twists and turns in our feelings and suggests actions to maintain our forward momentum despite obstacles.

The No-Pain Prescription for Change: Feeling and Learning

In his classic book *The Language of Feelings* (1976), psychiatrist David Viscott states that, "Our feelings are our reaction to what we have perceived through the senses and they shape our reaction to what we will experience in the future." He notes that emotional pain has only a few causes: Emotions stuck in the past are experienced as anger; anger held over time is felt as guilt; anger and guilt suppressed for an extended period turn into depression; and emotions projected into the future become anxiety. The key to moving forward in any life change is to release the hurt stuck in the past and the fear and angst projected into the future. This letting-go process moves us completely into the present moment, where we can take action with clarity.

Movies enliven our senses and instantly recreate sensory memories, like the smell of baking cookies or the sound of music that was popular during our teen years. Emotionally, pain increases when we resist the opportunities our life presents us. If we fail to take action and wait, things usually become more intense. For example, many people who become caught in corporate downsizings and layoffs admit they knew it was coming but refused to take action until it was too late. This is the universal nudge that shepherds us along, even if we are kicking and screaming. Escalated into a crisis situation, we have no choice but to release denial and concentrate on the immediate critical alternative actions in the present.

As the pain intensifies, we have several choices: a) continue resisting, b) release the 5% that holds us back, and c) open ourself to new ways to move forward. The antidote for the ache lies in ceasing the struggle, finding the courage to face our worst fears, and expanding our possibilities.

The Completely Intelligent Way to Change

Recent theories about learning and creativity, developed by Howard Gardner and Luiz Machado and popularized by Daniel Goleman, suggest there are seven intelligences. In our culture we tend to emphasize only two: the logical-mathematical and linguistic, commonly measured by IQ tests. Machado groups these two together and labels them the Small Intelligences. The other five intelligences are visual-spatial, musical, interpersonal (storytelling), kinesthetic (moving), and intrapsychic (inner guidance). Machado refers to these five together as the Great Intelligence. Goleman focuses on interpersonal intelligence, which he labels emotional intelligence.

Working with Luiz Machado, Noam Chomsky, the noted linguist, developed a way to measure the brain's ability to process information. Using a computer analogy, he found the Small Intelligence operates at 40 bits per second and in series. Information is processed like a logical computer sequence—if this, then that—and solutions are sought in known relationships. In times of accelerated change and the destructuring of old forms, this either/or approach leads to permanent confusion and processing overload because the answers lie in new, previously unknown interrelationships. This either/or process fuels our two basic fears of loss of the familiar and entrapment.

The Great Intelligence employs another method of information processing. It operates at much higher speeds, from 1 million to 10 million bits per second, and in parallel, like a massive parallel processing computer. All possible combinations of outcomes are evaluated simultaneously and the most elegant solution is selected. The problem is that this both/and approach, which requires the least amount of effort for the maximum result, may not make sense to the logical way of thinking because it may not be a previously known association. This may be one explanation for our feelings of conflict during life changes, when certain actions seem logically correct yet impossible to do because our "heart" is not in it.

The profound difference in learning speeds between the Small and Great Intelligences can be illustrated by the time required to learn a foreign language at an intermediate college level. Using the conventional approach, proficiency is achieved in two years. With the Great Intelligence accelerated learning approach, competency is reached in only six weeks.

Life's Changes Are Not Logical: That's the Point

To truly comprehend the nature of each stage of emotional change, you have to jump off your Small Intelligence treadmill for a while. Remember, the logical and linguistic intelligences view events in an orderly fashion of "if this, then that" and look for known relationships. If an association is not previously known, it cannot exist to these intelligences. Thus, emotions weaving webs of seemingly unrelated variables remain elusive and incomprehensible. Perhaps this is one reason emotional transitions are called vague, indefinite terms like "the void."

Both emotions and the Great Intelligence are accessed through the five senses of sight, sound, taste, touch, and smell, as shown in Figure 1. The *visual-spatial intelligence* is triggered by pictures, colors, and symbols. The *musical intelligence* is activated by sounds and music. The *interpersonal (storytelling) intelligence* is fired by tales illuminated with detailed descriptions of sensual experiences. The *kinesthetic (moving) intelligence* is ignited by physical body movement and/or sights of people in athletic or artistic movement. The *intrapsychic (inner guidance) intelligence* is enlivened by closed-eye techniques, like visualization, meditation, or prayer. For greater impact, the five Great Intelligences may be combined in a variety of ways. For example, dance and opera combine visual, movement, music, and storytelling. Viewing movies while eating aromatic finger foods activates all five senses and charges up the Great Intelligence, opening the mind's eye to new possibilities and choices.

Intelligence	Sense	Organ	Activators
Visual-Spatial	Sight	Eyes	Color Symbols Images
Musical	Sound	Ears	Music Mathematics Sounds
Interpersonal (storytelling)	Taste	Tongue	Stories Jokes Parables Eating/Drinking
Kinesthetic (Moving)	Touch	Skin	Athletics Exercise Yoga Massage
Intrapsychic (Inner Guidance)	Smell	Nose (closed eyes)	Visualization Meditation Aromatherapy

Figure 1:
The Great Intelligence

The challenge is learning to trust the elegant solutions offered up by the Great Intelligence. Remember that it computes all possible answers and selects the most elegant one that requires the least amount of effort for the maximum effect. It may be difficult to accept at first because the solution is not a formerly known connection. The Small Intelligence rejects it because it is not logical and does not make historical sense.

Inspiring movies can help stoke your courage through the most illogical stages of transition. Somehow, experiencing a movie character's ups and downs throughout an entire cycle of transition is reassuring. It is a safe way to explore alternative paths that might be too intimidating to try in the "real" world. Here is a chance to step out of our slow, narrow, logical labyrinth of frustration and worry. A visit without limits to our emotional dimensions may, in fact, unveil the most creative, easiest, and fastest way to move through our current life change.

The key is to focus on what we are learning on our journey. Remember, just like the hero or heroine, we will always achieve what we need—that is, the understanding and wisdom. Problems sometimes arise when our needs differ from our desires. The secret to fulfilling our dreams is to remain focused on the qualities of our goals and welcome any outcome. Take the Jamaican track star in *Cool Runnings* who is inadvertently disqualified from the Summer Olympics; he redirects his talents into organizing the first Jamaican bobsled team for the 1988 Olympics. Called "nonattachment" in the spiritual tradition, this ability to surf with the shifting waves of events allows time for the inner emotional integration in the ebb periods and the outer progress and accomplishment in the flow periods. If we know how the entire cycle of emotional transition works, we can choose to let go of our attachment to any one form of our goals, relax, and ride the tides of change with an attitude of receptivity and adventure.

CHAPTER 3

The Moving Picture of Change

The Geometry of Emotions

In ancient times, there was no distinction between the sciences, the arts, and spiritual pursuits. The modern cinema derives from the ancient Greek spring equinox celebration of death and rebirth. In honor of the god Dionysus, a full day of theater was provided by the priests and civic leaders at the local amphitheater. It consisted of three tragedies in five acts, a satire before noon, a midday meal, a nap, and a comedy before sunset. The tragedies were intended to teach moral principles and provide an intellectual catharsis. The satire, literally men dressed in animal skins to look like satyrs, provided relief from the seriousness of the tragedies with a spoof of the morals. After the only meal of the day and a siesta, the Hellenic festivities concluded on a lighter, upbeat note with a comic drama.

> *Film is evolving into a visual language and we must learn to read the pictures.*
>
> ***JEAN-LUC GODARD***

Now is a time to rediscover the interconnectedness between the scientific, artistic, and spiritual principles. Let us examine the application of the geometric principles of the Pythagorean theorem to the construction of a 120-minute movie screenplay.

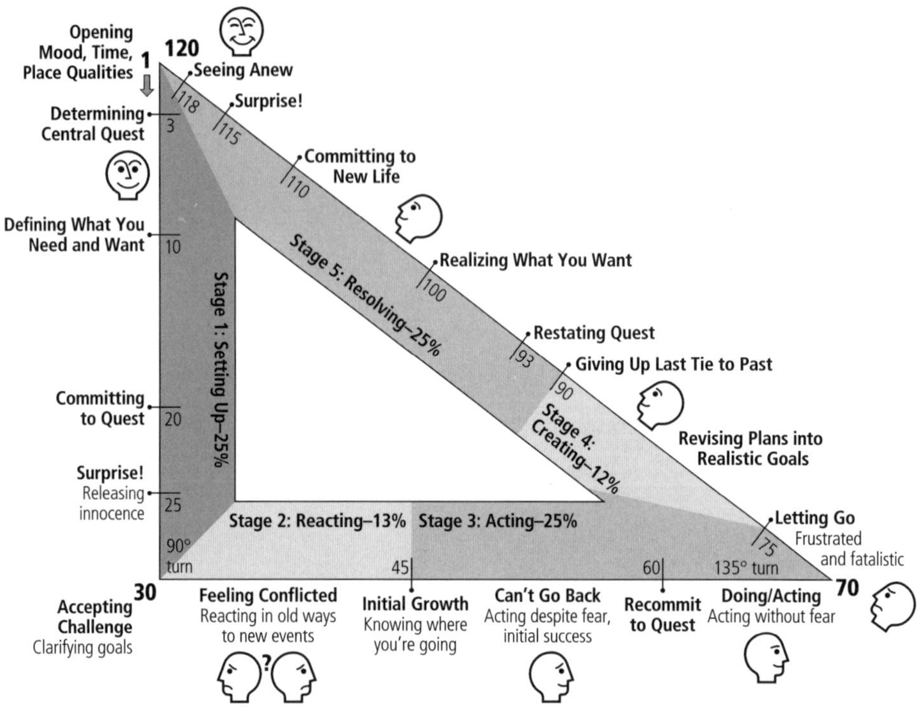

Figure 2:
The Moving Picture of Change: How a screenplay mirrors real-life emotional transitions

The right-angle triangle totals 120 degrees, with 30 degrees in the first leg, 40 degrees in the second leg, and 50 degrees in the third leg. Laying out the screenplay on a right-angle triangle unveils an entirely new perspective of the spiritual and emotional nature of one complete cycle of a life change, from beginning to end, in five stages. Called The Moving Picture of Change in this book, it visually depicts why some transition points feel more intense than others. See Figure 2.

There are four immediate benefits to employing movies and their screenplays as an analogy for understanding the emotions of a life passage. First, watching a favorite movie can make you feel better. It provides an opportunity for emotional catharsis through the release of tears of laughter and/or sadness. Second, if you are very honest about how you are feeling at this exact moment, you can identify which of the five emotional stages you are in. Awareness of where you are now is the first step to moving forward. It can lift your confusion and clarify your options about what to do next. It can suggest actions to propel you onto the next stage. Third, it provides a perspective on how much time is devoted to each segment of the emotional journey. It offers comfort by showing that no stage lasts forever, no matter how dismal it may feel in the moment. You can relax and begin to enjoy your life as a journey. Fourth, it may be much easier to understand how to resolve a movie character's dilemma than your own situation. Then you can evaluate how those solutions might apply to your challenge.

Think of this approach as suddenly having a light switched on after you have been bumping and bruising your way around an unlit attic full of furniture. Now you can see that there have been clear exit paths all along. There is no more need to struggle or hurt yourself in moving forward.

Shifting Your Perspective

Take a few minutes to gain the experience of the way your attitudes and perspectives shift as you undergo your life change. First, move around a room in a right-triangle formation and pay close attention to how the room appears from each vantage point. As shown in Figure 2, the Pythagorean right-angle triangle contains three sides in 3:4:5 proportion. You will march around an imaginary triangle that consists of three steps, a left turn, four steps, a left turn, and five steps, returning to your original starting point. Ready?

- Take three steps forward, looking straight ahead.
- Turn 90 degrees to the left. As you swing around, observe the new parts of the room that come into view.
- Walk four steps forward.
- Turn 135 degrees to your left. What new items and parts of the room have come into view in this last leg?
- Take five steps and return to the original starting point.

Now that you have been all around the room, what has changed from your initial impression? Like moving around a triangle, any life change is a continual learning process of observation and adjustment to an ever-shifting perspective. Sometimes, you move along with your focus straight ahead and obvious. Other times, you hit a turn and everything alters.

Five Stages of Emotional Transition

The modern rules of screenplay writing provide the structure to keep a story compelling and moving forward. The typical screenplay is written to be 120 minutes in length, but the actual running time may vary slightly. Note that the mathematical proportions still hold for any running time. Movie screenplays are divided into three acts that have a total of five stages. The first act is 30 minutes in length and equals one part. The second act is twice as long, at 60 minutes, and represents a total of three parts. The third act is 30 minutes in length and equals one part. Visually, the steps and transition points of the three acts are detailed in Figure 2 and summarized in Figure 3.

ACT ONE: Preparing

Sometimes called the set up, Act One of a movie lasts 30 minutes and occupies the first 25% of the movie's total length. Its focus is establishing the mood, time, and place of the quest of the main character, who is feeling optimistic about his or her ability to achieve dreams and fulfill needs. The hero or heroine commits to a goal with a certain innocence. Toward the end of the first act, the main character is usually surprised by an unexpected event that requires him or her to release some of their idealism and become more practical about how the quest will be accomplished. The main character's quest can be described as a journey of learning how to obtain what is required and what is needed. In this first stage, all actions are directed at preparing and refining exactly what it is that he or she craves and needs. At the end of Act One, there is an event that challenges the main character and requires a clarification of plans once and for all. Spun around in a 90-degree turn, he or she prepares for the challenge of overcoming the obstacles placed in the way of achieving the goal.

ACT TWO: Reacting, Acting, and Creating

Lasting 60 minutes, or 50% of the transition time, Act Two incorporates emotional stages two, three, and four. It is devoted to learning how to overcome obstacles and experimenting with different ways to achieve goals in emotional stages two, three, and four. This occurs in three levels of learning that defy the traditional logic of "focus, focus, focus" as the only way to manifest our desires. It is a more complex process of emotional evolution moving from reacting to acting into creating. The main character must learn to stop reacting in old ways, start acting despite fears, let go of specific idealistic outcomes, and create realistic plans based on accumulated know-how. In screenplay writing, the second act is said to be the most difficult to write. In real life, it is the most challenging, confusing, and uncomfortable time.

Reacting

The main character starts off in the second act feeling conflicted about his or her ability to take on the challenge and overcome obstacles. This head-spinning sense of conflict derives from the psychic reluctance to release old ways of behaving which have worked in the past but may no longer be appropriate for achieving new goals. This stubbornness clouds our ability to see exactly what is happening in the current moment. The way out of this reacting stage is to break old behavior patterns that do not serve the new purpose, stop looking back to the past, and start responding to events as they occur. Fortunately, this is a short stage lasting 15 minutes on screen, or 13% of the time. If it seems to drag during the 15 minutes in a movie, no wonder it can feel interminable in real life. This stage ends with a sudden understanding about one's direction and prepares the way for the next stage.

Acting

The sense of initial spiritual clarity signals the shift from stage-two reacting into stage-three acting. The acting segment takes 30 minutes, or 25% of the time, and is divided into three parts. The first part is clouded with a hesitancy to act due to an overriding sense of fear. There is a longing that we cannot go back to the way things were before. Despite initial success, fear lurks as an invisible wall. The only thing we can do is feel the anxiety and forge ahead.

At the halfway point, 60 minutes into the drama, there will be something that renews the sense of commitment to the quest, despite the mixed results occurring thus far. In *Gone with the Wind,* this is the point when a war-ravaged Scarlett O'Hara holds a carrot to the sky and swears, "As God is my witness, I will never go hungry again." Although external events may not change much at first, the restored dedication pushes the fear aside. With new resolve and more wisdom, the protagonist knows what actions must be taken and does them without fear.

Then comes the dizzy, logic-defying turn that signals the last segment of the acting stage. It is the secret to making our dreams come true in a way that is incomprehensible to our Small Intelligence. In a 135-degree turn, back over the left shoulder, any attachment to preconceived ideas about the quest's specific outcomes must be released. That's right, let go. Undoubtedly, this creates a flustered, frustrated, and fatalistic sense about our ability to achieve anything. Fortunately, this is the shortest duration, lasting only five minutes or 3% of the time. But it is a pivotal transition point of release and adjustment. The initial naïveté and innocence from emotional stage one must be shed. The truth is, we always get what we need, which is learning, but it may not match what we desire.

This is the crucial life change interval when we focus on releasing and resolve our differences between necessities and desires.

Creating

The last segment of the second act turns very practical. It takes 10 screen minutes, or 12% of the transition time. Now the main character has released his or her attachment to naive hopes and restates goals into specific outcomes that he or she has the skills to implement. Pie-in-the-sky fantasies are replaced with an action plan that establishes a realistic time frame to accomplish desired objectives. There is a sense of knowingness about what actions to take and a renewed confidence about what we can expect. The fruits of all the learning and experimenting are now preparing to bloom. The shift into the final emotional stage of the third act begins with a final release of the last vestiges of past behavior.

ACT THREE: Resolving

The third act, also known as the "resolution," is the fifth and last emotional stage of resolving. It takes 30 minutes of screen time, or 25% of the time, and often mirrors the steps of the first act. This concludes the quest initiated in the first act by resolving it from a new, knowledgeable perspective. It is accomplished in three steps. First, the original desires are realized—perhaps in a form not envisioned at the beginning of the quest. Next, there is an emotional commitment to a new way of life, with emphasis on the flow of events and a new openness to life's opportunities. Finally, there is a surprise that is usually much better than could be imagined at the outset. We start to understand how to accomplish our desires from a new perspective of nonattachment and begin to enjoy the journey. There is a renewed trust and sense of adventure that everything that is needed will be provided along the way.

Figure 3 summarizes the five stages: the focus of each stage, the percentage of time for each stage, the feelings experienced, and the indicated actions required to move on to the next step.

Figure 3: **The Five Stages of Emotional Change**

Act/Stage	Focus	Percent Time	Emotional Feeling	Indicated Actions
ACT ONE **Stage One**	**Preparing Quest**	25%	Optimistic & innocent	Prepare Clarify wants & needs
ACT TWO	(90° Turn) **Overcoming Obstacles**		Ready to take on challenges	Clarify goals and plans
Stage Two	**Reacting**	13%	Conflicted	Break old behavior patterns
Stage Three	**Acting**	25%		
	Fearful	10%	Can't go back	Act despite fears
	Acting without fear	12%	Renewed commitment	Continue acting
	(135° Turn)			
	Letting Go	3%	Frustrated; confused	Release old ideas & forms
Stage Four	**Creating**	12%	Knowing how to solve quest practically	Revise plans into achievable goals based on know how
ACT THREE	**Resolving**			
Stage Five	Resolving quest	25%	Committing to new way	Solve quest in new ways Get what you need: learning

The Moving Picture of Change Exercises

Exercise One: "How Are You Feeling?" Quiz

If you are very honest about your feelings at this time, you can identify which stage of your transition you are in. This will help you clarify your position and suggest actions to move you forward. Which of the following statements best describes how you feel right now about making a major change in your life?

- ☐ I'm ready for the adventure of making a major change in my life.
- ☐ I know what I want and what I need to make a major change in my life.
- ☐ I feel clear about my goals and ready for the challenges of achieving my desires.
- ☐ I feel conflicted between my old ways of accomplishing things and the new goals I want to achieve.
- ☐ I feel I can't go back to the way things were in the past, although at times I'd like to. I feel fearful about taking actions to move ahead.
- ☐ I feel a renewed sense of commitment to taking on the challenges of making a major change.
- ☐ I feel like I'm having to let go of everything I've worked so hard for. I feel frustrated that nothing is happening the way I expected it to.
- ☐ I feel like I realistically know how to achieve my desires. I'm ready to revise my plans and incorporate all that I've learned so far.
- ☐ I feel like I'm finally seeing the fruits of what I've wanted for so long.
- ☐ I feel like I'm ready to commit to a whole new way of experiencing my life.
- ☐ I feel like I've achieved what I wanted and got what I needed in a major life change.

Look back to Figure 3 on page 41. Compare how you feel right now about your transition to the emotional feeling column. What stage are you in? What is the indicated action to move you into the next stage? List three actions you could take right now. List three obstacles that prevent you from engaging in those activities right now. Note and view at least three movies that would inspire you to overcome your obstacles in new inventive ways.

See Exercise Three to determine your results.

Exercise Two: Experiencing All Five Stages

- Review the Guide to Laugh and Cry Movies on page 139 and select several films that run for about 120 minutes. For example, try *The Ballad of Little Jo* (page 145), *Boys on the Side* (page 150), *The Five Heartbeats* (page 165), or *Philadelphia* (page 186).
- Discover and experience the five emotional stages by viewing each movie and noting the time in minutes and what is happening to the main character in each segment. Pay attention to the focus of the main character's quest and the obstacles he or she must overcome to obtain it.
- Think about the main character's actions to achieve what he or she wants. Note how that differs from what the character needs. Note any insights about how to overcome obstacles in your own personal transition.
- Based on the movie's ending, how could you rescript your own life change for a more uplifting conclusion?

Exercise Three: Identifying Your Current Stage

- View the sights and sounds of the film *Bull Durham* several times. Indulge yourself in some favorite finger food treats to activate your taste, touch, and smell.
- Review Chapter 4: Viewing Bull Durham.
- Compare your How Are You Feeling Quiz check box with the movie. What stage best matches your feelings right now?
- Confirm the answer by referring to Figure 2. Evaluate what stage you are currently in.
- Check Figure 3 Indicated Actions column for suggestions about your choices for moving forward.
- What new insights does this offer about your transition?

CHAPTER 4
Viewing *Bull Durham*

Bull Durham, with a running time of 108 minutes, provides a perfect example of the transformative learning process in a screenplay. It's an upbeat, raucous look at sex and the underbelly of professional baseball. The main character, Annie Savoy, played by Susan Sarandon, seeks a romance with a boy for the baseball season and ends up with a man, possibly for life.

Bull Durham demonstrates the power of third act bookending. In screenplay parlance, "bookending" is a technique in which the third act is a mirror image of the first act. There is a good reason for this. In *Bull Durham,* for example, the original ending bombed with test audiences. Writer/director Ron Shelton, who played minor league baseball in his youth, started to write a tale of a washed-up older pitcher named Crash Davis, played by Kevin Costner, who just cannot give up the game until he sets a league record. The first ending had Crash leaving town after being fired, without interacting with Annie Savoy, the film's narrator. That first ending did not resolve Annie's quest to have a monogamous relationship with one of the promising young boys for the season. Parts of the third act were reshot to mirror the first act, scene for scene, with heart-warming results.

Here's a recap of the key plot points of *Bull Durham.* You may want to view the movie several times so that you understand the emotional rhythm of the transition points in each emotional stage. Note Annie's changing perspective on how she can achieve the qualities of her quest "to feel pretty and safe."

ACT ONE: Preparing Annie's Quest for a Boy for the Season

Emotional Stage One: Setting Up

Minutes 1 - 27

% of Elapsed Time = 25% (27 minutes of 108 minute total)

% of Cumulative Run Time = 25%

minute 1-3
elapsed time: 2%

Opening Mood, Time, and Place

The opening collage of baseball stills narrated with a voice-over of Annie explaining the analogy between baseball and life using Walt Whitman poetry sets a lyrical mood.

minute 3
elapsed time: 1%

Determining Central Quest

Cut to live action. Annie is getting dressed to go to the opening game of the baseball season in Durham, North Carolina. Then she walks to the ballpark to begin her search for a boy for the season who will make her "feel pretty and safe."

minutes 9-13
elapsed time: 4%

Defining Her Wants and Needs

Annie takes notice of the hot new pitcher, Ebby Calvin LaLoosh, played by Tim Robbins, and asks the baseball groupie, Millie, for her opinion on how he is in bed. Crash Davis, an aging pitcher, is hired to coach and season Ebby's 100-mile-an-hour, but out-of-control, pitching arm. When informed of his task, Crash is tempted to quit because he feels he is too old, but he can't until he achieves his own quest for breaking the league hitting record. He and Ebby and the team go to a local bar after the game and meet Annie (at minute 13). Crash and Ebby get into a fight over dancing with Annie. Crash knocks Ebby down.

minutes 18-19
elapsed time: 2%

Committing to the Quest

Annie invites both Ebby and Crash to her home for a drink, where she explains her rules for trying out different men for a few weeks before she selects her man for the season.

minutes 22-24
elapsed time: 2%

Surprise! Releasing of Innocence

Crash refuses to play Annie's selection game her way. He leaves Annie's house saying he is not interested in a woman who is interested in a boy. Annie can't believe Crash won't play her game. It is the first time anyone has turned her down for a date. Her seductive mood ruined, she spends the night platonically reading Ebby poetry by Walt Whitman. She has de facto selected Ebby, caught in her own rules of monogamy for the season.

minute 27
elapsed time: 1%

The 90-Degree Turn—Accepting the Challenge and Clarifying Goals

Even though Annie would prefer to be with Crash for the season, she is determined to win at her own game so she commits to Ebby, whom she nicknames Nuke.

ACT TWO: Overcoming the Obstacles to What Annie Wants

Emotional Stage Two: Reacting

Minutes 28 - 41
% of Elapsed Time = 13% (13 minutes of 108 minute total)
% of Cumulative Run Time = 38% (25% + 13%)

minutes 28-41
elapsed time: 13%

Feeling Conflicted and Reacting in Old Ways to New Events

At a ball game Annie receives a note from Crash saying that he wants to make love to her (minute 30). They meet at a batting cage the next day (minute 31). Annie reiterates that she has decided to be with Nuke for the season. She states her purpose is to give inexperienced young men life's wisdom and help them get to the major leagues. Crash agrees he has the same goal for Nuke. A rivalrous tension arises between Crash and Nuke about Annie's choice of Nuke for the season. The coaching staff is pleased that Annie has selected Nuke, knowing this means he will have a good season.

Emotional Stage Three: Acting

Minutes 42 - 71
% of Elapsed Time = 25%
% of Cumulative Run Time = 63% (25% + 13% + 25%)

minutes 42-53
elapsed time: 10%

Acting Despite Fear with No Going Back

Annie moves forward in her relationship with Nuke and gives him garters as a send-off gift for a long road trip. Like a good experiential teacher, she feels that it will increase his body awareness while he is pitching.

halfway point:
minutes 54-67
elapsed time: 12%

Recommitting to the Quest

Early one morning, Annie picks up Nuke after a losing streak on the road. She takes him home for a quick coaching session, playing catch in her backyard. Offhandedly, she suggests celibacy as a way to preserve his pitching energy for that night's game. She also recommends that he take all Crash's calls, which he has been avoiding.

It gets a little complicated when an unprecedented winning streak forces Annie to keep her promise and give up sex with Nuke. Crash advises Nuke not to mess with a winning streak.

minutes 68-71
elapsed time: 3%

Letting Go—135-Degree Turn

Annie, frustrated sexually by the interminable winning streak, tries to seduce Nuke in her kitchen. Nuke refuses. He says Crash told him not to have sex with her.

Emotional Stage Four: Creating

Minutes 72 - 82
% of Elapsed Time = 12%
% of Cumulative Run Time = 75% (25% + 13% + 25% + 12%)

minutes 72-80
elapsed time: 9%

Revising Her Quest as a Problem She Can Solve

Furious at Crash, she storms over to his boarding house to confront him about messing with her sex life. Annie declares she really wants him. She understands Crash is scared about this possibility because he knows that she is not just another baseball groupie. At minute 73, the Durham Bulls finally lose a game, but Annie realizes Nuke isn't the right man for her—Crash is.

minutes 81-82
elapsed time: 3%

Giving Up Last Tie to the Past

After the winning streak, Nuke realizes his dream. He is called to the Show (the major league team). He wants to sleep with Annie, but she rebuffs him. Annie restates her desire to sleep with Crash.

ACT THREE: Resolving Annie's Quest

Emotional Stage Five: Resolving

Minutes 83 - 108
% of Elapsed Time = 25%
% of Cumulative Run Time = 100%

minutes 83-90
elapsed time: 7%

Bookending the First Act

Nuke goes to find Crash to tell him about his good fortune. Crash is getting drunk at the local pool hall after getting kicked out of the game. Crash breaks a mirror (Nuke broke a window in the first act fight scene). They fight. Ebby knocks Crash down—the reverse of the first act.

minutes 91-99
elapsed time: 8%

Realizing What She Wants

The next game, Crash gets fired, although he is told of a coaching position next season if he is open to managing. He gets drunk and goes to Annie's house to make love with "long, slow, wet kisses that last for three days," as he stated in the Act One scene at Annie's house.

minutes 100-103
elapsed time: 3%

Committing to a New Life

Crash leaves Annie to fulfill his goal of breaking the league home run record, which he accomplishes after joining another team. Annie cleans up her house, resolving to give up boys in future seasons. She goes to the final game of the season in the rain.

minutes 104-106
elapsed time: 3%

Surprise! Getting What She Needs

Annie returns from the ballpark. She is surprised to find Crash on her porch swing. He says he is quitting baseball as a player and thinking about becoming a manager. Annie tells him she is quitting too—boys, that is, not baseball. She realizes she has something much better than a boy for the season who makes her feel pretty and safe. She has a man after the baseball season, possibly for life.

minutes 105-108
elapsed time: 4%

Seeing Anew

Annie and Crash dance together in her living room. Crash doesn't want to think; he just wants to be. Annie's voice reads more Walt Whitman poetry as the movie ends.

CHAPTER 5

Creating a Happier Ending to Your Life Change

Everybody wants to be Cary Grant.

*Even **I** want to be Cary Grant.*

ACTOR CARY GRANT (ARCHIBALD A. LEICH)

The true nature of a life passage is an unhurried, reiterative process of gradual release and re-integration focused by desire. Little by little, attitudes and beliefs that do not support new goals are chipped away and replaced with fresh ones that do. Successful change is eased by seeking like-minded people who support your shifts and by mentors who show the way.

Here are a few games you can play with your favorite movies to help you have more fun embracing the challenges of your quest. Choose only those exercises that address your specific situation and challenges.

Back to the Future: If You Can't Go Forward, Go Back and Improve Your Past

The key to successful personal change is to release the past and move yourself into the present; then, each day can begin anew. Many people reach a point in their transition where they simply cannot go forward. The old emotional and mental baggage has ground them to a halt. If they keep holding on, the release is even more painful.

Back to the Future suggests an inventive approach to trashing attitudinal luggage. In the film, Michael J. Fox's character goes back in time to straighten out his parents' self-esteem issues in high school before he was born. The before and after difference in his parents' lifestyle is amazing, refreshing, and inspiring for all of us.

This is an entertaining exercise to do with your parents. Therapist Barbara Sher, author of *I Could Do Anything If I Only Knew What It Was* (1994), believes one of the keys to discovering what you want to do in your life is to start by figuring out what your parents' unfulfilled aspirations were. For example, what did your mother and father really want to be? What were their dreams? What would their lives have been like if they had fulfilled their dreams? Would you have been part of their new lives? How would your life be different if they had actualized their desires?

Exercise: Improving Your Past

Step 1: Watch *Back to the Future* a few times.

Step 2: At the conclusion of each viewing, note any thoughts and insights you have about your own life change.

Step 3: Note actions you could take to make your parents' lives better in the past and in the present.

Step 4: What choices and opportunities would be available to you now if your parents' lives had changed before you were born?

Step 5: If your parents are living, ask them what they would have done differently with their lives during your childhood. Ask what changes they would make in their lives now.

Step 6: Note any family beliefs and feelings that may be restricting you now. For example, a belief that you cannot make money doing what you love may make it difficult to start your own business. Consider ways to release those attitudes now.

The Turnaround: Making Your Wes Craven Horror Story into a Ron Howard Comedy

In movie business terminology, a movie project is "in turnaround" when a producer cannot assemble the right team of stars, writers, and directors and releases it for someone else to repackage. Film production is a collaborative effort. The mood, time, and place of a movie, even its central quest, can be altered dramatically, depending on the final creative group.

If you don't like how your transition is going—if it is too much of a struggle or it is too painful—consider a turnaround. Change the script or the direction or both, as a producer might change the writer or director to make a project more salable.

We may not be able to control our current circumstances, but we have a choice about how we react. One of the best ways to shift our feelings is to laugh. Linguistically, the word "humor" derives from a Germanic root word that means "to break up ice." That may be the source of the term "to crack up," meaning to make one laugh. Do you want to play it alone and scared, or do you want to be able to laugh about your learning, pick yourself up, dust yourself off, and start again with a new support team?

Here's a way to crack up your fears and cast new light on your dilemma.

Exercise: Gathering Your Support Team

Step1: View an uplifting movie about teamwork; for example, *Sneakers.*

Step 2: Evaluate the people assisting you in your transition. Are they supporting your efforts with positive suggestions? Are they negating every move you make? What would happen if you put the "yes, but..." naysayers on a Flying Dutchman ship that never returns? Consider where to find like-minded champions who provide "yes, and..." support on your path.

Step 3: Who is directing your drama right now? Do you need to change direction? What famous director could revitalize your quest? How would your experiences be different if Ron Howard, with his great sense of humor, were supervising your story instead of horror-movie director Wes Craven?

Step 4: Who is writing your tale right now? Do you need a script doctor to rewrite the story of your quest without the horror? What celebrated writer would you select to retell your drama? What if Mel Brooks were telling your story instead of Anne Rice? How would it change? Would you change your quest? Would you change the qualities and the feelings that you want and need?

Step 5: Take three of the most frightening experiences of your current life change and retell the events with a humorous, upbeat ending.

Bookend Your Tragic First Act with a Feel-Good Third Act

Baby Boom is a good example of "bookending," a screenwriting device where the third act is a mirror image of the first act. The film opens with Diane Keaton charging into her Manhattan management-consulting firm in search of power in a traditionally "male" way—through a partnership in the firm. The last shot shows Diane, owner of a successful baby food company, in a chair rocking her daughter in her Vermont living room. Her quest ended up much better than she first imaged it would. She found power in a more balanced, "female" way.

If you have set up your first-act quest but things are not going according to plan, here is an opportunity to use the bookending exercise to sustain hope and improve your goal. Use this exercise every time you feel anxious about the future or are stuck in the present. Each time you do this exercise you have an opportunity to incorporate your new learning into your goal, creating a more positive conclusion.

Exercise: Bookending a Feel-Good Ending

Step 1: View a few of your favorite upbeat movies to fully understand the mirror-image effect of the first and third acts. Note the difference in the main character's emotional understanding between the opening and closing shots.

Step 2: What does the opening shot of your current life change look like? What is the mirror opposite of that? How can you improve that image?

Step 3: Map out the first-act events of your quest. Note the mood, time, and place when you started. What were your feelings at that time? What problem in life was this quest going to solve? What did you decide you wanted? What did you feel you needed? What occurred when you committed to your quest? Were there any surprises? How did you release your naïveté?

Step 4: List your negative first-act events. Take each event and note its positive opposite. Now rescript your third act with these upbeat outcomes.

Step 5: Improve and enrich this new scenario to make it even better.

Turn Your Quest into a Realistic Goal: *Rocky's* Secret of Letting Go

One of the secrets to making your dreams come true seems counterintuitive. You must let go and release your attachment to a specific outcome or form of your dream. You have worked long and hard, trying out different ways to overcome unimaginable obstacles to what you want. Now you have to bury the attitude that "When I have it, then everything will be okay." You've learned a few things. You have a different perspective on how to accomplish your goals. You are more grounded in practical experience. For example, in the film *Rocky*, just before the big fight, Rocky realizes his goal of beating Apollo Creed is impossible. He gives up his dream of winning and makes a new commitment to "go the distance" with Apollo, an outcome no fighter had ever accomplished and something he might have the skills to achieve.

Exercise: Transforming Your Quest

Step 1: View *Rocky* at least twice.

Step 2: What is your quest about—learning to trust yourself, learning to love yourself, learning to express your power? What have you learned so far about achieving your goal? What steps can you take to make it more practical?

Step 3: What do you want and what do you need to achieve your quest? What are three different positive outcomes to your quest that would fulfill what you want? What are three positive ways to achieve what you need? How could you make each one even better?

Step 4: How would your quest be transformed if you were to overhaul it from an idealistic "beat the champion" pursuit into a more realistic "go the distance" challenge that you know you have the skills to accomplish?

Avoid the *Groundhog Day* Syndrome: Take Your Lesson Now

Do you find yourself constantly in frustrating situations, most of which seem strangely familiar? You may be experiencing the *Groundhog Day* syndrome. In that movie, Bill Murray plays a conceited TV weather reporter who has to keep repeating the same day over and over again until he learns his lesson about treating people considerately. Unfortunately, in real life, we don't have the luxury of repeating the same day without consequences.

The core of all of life's changes is learning to see things in new ways. We always get the education we need in any transition and we have the choice to take our lesson now or later. If we choose not to take it now, another opportunity comes around again. There is a catch: The experience usually becomes more painful and difficult each time we repeat the process.

Exercise: Taking Your Lesson Now

Step 1: Watch *Groundhog Day* at least twice.

Step 2: Note any situations in your life that seem to be repeating themselves. Is there something that you are avoiding?

Step 3: List at least three ways that you can change your response to your repetitive circumstances. Reflect on Bill Murray's comic daily scenarios for new ideas about making new choices in your own situation.

The Wayne and Garth Reality Check: Improving Your Self-Esteem

The geeky characters of Wayne and Garth, created by Mike Myers and Dana Carvey on *Saturday Night Live,* represent a silly take on teenage heavy-metal fans' fantasy of rubbing elbows with the famous. These access-cable TV hosts from suburbia lack the self-esteem and the talent to comfortably enjoy their dreams come true. Every time Wayne and Garth are in the presence of well-known musicians, they start bowing down, groveling, and chanting, "We are not worthy. We are not worthy."

If you find yourself seriously questioning whether you belong where you think you want to be, then try the next exercise.

Exercise: Improving Your Self-Esteem

Step 1: Watch *Wayne's World* at least twice.

Step 2: Note the main characters' responses to realizing their dreams. How similar are your own feelings of uncertainty about pursuing your quest?

Step 3: List three actions you can take to improve your sense of worth in following your dreams.

Step 4: How would you feel if you did not act on your quest?

Step 5: How will you feel when you do achieve it? Visualize yourself after you have accomplished your goal.

The *Full Monty* Strategy: Transforming Your Obstacles

The secret to achieving your dreams is to concentrate on what you do want and welcome the challenges along the way. Like the out-of-work blokes in *The Full Monty*, sometimes it is difficult to muster up the courage to face your obstacles and move through them in an inventive way. Viewing inspiring movies can help open up creative ways to break down the barriers.

Exercise: Transforming Your Obstacles

Step 1: View a favorite movie that inspires you; for example, *The Full Monty.*

Step 2: When you complete the film, close your eyes and visualize the outcome you desire at the conclusion of your quest. Allow your senses to develop a complete picture—the sights, sounds, taste, smell, and touch you will have in the end.

Step 3: Keep your eyes closed. Allow a sensory portrait of your major obstacle to develop. Now play with ways to dissolve and transform it. For example, you might see yourself boxed into a corner with no way out. You could then turn the walls into cardboard and cut a door for an exit.

Step 4: Open your eyes. Write down your observations about breaking through your obstacles.

Step 5: Observe how the main characters in the film moved through their challenges. Compare it with your own situation. Note any new ideas you have for solving your immediate challenges.

CHAPTER 6

Enjoying the Adventure of Life-Long Learning Cycles

A Major Learning Cycle Shift Happens About Every 30 Years

As life expectancy improves, we can expect to live into our 70s and 80s in good health. We need to draw a new picture of growing and learning throughout a long, productive lifetime. Movies may help us create a more realistic picture of our life passages.

> *From birth to age 18, a girl needs good parents. From 18 to 35, she needs good looks. From 35 to 55, she needs a good personality. From 55 on, she needs good cash.*
>
> **SOPHIE TUCKER**

We live in a time when the universal truth incorporating art, science, and spirit is being rediscovered. The structure of classic Greek drama has been adapted for the movie screenplay. The ancient principles of the Pythagorean theorem have been reaffirmed by the new science of fuzzy logic. The life-cycle wisdom of Kabbalah and Hindu teachings are being reconfirmed by best-selling authors like Gail Sheehy and Deepak Chopra.

If we apply the modern psychological understanding of the focus of each life stage to the Pythagorean triangle, an interesting pattern of cumulative learning emerges, in long-term cycles of about 30 years. Each shift from one cycle to the next provides the emotional fuel for our lifelong adventure. Each change is a simultaneous ending of the old and beginning of the new. These overlap periods, which may take several years, might explain why life transitions feel so disagreeable. There is an inherent conflict between completing and letting go of the past and moving forward and embracing the future.

Our first cycle, from birth to our late 20s, tests the range of our talents and abilities. In our mid-to-late 20s, we make our first major shift in focus. Remember when you didn't trust anyone over 30—until you became one of them?

In our second cycle, from our late 20s to mid-50s, we seek to maximize the power of all the talents and abilities we have. In *Creating Minds* (1993), a study of creative people who revolutionized their fields, Howard Gardner found that major creative breakthroughs take about 10 years and culminate over 30 years at this time of life.

In the third cycle, from our mid-50s to early 80s, we integrate our talents and abilities into a unique individual expression, using the least amount of effort for maximum return. See Figure 4 on page 62.

Why Men Like Action and Women Like Romance and Other Sexual Stereotypes

Universally, each person's life-long quest is a search for wholeness. We explore by shifting the balance between our inner female and inner male, regardless of sexual orientation. A common story device is to create characters who play against society's sexual expectations. Film director Howard Hawkes turned the gender-bending approach into an outstanding career with memorable films such as *His Girl Friday* and *I Was a Male War Bride.* Real life is a bit more complex. One person's dream is another's nightmare. The documentary *Paris Is Burning* shows a gay black man in Harlem whose dream is to be dependent on a rich man. The Victorian heroine in *The*

Ballad of Little Jo, who must pose as a man to achieve her independence, holds the exact opposite viewpoint.

In her book *How to Write a Movie in 21 Days* (1988), Viki King points out that men and women characters learn their lessons differently: "His test tends to pit him against his own life's circumstances. Her test tends to pit her sense of herself against her relationships."

Many men choose to learn their lessons through action-oriented life tests, in which they decide if they have passed. Films like *Cliffhanger* engage male fantasies about overcoming physical jeopardy. Men can compare their own life trials to those of the movie hero. On the other hand, women often select lessons that experiment with their relationships. Women place themselves in jeopardy with their parents, their lovers, their children, or their co-workers. Women seek totality through the successful resolution of cooperative efforts. The different learning strategies of men and women are most pronounced in the second learning cycle.

> *Parents are the bones on which children sharpen their teeth.*
>
> **PETER USTINOV**

These differences may be reflected in people's tastes in films. A hilarious scene in *Sleepless in Seattle* shows people's different emotional responses to courage-under-fire and lost love: Two men get choked up over how the final scene in *The Dirty Dozen* always makes them weep; two women tearfully reminisce about how the ending scenes in *An Affair to Remember* always make them cry.

Figure 4:
The Life-Long Learning Cycles

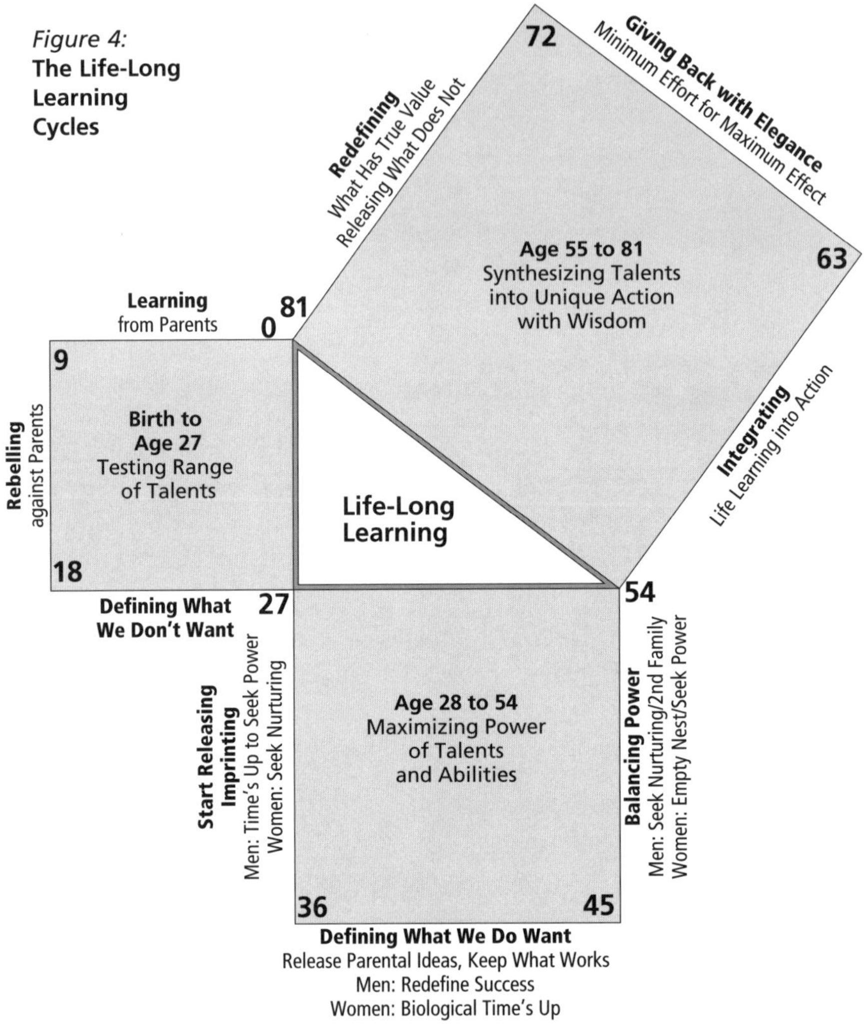

The Long-Term Learning Dramas

Testing the Range of Your Abilities

The first long-term cycle is spent learning and defining ourselves in relationship to our parents and mentors. The birth-to-nine-years phase is focused on absorbing lessons from our parents, family, caretakers, and mentors—that is, our "tribe" in anthropological terms. *Irreconcilable Differences* takes an amusing look at the end of this life stage. The nine-year-old main character wants to divorce her neglectful, career-obsessed parents and live with her loving Hispanic nanny.

The second stage, from age 10 to 18, is devoted to rebelling against one's tribe. In this stage, we test the entire range of our talents and abilities, both negatively and positively. The only approval we seek is from our peers. These teenage years drive many parents and loved ones to distraction. Remarkably, many people make major career and schooling decisions at this time. Well-told teenage tales like *Back to the Future, Lucas,* and *American Graffiti* permit us to revisit the emotions of those heady and sensitive high school years. They provide opportunities to gain new perspectives on the life choices we made as teenagers.

The third phase, from age 19 to 27, is dedicated to defining what we do not want, using our tribe as a reference point. Those who deferred their career decisions must commit by their early 20s. *Breaking Away* and *Mystic Pizza* are two stories about boys and girls puzzling over the course of their lives after high school. *Diner* and *Reality Bites* describe the period of uncertainty occurring after college. *The Big Picture* and *She's Gotta Have It* focus on the period of the mid-20s. *Desperately Seeking Susan* and *The Night We Never Met* examine the late 20s, just before the major shift into the next long-term cycle.

Maximizing Your Power

The second cycle, from our late 20s to mid-50s, is devoted to determining how to maximize all our talents and abilities. It is a gradual process of releasing the tribal imprinting that does not work for us personally. This time centers on defining what we do want in our lives. We attract a new support group. We figure out how to balance our power.

Men and women embark on two dramatically divergent paths during this second life passage. Each sex pursues power in a unique way. In part, this explains why older men and younger women often find each other attractive. Both are seeking nurturing, similar to the financial planner and stewardess characters in Alan Alda's *The Four Seasons.* Both younger men, age 27 to 36, and older women, age 45 to 54, seek to express the power of their own abilities, like the young lawyer and his older painter girlfriend in the film *In Love with an Older Woman.*

In the 28-to-36 phase, we reevaluate the usefulness of our tribal teachings for optimizing our power. This is the time to let go of those beliefs and emotions that inhibit us. At this stage, men have a biologically driven sense of urgency that their time to seek power may be up. Many hard-charging business executives are ready to sacrifice everything to climb the ladder of success, similar to the experience of the advertising executive character played by Tom Hanks in *Nothing in Common.* Women choose between two options in this phase. Some seek nurturing through relationships and children, like the character played by Mary Steenburgen in *Parenthood.* Others emulate their male counterparts in an aggressive pursuit of traditionally masculine-style power, such as the television producer played by Holly Hunter in *Broadcast News.*

> *Make him an offer he can't refuse.*
>
> **MARIO PUZO'S GODFATHER**

Michael Apted offers a real-life perspective. In his documentary film series created for the BBC, he has been following a group of English children since they were age 7, reporting on their progress every seven years. The latest installments are *28 Up* and *35 Up*. This fascinating study demonstrates that the 7-year-old children's dreams are, for the most part, actualized by the time they reach the age of 35.

The period from age 37 to 45 is the time of the so-called midlife crisis. In truth, it is a period of realigning our outer pictures of who we are with our deepest desires. Old beliefs and emotions are released as we adjust our focus inwardly. Men, and women taking on the traditional roles of men, redefine success, status, and security in completely new terms. *The Big Chill* is a meditation on the challenge of releasing old ways and moving forward. Women who chose the male-defined success track may feel their biological time is running out and may consider starting a family, such as the character played by Mary Kay Place in *The Big Chill*. The farmer played by Kevin Costner in *Field of Dreams* is propelled into action because he does not want to end up just like his father. People may rearrange their relationships and select more appropriate partners for this time in their lives. In *Mrs. Doubtfire*, the success-driven career mother played by Sally Fields rejects her happy-go-lucky actor husband, played by Robin Williams, and chooses the more financially stable character played by Pierce Brosnan.

From age 46 to 54, the expression of our aptitudes and expertise is adjusted for personal satisfaction, without concern for what others think. Singer Paul Simon's semiautobiographical film *One Trick Pony* examines this awkward process for a professional singer. At this time, men seek the nurturing they suppressed earlier, similar to the character played by Harrison Ford in *Regarding Henry,* who reestablishes a relationship with his 12-year-old daughter. Women whose children have grown have the time to focus on their own strengths and interests, like the heroine in *Rosalie Goes Shopping.* Some may find the support of a younger man, such as the character played by Ellen Burstyn in *Resurrection.*

Synthesizing Your Talents Into Elegant Action

The third cycle, from age 55 to 81, can be the most productive time of life. It is during this period that we can integrate all our talents and experiences into their own unique application. Contrary to popular impression, this is the time of life when we excel in an elegant way, using the least amount of effort for the maximum return to achieve our goals. We figure out how to get exactly what we want without struggle. It is a time to give back to others and help others avoid the struggles we went through.

> *The moments of connecting are what count. And not needing to win anymore.*
>
> **NORMAN LEAR AT AGE 70**

Creative people do not retire. They switch to new mediums of expression to accommodate new interests. But initially this cycle, which starts in our mid-50s, can be a confusing, frustrating, and disconcerting time. Our energy must be redirected from maximizing our strengths into synthesizing all our talents and abilities. It is a period of gathering all the seemingly unrelated skills and interests we have acquired over the years and bringing them together in a whole new way that is uniquely our own. Fred Astaire shifted his energy to television in his late 50s. Working with the United Nations, Audrey Hepburn turned her attention to feeding starving children (as a girl, she had gone hungry during World War II).

The first stage of this cycle, from 55 to 63, is devoted to integrating our learning, combining all our different skills, and creating a unique set of qualifications. For example, actors who played leading roles in their youth use this time to shift into character roles. Jimmy Stewart went from romantic comedy leads to playing abrasive Western villains. Other actors turn their attention behind the camera to directing and producing. Robert Redford developed an outstanding reputation as a director for *A River Runs through It* and *Quiz Show.* For those who resist transition this stage can be increasingly painful. The over-the-hill secret service character played by Clint Eastwood in the film *In the Line of Fire* depicts the complications created by a reluctance to move into this next life stage. C. S. Lewis, portrayed by Anthony Hopkins in *Shadowlands,* shows our hesitancy at this age to open our hearts to new relationships.

The second segment of this cycle, from age 64 to 72, may lead to refining our craft and selecting mediums more appropriate to our interests. The master tap dancers in *Tap* continued to practice their art and show off their footwork to each other and the younger dancers. The 65-year-old investigative reporter character played by Robert Preston in *Finnegan Begin Again* stayed with his newspaper, despite his demotion to the lonely hearts column, and found time for an unexpected romance. Stan Laurel and Oliver Hardy returned to their English music-hall roots when their films waned in popularity. Paul Newman has grossed more revenue in his food business, operated for charity, than in all his movies combined.

The final segment of this cycle, from age 73 to 81, is a time when we only act on what has true value for us. The 72-year-old Betty Friedan entitled her study of vital people over age 65 *The Fountain of Age* (1993). This is the time to tap into a self-renewing vitality and clarity. Ruth Gordon blossomed as a character actress portraying kooky women in this life stage, like Maude in *Harold and Maude* and the mother in *Where's Poppa?* The film *Cocoon* has fun with the prospect of immortality for this age group. A romantic lead early in his career, Don Ameche played dinner theaters from his mid-40s into his 70s, before revitalizing his movie career at age 75 with *Trading Places.* Jessica Tandy obtained many choice roles in her late 70s and early 80s, including award-winning performances in *Driving Miss Daisy* and *Fried Green Tomatoes.*

Enjoying the Fruits of Elegance

For the years beyond our early 80s, George Burns, Bob Hope, Katharine Hepburn, and Lillian Gish inspire us with the possibilities given a long, healthy, and productive life. This is the time to savor the spirit of the moment, look forward to each day, welcome the challenges, act with the least amount of effort, and thoroughly enjoy the maximum rewards.

> *How can I die? I'm booked.*
>
> GEORGE BURNS

The Gifts of a Life-Long Adventure

Each cycle of life offers a new phase of learning. Our perspective on our life is like a camera, focusing close up on the intimate details, then suddenly pulling back for a breathtaking panorama. The focus of each period is constantly being adjusted to examine the small and the large issues. Shifting from one cycle to the next requires the disconcerting process of simultaneously completing and releasing past concerns while moving forward and being open to new challenges. We can use movies as a tool to help ourselves make the shift, drawing inspiration from a cinematic technique called a "transitional effect" to end one scene and start another. Try a "fade out," a "dissolve," or a "wipe" to move on.

It's our choice to accept or not the lessons of our life's learning stages. We can wallow in "why me?" self-pity, holding on to the past for dear life, refusing to refocus—or we can take a resilient show-business attitude of "what's next?" If we embrace the challenges, move through them, and welcome any outcome, our life changes will be filled with inspiration and joy. Only we can decide how we will play out our life story—as a tragedy, a drama, a satire, a comedy, or an adventure.

NOTES

CHAPTER 7

Guide to Laugh & Cry Movies

The Laugh & Cry Rating System

This chapter gives you a list of 501 movies. Each movie is rated with its after-view feelings. The life changes addressed by each film are listed as well.

After-View Feeling

These icons tell you how you'll feel when you've finished watching that film.

- Feel Better/Uplift
- Laughing Release
- Crying Release
- This icon indicates Violent Content

Work & Prosperity

Loving Your Work
Realizing Dreams
Balancing Work & Family
Collaborating w/ Colleagues
Destructuring Workplace

Relationships

Lovers & Mates
Lovers
Married Couples
Two-Career Couples
Divorced Couples

Family
Parent/Child
Working Parents
Single Parent
Multi-Generation Family
Siblings
Elder Care

Friends & Colleagues
Friends
Colleagues & Co-Workers

Professional
Teacher/Student
Boss/Employee
Leader/Follower

Love of Self
Self-Esteem
Breaking Old Patterns

Finding Love

Teen Years
College Years
20s
Age 28 to 54
Age 55 to 81
Over 81
Radical Age Difference
Same Sex

Transitions

Birth to 27: Testing Range of Talents
Pre-Teen Years
Teen Years
College Years
20s

28-54: Maximizing Power
20s to 30s Passage
Mid-Life Crisis 30s & 40s

55 to 81: Synthesizing Wisdom
Mid-50s Passage
60s & 70s
After Retirement

Relationship Transitions
Courting
Living Together/Moving In
Marrying
Divorcing
Moving Out/Separating
Losing Mate
Becoming Parent

Work Transitions
Landing First Job
Achieving Career Goals
Changing Careers
Losing Job
Surviving Downsizing

Overcoming Obstacles

Sexual Prejudice
Racial Prejudice
Class Prejudice
Age Prejudice
Physical Abilities
Mental Abilities
Cultural Abilities
Loss
Entrapment
Creative Expression
War
Adventure

How to Use the Life's Changes Cross-Index

Here's a sample of the Life's Changes Cross-Index that appears in this chapter. Movies are listed alphabetically by title. Once you find the movie you want, read across to find the after-view feeling icon, and which life changes are addressed in the movie.

Life Changes

***Release date** and **run time** in minutes.*

***Title** A boldface title indicates a plot description in Chapter 8.*

***After-View Feeling** These icons tell you how you'll feel when you've finished watching the film*

Feel Better/Uplift

Laughing Release

Crying Release

After-View Feeling	Movie Title	Date/ Run Time	Work & Prosperity	Relationships	Finding Love	Transitions	Overcoming Obstacles
	Big Chill, The	1983/108	Realizing Dreams	Lovers Friends Two-Career Couples	28-54	Mid-Life Crisis 30s & 40s	Loss
	Big Easy, The	1987/106	Collaborating w/ Colleagues	Lovers Colleagues & Co-Workers	28-54	20s to 30s Passage	Sexual Prejudice Adventure
	Big Night	1995/105	Realizing Dreams Loving Your Work	Siblings		Achieving Career Goals	Creative Expression
	Big Picture, The	1974/90	Collaborating w/ Colleagues	Lovers Colleagues		20s Landing First Job	Creative Expression

After-View Feeling	Movie Title	Date/ Run Time	Work & Prosperity	Relationships	Finding Love	Transitions	Overcoming Obstacles
	Adam's Rib	1950/101	Balancing Work & Family Destructuring Workplace	Two-Career Couples		Mid-Life Crisis 30s & 40s	Sexual Prejudice
	Adventures of Priscilla, Queen of the Desert, The	1994/102	Collaborating w/ Colleagues				Sexual Prejudice
	Affair to Remember, An	1957/115		Lovers	28-54	Courting	Loss
	Airplane!	1980/88	Collaborating w/ Colleagues	Colleagues & Co-Workers Lovers Breaking Old Patterns	28-54	Losing Mate	Adventure
	Airplane II: The Sequel	1982/85					
	Aladdin	1992/90	Realizing Dreams	Parent/Child Lovers	Teen Years	Teen Years Moving Out/Separating	Class Prejudice Entrapment
	All the President's Men	1976/135	Collaborating w/ Colleagues Loving Your Work	Colleagues & Co-Workers Boss/Employee		20s Achieving Career Goals	Adventure
	Amadeus	1984/158	Realizing Dreams	Colleagues & Co-Workers Parent/Child		20s to 30s Passage	Creative Expression
	American Graffiti	1973/112		Friends Lovers	Teen Years	Teen Years Moving Out/Separating	Loss
	American President	1995/120	Balancing Work & Family	Lovers	28-54	Courting	Entrapment

After-View Feeling	Movie Title	Date/ Run Time	Work & Prosperity	Relationships	Finding Love	Transitions	Overcoming Obstacles
Feel Better/Uplift, Violent Content	Angels and Insects	1995/116	Loving Your Work	Lovers Married Couples		Achieving Career Goals Courting	Entrapment
Feel Better/Uplift, Laughing Release	**Annie Hall**	1977/95		Breaking Old Patterns Lovers	28-54	Late 20s to 30s Passage Courting	Entrapment
Violent Content	**Apocalypse Now**	1979/150		Colleagues & Co-Workers Leader/Follower			War
Feel Better/Uplift	Apollo 13	1995/140	Realizing Dreams	Colleagues & Co-Workers		Achieving Career Goals	Adventure
Feel Better/Uplift, Laughing Release	Associate, The	1996/113	Realizing Dreams Collaborating w/ Colleagues	Boss/Employee Colleagues & Co-Workers		Achieving Career Goals	Sexual Prejudice
Feel Better/Uplift	Atlantic City	1981/104	Collaborating w/ Colleagues	Lovers	28-54	Achieving Career Goals	
Feel Better/Uplift, Laughing Release	**Austin Powers**	1997/88	Loving Your Work	Lovers	20s 28-54	Achieving Career Goals	Adventure
Feel Better/Uplift, Crying Release	**Avalon**	1990/126	Realizing Dreams	Multi-Generation Family		20s to 30s Passage Mid-Life Crisis 30s & 40s After Retirement	Cultural Abilities
Feel Better/Uplift, Laughing Release	**Babe**	1995/85	Realizing Dreams Collaborating w/ Colleagues	Boss/Employee Colleagues & Co-Workers		Achieving Career Goals	Physical Abilities
Feel Better/Uplift, Crying Release	**Baby Boom**	1987/103	Balancing Work & Family	Single Parent Lovers Boss/Employee	28-54	Changing Careers Becoming Parent Mid-Life Crisis 30s & 40s	Sexual Prejudice
Feel Better/Uplift, Laughing Release	**Back to School**	1986/94	Realizing Dreams	Parent/Child Lovers	28-54	Mid-50s Passage College Years	Age Prejudice

After-View Feelings Key: Feel Better/Uplift Laughing Release Crying Release Violent Content **Boldface** See description in Chapter 8

After-View Feeling	Movie Title	Date/ Run Time	Work & Prosperity	Relationships	Finding Love	Transitions	Overcoming Obstacles
	Back to the Future	1985/116	Realizing Dreams	Parent/Child Self-Esteem Lovers	Teen Years	Teen Years	Entrapment
	Back to the Future, Part II	1989/107					
	Back to the Future, Part III	1990/118					
	Backbeat	1993/100		Friends		20s Landing First Job	Creative Expression
	Bad and the Beautiful, The	1952/118	Collaborating w/ Colleagues	Colleagues & Co-Workers		Achieving Career Goals	Creative Expression
	Bagdad Cafe	1988/91	Collaborating w/ Colleagues	Boss/Employee		Mid-Life Crisis 30s & 40s Moving Out/Separating	Entrapment
	Ballad of Little Jo, The	1993/120	Realizing Dreams	Breaking Old Patterns Lovers		Changing Careers	Sexual Prejudice
	Barbarians at the Gate	1993/107	Realizing Dreams	Colleagues & Co-Workers	28-54	Achieving Career Goals	Creative Expression
	Barcelona	1994/102	Realizing Dreams	Lovers	28-54	Courting	Cultural Abilities
	Batteries Not Included	1987/106			20s	After Retirement	Entrapment
	Beaches	1988/123	Realizing Dreams	Friends Breaking Old Patterns	55-81	Teen Years 20s Mid-Life Crisis 30s & 40s	Loss
	Beautiful Dreamers	1992/108	Realizing Dreams	Siblings Friends		Achieving Career Goals	Mental Abilities

After-View Feeling	Movie Title	Date/ Run Time	Work & Prosperity	Relationships	Finding Love	Transitions	Overcoming Obstacles
Feel Better/Uplift, Laughing Release	**Beautiful Girls**	1996/110	Realizing Dreams	Lovers Friends		20s to 30s Passage	Entrapment
Feel Better/Uplift	**Beauty and the Beast**	1991/84		Parent/Child Lovers	28-54	Living Together/Moving In	Physical Abilities Entrapment
Feel Better/Uplift	**Before Sunrise**	1995/101		Lovers	20s	College Years	Adventure
Feel Better/Uplift	**Being There**	1979/130	Collaborating w/ Colleagues	Leader/Follower	College Years	Changing Careers	Mental Abilities
Feel Better/Uplift	**Benny & Joon**	1993/98		Siblings Lovers	20s	Moving Out/Separating	Mental Abilities
Laughing Release, Violent Content	**Beverly Hills Cop**	1984/105	Collaborating w/ Colleagues	Colleagues & Co-Workers		20s to 30s Passage	Loss
Feel Better/Uplift, Laughing Release	**Big**	1988/102	Realizing Dreams	Lovers Boss/Employee Friends	Radical Age Differences	Changing Careers	Physical Abilities Adventure
Feel Better/Uplift	**Big Chill, The**	1983/108	Realizing Dreams	Lovers Friends Two-Career Couples	28-54	Mid-Life Crisis 30s & 40s	Loss
Feel Better/Uplift, Violent Content	**Big Easy, The**	1987/106	Collaborating w/ Colleagues	Lovers Colleagues & Co-Workers	28-54	20s to 30s Passage	Sexual Prejudice Adventure
Feel Better/Uplift, Laughing Release	**Big Night**	1995/109	Realizing Dreams Loving Your Work	Siblings		Achieving Career Goals	Creative Expression
Feel Better/Uplift, Laughing Release	**Big Picture, The**	1989/95	Realizing Dreams Collaborating w/ Colleagues	Lovers Colleagues & Co-Workers	20s	20s Landing First Job	Creative Expression

After-View Feelings Key: Feel Better/Uplift · Laughing Release · Crying Release · Violent Content · **Boldface** See description in Chapter 8

After-View Feeling	Movie Title	Date/ Run Time	Work & Prosperity	Relationships	Finding Love	Transitions	Overcoming Obstacles
	Birdcage, The	1995/120		Lovers Married Couples Parent/Child	20s 28-54	Living Together/Moving In Courting	Sexual Prejudice
	Blazing Saddles	1974/90	Collaborating w/ Colleagues	Colleagues & Co-Workers Leader/Follower		Changing Careers	Adventure
	Bodyguard, The	1992 /130	Balancing Work & Family	Lovers Boss/Employee	28-54	Changing Careers	Entrapment
	Boys On the Side	1995/120		Friends Lovers	Same Sex 20s 28-54	Living Together/Moving In	Loss
	Breaker Morant	1980/107	Collaborating w/ Colleagues	Boss/Employee		Losing Job	Class Prejudice Cultural Abilities War
	Breaking Away	1979/100	Realizing Dreams	Friends Working Parents	Teen Years	Teen Years	Class Prejudice
	Breaking In	1989/95	Collaborating w/ Colleagues	Colleagues & Co-Workers		Landing First Job	Entrapment
	Brideshead Revisited	1981/540		Lovers Friends Multi-Generation Family	College Years 28-54 Same Sex	College Years Mid-Life Crisis 30s & 40s	Class Prejudice
	Bridges of Madison County	1995/135		Lovers	28-54	Courting	Entrapment
	Brief History of Time, A	1992/85	Loving Your Work	Colleagues & Co-Workers		Achieving Career Goals	Physical Abilities

After-View Feeling	Movie Title	Date/ Run Time	Work & Prosperity	Relationships	Finding Love	Transitions	Overcoming Obstacles
Feel Better/Uplift	**Broadcast News**	1987/125	Destructuring Workplace Balancing Work & Family	Lovers Colleagues & Co-Workers	28-54	20s to 30s Passage	Sexual Prejudice
Feel Better/Uplift	Bronco Billy	1980/117	Realizing Dreams	Colleagues & Co-Workers		Achieving Career Goals	Creative Expression
Feel Better/Uplift, Laughing Release	**Brother From Another Planet, The**	1984/109		Lovers Colleagues & Co-Workers	28-54	Changing Careers	Racial Prejudice Entrapment
Feel Better/Uplift, Laughing Release	**Brothers McMullen, The**	1994/98		Siblings Married Couples Lovers	20s	Courting Living Together/Moving In	Entrapment
Feel Better/Uplift	**Buddy Holly Story, The**	1978/113	Realizing Dreams	Colleagues & Co-Workers		20s Landing First Job	Creative Expression
Feel Better/Uplift, Laughing Release	**Bull Durham**	1988/108	Realizing Dreams Collaborating w/ Colleagues	Lovers Colleagues & Co-Workers	28-54 Radical Age Differences	Landing First Job Losing Job Courting	Adventure
Feel Better/Uplift, Laughing Release, Violent Content	**Bullets Over Broadway**	1995/95	Collaborating w/ Colleagues	Colleagues & Co-Workers		Landing First Job	Creative Expression
Feel Better/Uplift	Butch Cassidy and the Sundance Kid	1969/112	Collaborating w/ Colleagues	Friendship Lovers Colleagues & Co-Workers	28-54	Mid-Life Crisis 30s & 40s	Adventure Entrapment
Feel Better/Uplift	Bye Bye Blues	1989/116	Balancing Work & Family	Colleagues & Co-Workers Single Parent		Landing First Job Losing Mate	Sexual Prejudice Creative Expression War

After-View Feelings Key: Feel Better/Uplift · Laughing Release · Crying Release · Violent Content · **Boldface** See description in Chapter 8

After-View Feeling	Movie Title	Date/ Run Time	Work & Prosperity	Relationships	Finding Love	Transitions	Overcoming Obstacles
	Bye Bye, Love	1994/107		Divorced Couples Parent/Child Single Parent	28-54	Divorcing Courting	
	Can't Buy Me Love	1987/94	Realizing Dreams	Lovers Friends Self-Esteem	Teen Years	Teen Years Courting	Class Prejudice
	Casablanca	1942/102	Collaborating w/ Colleagues	Lovers Colleagues & Co-Workers Breaking Old Patterns Friends	28-54	Changing Careers	War Loss
	Celluloid Closet, The	1995/102	Loving Your Work Collaborating w/ Colleagues	Colleagues & Co-Workers Boss/Employee		Achieving Career Goals	Sexual Prejudice Creative Expression
	Cemetery Club	1992/107		Breaking Old Patterns Lovers Friends	55-81	Losing Mate 60s & 70s	Loss
	Chances Are	1989/108		Lovers Parent/Child	20s Radical Age Differences	Losing Mate	Loss
	Chaplin	1992/144	Collaborating w/ Colleagues Balancing Work & Family	Lovers	20s 28-54 55-81	Achieving Career Goals	Creative Expression
	Charade	1963/114		Lovers	28-54	Losing Mate	Adventure

After-View Feeling	Movie Title	Date/ Run Time	Work & Prosperity	Relationships	Finding Love	Transitions	Overcoming Obstacles
Feel Better/Uplift	**Chariots of Fire**	1981/123	Realizing Dreams Collaborating w/ Colleagues	Colleagues & Co-Workers		College Years	Class Prejudice
Feel Better/Uplift	Children of a Lesser God	1986/110		Teacher/Student Lovers	20s		Physical Abilities
Feel Better/Uplift	**Circle of Friends**	1994/96		Lovers Friends	20s	Courting	Entrapment
Feel Better/Uplift	Citizen Kane	1941/119	Loving Your Work Collaborating w/ Colleagues	Boss/Employee		Achieving Career Goals	Creative Expression
Feel Better/Uplift, Laughing Release	**City Slickers** **City Slickers II: The Legend of Curly's Gold**	1991/112 1994/116	Realizing Dreams	Breaking Old Patterns		Mid-Life Crisis 30s & 40s	Adventure
Feel Better/Uplift, Crying Release	Clara's Heart	1988/108		Divorced Couples Child/Mentor Teacher/Student		Teen Years	Loss
Crying Release	Class of '44	1973/95		Friends	College	College Years	
Feel Better/Uplift, Laughing Release	**Clerks**	1994/92	Collaborating w/ Colleagues	Boss/Employee	20s	Landing First Job	Entrapment
Feel Better/Uplift, Violent Content	Cliffhanger	1993/118	Loving Your Work	Colleagues & Co-Workers		Achieving Career Goals	Adventure
Feel Better/Uplift, Violent Content	Close Encounters of a Third Kind	1977/135	Collaborating w/ Colleagues	Breaking Old Patterns Colleagues & Co-Workers			Cultural Abilities

After-View Feelings Key: Feel Better/Uplift · Laughing Release · Crying Release · Violent Content · **Boldface** See description in Chapter 8

After-View Feeling	Movie Title	Date/ Run Time	Work & Prosperity	Relationships	Finding Love	Transitions	Overcoming Obstacles
	Clueless	1995/113		Parent/Child Breaking Old Patterns	Teen Years	Teen Years Courting	
	Coal Miner's Daughter, The	1980/125	Realizing Dreams	Breaking Old Patterns	Teen Years 20s 28-54	Achieving Career Goals	Creative Expression Sexual Prejudice
	Cocoon	1985/115	Collaborating w/ Colleagues Realizing Dreams	Colleagues & Co-Workers Multi-Generation Family	55-81	After Retirement	Age Prejudice Physical Abilities
	Cold Comfort Farm	1994/104		Multi-Generation Family Lovers	20s	Living Together/Moving In	Entrapment
	Cold Sassy Tree	1989/97	Loving Your Work Realizing Dreams	Lovers Multi-Generation Family	Radical Age Differences	Living Together/Moving In Marrying	Sexual Prejudice Entrapment
	Color Purple, The	1985/155	Realizing Dreams	Self-Esteem Friends Multi-Generation Family	28-54	Teen Years Marrying	Sexual Prejudice Entrapment Loss
	Conrack	1974/111	Loving Your Work	Teacher/Student		Landing First Job	Creative Expression
	Contact	1997/120	Realizing Dreams	Lovers Colleagues & Co-Workers	28-54	Achieving Career Goals	Adventure
	Cool Runnings	1993/98	Realizing Dreams Collaborating w/ Colleagues	Colleagues & Co-Workers		Changing Careers	Physical Abilities Adventure
	Corrina, Corrina	1994/115		Parent/Child Lovers	28-54	Courting Losing Mate	Loss Racial Prejudice
	Cousin Bobby	1991/70	Realizing Dreams	Multi-Generation Family		Achieving Career Goals	

After-View Feeling	Movie Title	Date/ Run Time	Work & Prosperity	Relationships	Finding Love	Transitions	Overcoming Obstacles
Feel Better/Uplift	**Cousins**	1989/110	Balancing Work & Family	Lovers	28-54	Moving Out/Separating Courting	Entrapment
Feel Better/Uplift, Laughing Release, Violent Content	"Crocodile" Dundee	1986/98	Loving Your Work	Lovers Boss/Employee	28-54		Class Prejudice Adventure
	"Crocodile" Dundee II	1988/110					
Feel Better/Uplift	**Crossing Delancy**	1988/97		Lovers	28-54	Courting	Class Prejudice
Crying Release	**Cry, The Beloved Country**	1995/109		Parent/Child Breaking Old Patterns			Racial Prejudice
Crying Release	Cure, The	1995/99		Friends		Pre-Teen Years	Loss
Feel Better/Uplift	Cutting Edge, The	1992/101	Loving Your Work Collaborating w/ Colleagues	Lovers Colleagues & Co-Workers	20s	Changing Careers	Creative Expression Class Prejudice
Feel Better/Uplift, Crying Release, Violent Content	**Dances with Wolves**	1990/181	Collaborating w/ Colleagues	Lovers Colleagues & Co-Workers	28-54	Changing Careers	Racial Prejudice
Feel Better/Uplift	Dangerous Liaisons	1988/120		Colleagues & Co-Workers Lovers	28-54 Radical Age Differences	Teen Years Mid-Life Crisis 30s & 40s	Entrapment
Feel Better/Uplift	Dangerous Minds	1995/99	Loving Your Work	Teacher/Student		Teen Years	Cultural Abilities
Crying Release	Dark Victory	1939/106		Lovers	28-54	Mid-Life Crisis 30s & 40s	Physical Abilities
Feel Better/Uplift, Laughing Release	**Dave**	1993/110	Collaborating w/ Colleagues Balancing Work & Family	Lovers Colleagues & Co-Workers	28-54	Changing Careers	Adventure

After-View Feelings Key: Feel Better/Uplift · Laughing Release · Crying Release · Violent Content · **Boldface** See description in Chapter 8

After-View Feeling	Movie Title	Date/ Run Time	Work & Prosperity	Relationships	Finding Love	Transitions	Overcoming Obstacles
	Dead Again	1991/107	Collaborating w/ Colleagues	Breaking Old Patterns Lovers Married Couples	28-54	Losing Mate	Loss
	Dead Poets Society	1989/128	Realizing Dreams	Parent/Child Teacher/Student		Teen Years	Entrapment Creative Expression
	Deep Cover	1992/112	Loving Your Work Collaborating w/ Colleagues	Colleagues & Co-Workers		Changing Careers	Adventure Entrapment
	Desk Set	1957/103	Realizing Dreams	Lovers Colleagues & Co-Workers	28-54	Surviving Downsizing	Sexual Prejudice Loss
	Desperately Seeking Susan	1985/103		Lovers Friends	20s	20s to 30s Passage Moving Out/Separating	Entrapment Adventure
	Devil in a Blue Dress	1995/102	Collaborating w/ Colleagues	Colleagues & Co-Workers		Losing Job	Racial Prejudice
	Diary of a Hit Man	1992/91	Realizing Dreams	Breaking Old Patterns Colleagues & Co-Workers	28-54	Mid-Life Crisis 30s & 40s Divorcing	Entrapment
	Diary of a Mad Housewife	1970/95		Self-Esteem Married Couples	28-54	Mid-Life Crisis 30s & 40s	Sexual Prejudice Entrapment
	Diner	1982/110		Lovers Friends	20s	College Years Moving Out/Separating	Loss Sexual Prejudice
	Dirty Dancing	1987/100	Realizing Dreams Loving Your Work	Parent/Child Lovers	Teen Years	Teen Years	Class Prejudice Physical Abilities
	Dirty Dozen	1967/150	Collaborating w/ Colleagues	Colleagues & Co-Workers		Changing Careers	Entrapment War

After-View Feeling	Movie Title	Date/ Run Time	Work & Prosperity	Relationships	Finding Love	Transitions	Overcoming Obstacles
Crying Release, Violent Content	Doctor Zhivago	1965/180	Realizing Dreams	Lovers Colleagues & Co-Workers	28-54		War Loss
Feel Better/Uplift, Crying Release, Violent Content	**Dominick and Eugene**	1988/111	Balancing Work & Family	Siblings Lovers	20s	Moving Out/Separating 20s to 30s Passage	Mental Abilities
Feel Better/Uplift	**Don Juan deMarco**	1995/92		Married Couples Lovers Teacher/Student	20s 55-81	After Retirement Courting	Entrapment
Feel Better/Uplift, Laughing Release	Down and Out in Beverly Hills	1986/103	Balancing Work & Family	Breaking Old Patterns Friends		Mid-Life Crisis 30s & 40s	Class Prejudice
Feel Better/Uplift, Laughing Release, Violent Content	**Dr. Strangelove**	1964/93	Collaborating w/ Colleagues	Colleagues & Co-Workers Leader/Follower			War
Feel Better/Uplift, Violent Content	**Dragon: The Bruce Lee Story**	1993/119	Realizing Dreams		20s	20s to 30s Passage Changing Careers	Racial Prejudice Physical Abilities
Feel Better/Uplift	Driving Miss Daisy	1989/99	Collaborating w/ Colleagues	Elder Care Boss/Employee Friends		60s & 70s After Retirement	Racial Prejudice Age Prejudice
Feel Better/Uplift	E.T.–the Extra Terrestrial	1982/115	Collaborating w/ Colleagues	Friends		Pre-Teen Years	Cultural Abilities
Feel Better/Uplift, Laughing Release	Earth Girls are Easy	1989/100		Breaking Old Patterns Lovers	20s	20s to 30s Passage	Cultural Abilities
Feel Better/Uplift, Laughing Release	**Ed Wood**	1994/127	Loving Your Work	Colleagues & Co-Workers		Achieving Career Goals	Creative Expression
Feel Better/Uplift	**Ed's Next Move**	1996/81		Lovers	20s	20s Courting	

After-View Feelings Key: Feel Better/Uplift Laughing Release Crying Release Violent Content **Boldface** See description in Chapter 8

After-View Feeling	Movie Title	Date/ Run Time	Work & Prosperity	Relationships	Finding Love	Transitions	Overcoming Obstacles
	Educating Rita	1983/110	Realizing Dreams	Teacher/Student	28-54	Mid-50s Passage	Class Prejudice
	El Norte	1983/141	Realizing Dreams	Siblings		Moving Out/Separating Changing Careers	Racial Prejudice War Adventure
	Electric Horseman	1979/120	Realizing Dreams	Lovers Breaking Old Patterns	28-54	Changing Careers	Entrapment
	Emerald Forest, The	1985/113		Parent/Child Breaking Old Patterns			Loss Cultural Abilities
	Emma	1996/120		Parent/Child Friends	20s	20s Courting	Class Prejudice
	Empire Strikes Back	1980/124	Realizing Dreams	Parent/Child Colleagues & Co-Workers	20s	Achieving Career Goals	Adventure
	Enchanted April	1992/97		Friends Self-Esteem Married Couples	28-54		Sexual Prejudice Entrapment Adventure
	English Patient, The	1996/162		Lovers Colleagues & Co-Workers	28-54	Courting	War
	Evening Star, The (Sequel to *Terms of Endearment.*)	1996/126		Multi-Generation Family		After Retirement	
	Excalibur	1981/140	Realizing Dreams Collaborating w/ Colleagues	Teacher/Student Lovers Colleagues & Co-Workers	20s		Adventure

After-View Feeling	Movie Title	Date/ Run Time	Work & Prosperity	Relationships	Finding Love	Transitions	Overcoming Obstacles
Feel Better/Uplift	Fabulous Baker Boys, The	1989/113	Collaborating w/ Colleagues	Lovers Colleagues & Co-Workers	28-54	Landing First Job Mid-Life Crisis 30s & 40s	Creative Expression
Feel Better/Uplift	**Fame**	1980/133	Realizing Dreams	Teacher/Student Colleagues & Co-Workers	Teen Years	Teen Years Landing First Job	Creative Expression
Feel Better/Uplift, Violent Content	Far and Away	1992/140	Realizing Dreams	Lovers	20s	20s Moving Out/Separating Landing First Job	Class Prejudice Entrapment
Laughing Release, Violent Content	Fargo	1996/97	Collaborating w/ Colleagues	Colleagues & Co-Workers			Sexual Prejudice
Violent Content	Fat Man and Little Boy	1989/126	Collaborating w/ Colleagues	Colleagues & Co-Workers Boss/Employee		Achieving Career Goals	War
Feel Better/Uplift, Laughing Release	**Father of the Bride (1950)**	1950/93		Parent/Child Married Couples	20s	Marrying	Loss
	Father of the Bride (1991)	1991/105			20s	Marrying Moving Out/Separating	Loss
	Father of the Bride Part II	1995/106				Mid-Life Crisis 30s & 40s Becoming Parent	Age Prejudice
Feel Better/Uplift	Ferris Bueller's Day Off	1986/103	Realizing Dreams	Teacher/Student Lovers	Teen Years	Teen Years	Entrapment
Feel Better/Uplift	**Field of Dreams**	1989/106	Realizing Dreams	Parent/Child Husband/Wife	28-54	Mid-Life Crisis 30s & 40s Changing Careers	Adventure Entrapment
Feel Better/Uplift, Laughing Release	**Finnegan Begin Again**	1984/112		Elder Care Lovers Breaking Old Patterns	Radical Age Differences	Changing Careers 60s & 70s	Age Prejudice Entrapment

After-View Feelings Key: Feel Better/Uplift · Laughing Release · Crying Release · Violent Content · **Boldface** See description in Chapter 8

After-View Feeling	Movie Title	Date/ Run Time	Work & Prosperity	Relationships	Finding Love	Transitions	Overcoming Obstacles
	Firm, The	1993/154	Collaborating w/ Colleagues	Boss/Employee	20s	Landing First Job	Entrapment
	First Wives Club, The	1996/104		Divorced Couples	28-54	Moving Out/Separating Divorcing	Loss
	Fish Called Wanda, A	1988/98	Collaborating w/ Colleagues	Lovers Colleagues & Co-Workers	28-54	Achieving Career Goals	Adventure
	Fisher King, The	1991/137	Realizing Dreams	Breaking Old Patterns Lovers	28-54	Mid-Life Crisis 30s & 40s Living Together/Moving In	Entrapment
	Five Easy Pieces	1970/98		Parent/Child Lovers	20s	Changing Careers 20s to 30s Passage	Entrapment
	Five Heartbeats, The	1991/120	Realizing Dreams Collaborating w/ Colleagues	Colleagues & Co-Workers		Achieving Career Goals	Racial Prejudice Creative Expression
	Flashdance	1983/96	Realizing Dreams	Colleagues & Co-Workers Lovers	Radical Age Differences	Achieving Career Goals	Class Prejudice Creative Expression
	Flirting with Disaster	1995/92		Parent/Child Married Couples		Becoming Parent	Loss
	For the Boys	1991/145	Realizing Dreams Collaborating w/ Colleagues	Colleagues & Co-Workers		Achieving Career Goals	Creative Expression
	Forever Young	1992/104		Lovers	20s	Losing Mate	Loss
	Forrest Gump	1994/142	Collaborating w/ Colleagues	Parent/Child Lovers Friends			Mental Abilities

After-View Feeling	Movie Title	Date/ Run Time	Work & Prosperity	Relationships	Finding Love	Transitions	Overcoming Obstacles
Feel Better/Uplift	Four Seasons, The	1981/107		Married Couples Divorced Couples Lovers	28-54	Divorcing Courting	Entrapment Loss
Feel Better/Uplift, Laughing Release	**Four Weddings and a Funeral**	1994/117		Friends Lovers Breaking Old Patterns	28-54	Marrying	Entrapment
Feel Better/Uplift	**Frankie Starlight**	1995/100		Parent/Child Lovers	28-54	Achieving Career Goals Courting Pre-Teen Years	Physical Abilities
Feel Better/Uplift	**French Lieutenant's Woman, The**	1981/124		Breaking Old Patterns Lovers	28-54	Moving Out/Separating	Sexual Prejudice Entrapment
Feel Better/Uplift, Laughing Release	Freshman, The	1990/102	Collaborating w/ Colleagues	Lovers Boss/Employee	20s	College Landing First Job	Entrapment
Feel Better/Uplift, Laughing Release	**Fried Green Tomatoes**	1992/130	Collaborating w/ Colleagues	Friendship Elder Care Self-Esteem	28-54	Mid-Life Crisis 30s & 40s	Racial Prejudice Entrapment
Feel Better/Uplift, Laughing Release	**Full Monty, The**	1996/90	Destructuring Workplace Collaborating w/ Colleagues	Colleagues & Co-Workers Married Couples Breaking Old Patterns		Losing Job Surviving Downsizing	Loss
Feel Better/Uplift, Laughing Release	**Gaby, A True Story**	1987/115		Parent/Child Lovers	Teen Years		Physical Abilities
Feel Better/Uplift	Gay Divorcée	1934/107		Lovers	28-54	Divorcing	Loss
Feel Better/Uplift	Gentleman's Agreement	1947/118	Loving Your Work	Colleagues & Co-Workers Friends			Racial Prejudice Entrapment

After-View Feelings Key: Feel Better/Uplift · Laughing Release · Crying Release · Violent Content **Boldface** See description in Chapter 8

After-View Feeling	Movie Title	Date/ Run Time	Work & Prosperity	Relationships	Finding Love	Transitions	Overcoming Obstacles
	George of the Jungle	1997/90		Lovers	20s	Courting	
	Get on the Bus	1996/121		Colleagues & Co-Workers Parent/Child Breaking Old Patterns			Racial Prejudice
	Get Shorty	1995/105	Realizing Dreams	Colleagues & Co-Workers Lovers		Changing Careers	Creative Expression
	Ghost	1990/122		Colleagues & Co-Workers	28-54		Loss Physical Abilities
	Ghost and Mrs. Muir, The	1947/104		Lovers Friends	28-54		Loss
	Ghostbusters	1984/107	Collaborating w/ Colleagues	Colleagues & Co-Workers Friends		Achieving Career Goals	Adventure
	Ghostbusters II	1989/102					
	Giant	1956/201	Realizing Dreams	Multi-Generation Family	20s 28-54 55-81	Achieving Career Goals	Class Prejudice
	Godfather, The	1972/175	Realizing Dreams Balancing Work & Family	Multi-Generation Family	20s 28-54 55-81	Achieving Career Goals Moving Out/Separating	Class Prejudice Entrapment Cultural Abilities
	Godfather, Part II, The	1974/200					
	Godfather, Part III, The	1990/161					

After-View Feeling	Movie Title	Date/ Run Time	Work & Prosperity	Relationships	Finding Love	Transitions	Overcoming Obstacles
Feel Better/Uplift, Laughing Release	**Gods Must Be Crazy, The**	1972/533		Parent/Child			Cultural Abilities Adventure
	Gods Must Be Crazy II, The	1980/109					
Feel Better/Uplift, Crying Release, Violent Content	**Gone with the Wind**	1939/222	Realizing Dreams		20s	Achieving Career Goals	Sexual Prejudice Loss War
Feel Better/Uplift, Violent Content	Good Man in Africa, A	1993/95	Collaborating w/ Colleagues	Lovers Multi-Generation Family		Achieving Career Goals	Entrapment
Feel Better/Uplift, Laughing Release, Violent Content	Good Morning Vietnam	1987/120		Boss/Employee Colleagues & Co-Workers	20s	Changing Careers	War Cultural Abilities
Feel Better/Uplift, Laughing Release	Goodbye, Columbus	1969/105		Lovers Boss/Employee	College Years	Marrying	Class Prejudice
Crying Release	Goodbye, Mr. Chips	1939/115	Loving Your Work	Teacher/Student		Achieving Career Goals	Creative Expression
Feel Better/Uplift, Crying Release	Gorillas in the Mist	1988/129	Loving Your Work Balancing Work & Family	Lovers Colleagues & Co-Workers	28-54	Achieving Career Goals	Loss Adventure
Feel Better/Uplift	**Grace of My Heart**	1996/116	Loving Your Work Balancing Work & Family	Two-Career Couples	20s 28-54	Achieving Career Goals Marrying	Creative Expression
Feel Better/Uplift, Laughing Release	Graduate, The	1967/105		Lovers Parent/Child	College Years	College Moving Out/Separating	Entrapment

After-View Feelings Key: Feel Better/Uplift · Laughing Release · Crying Release · Violent Content · **Boldface** See description in Chapter 8

After-View Feeling	Movie Title	Date/ Run Time	Work & Prosperity	Relationships	Finding Love	Transitions	Overcoming Obstacles
	Grass Harp, The	1995/107		Lovers Multi-Generation Family Siblings	55-81	Moving Out/Separating	Entrapment
	Great Santini, The	1980/118	Balancing Work & Family	Breaking Old Patterns Parent/Child Friends		Teen Years	Racial Prejudice Entrapment
	Green Card	1991/108	Realizing Dreams	Married Couples	28-54	Marrying	Creative Expression
	Grey Fox, The	1983/92	Collaborating w/ Colleagues	Lovers	55-81	Changing Careers 60s & 70s	Age Prejudice Entrapment
	Groundhog Day	1993/101	Collaborating w/ Colleagues	Breaking Old Patterns Lovers Colleagues & Co-Workers	28-54	Courting	Cultural Abilities
	Grumpy Old Men **Grumpier Old Men**	1993/104 1995/101		Friends Parent/Child Married Couples Lovers	55-81	Courting After Retirement	Loss Age Prejudice
	Happy Together	1990/102		Lovers	College Years	Living Together/Moving In	Creative Expression
	Hard Day's Night	1964/85	Collaborating w/ Colleagues	Colleagues & Co-Workers Friends	20s	Achieving Career Goals	Creative Expression
	Harold and Maude	1972/90		Self-Esteem Lovers	Radical Age Differences		Entrapment
	Harvey	1950/104		Friends Siblings		Moving Out/Separating	Mental Abilities
	Hear My Song	1992/104	Realizing Dreams Love Work	Lovers Colleagues & Co-Workers	28-54	Achieving Career Goals	Creative Expression

After-View Feeling	Movie Title	Date/ Run Time	Work & Prosperity	Relationships	Finding Love	Transitions	Overcoming Obstacles
Feel Better/Uplift, Crying Release	**Heart Like a Wheel**	1983/113	Balancing Work & Family Realizing Dreams	Two-Career Couples Parent/Child	28-54	Achieving Career Goals	Sexual Prejudice Loss
Feel Better/Uplift	**Hearts of Darkness**	1992/96	Loving Your Work Collaborating w/ Colleagues	Colleagues & Co-Workers		Achieving Career Goals	Creative Expression
Feel Better/Uplift	Heaven Can Wait (1943)	1943/112		Colleagues & Co-Workers	28-54		Loss
	Heaven Can Wait (1978)	1978/100			28-54		Loss
Feel Better/Uplift	Here Comes Mr. Jordan	1941/93		Colleagues & Co-Workers	28-54		Loss
Feel Better/Uplift, Laughing Release	His Girl Friday	1940/92	Balancing Work & Family	Divorced Couples	28-54	Courting Achieving Career Goals	Creative Expression Sexual Prejudice
Feel Better/Uplift	**Holiday**	1938/93	Realizing Dreams	Lovers Siblings	20s	Changing Careers	Class Prejudice Entrapment
Feel Better/Uplift, Laughing Release	Hollywood Shuffle	1987/82	Realizing Dreams	Colleagues & Co-Workers	20s	Achieving Career Goals	Racial Prejudice Creative Expression
Laughing Release	Home for the Holidays	1990/105		Multi-Generation Family Siblings Lovers			Sexual Prejudice Entrapment
Feel Better/Uplift, Crying Release	Home of Our Own, A	1993/104		Single Parent Parent/Child		Teen Years	Entrapment
Feel Better/Uplift, Laughing Release	Honey, I Shrunk the Kids	1989/101	Balancing Work & Family	Married Couples Parent/Child		Achieving Career Goals	Creative Expression

After-View Feelings Key: Feel Better/Uplift · Laughing Release · Crying Release · Violent Content · **Boldface** See description in Chapter 8

After-View Feeling	Movie Title	Date/ Run Time	Work & Prosperity	Relationships	Finding Love	Transitions	Overcoming Obstacles
	Hoop Dreams	1994/176	Realizing Dreams	Teacher/Student Self-Esteem		Teen Years College Years	Class Prejudice
	Hope and Glory	1987/118		Multi-Generation Family	Teen Years		War
	House Party	1990/100		Lovers Friends	Teen Years	Teen Years	Adventure
	How to Make An American Quilt	1995/109		Lovers	20s	Marrying	Entrapment
	I Love You to Death	1990/96		Parent/Child	28-54	Losing Mate	Entrapment
	I Was a Male War Bride	1949/105			20s	Marrying	Sexual Prejudice War
	I've Heard the Mermaids Singing	1987/87	Realizing Dreams	Boss/Employee		Achieving Career Goals 20s to 30s Passage	Creative Expression
	Impromptu	1991/107	Loving Your Work	Lovers	28-54	Achieving Career Goals	Sexual Prejudice Creative Expression
	In Love with an Older Woman	1982/100		Breaking Old Patterns Lovers	Radical Age Differences	Living Together/Moving In	Creative Expression Entrapment
	In & Out	1997/90		Lovers Parent/Child	28-54	Marrying	Sexual Prejudice
	In the Line of Fire	1993/128	Loving Your Work	Lovers	Radical Age Differences	Achieving Career Goals Retiring	Age Prejudice
	In the Mood	1987/99			Radical Age Differences	Marrying	Age Prejudice

After-View Feeling	Movie Title	Date/ Run Time	Work & Prosperity	Relationships	Finding Love	Transitions	Overcoming Obstacles
Feel Better/Uplift, Laughing Release	Incredibly True Adventure of Two Girls in Love, The	1995/95		Lovers Parent/Child	Teen Years	Teen Years	Sexual Prejudice
Feel Better/Uplift, Violent Content	**Indiana Jones**	1981/358	Loving Your Work	Parent/Child Teacher/Student		Achieving Career Goals	Adventure
	Indiana Jones and the Last Crusade	1989/127					
	Indiana Jones and the Temple of Doom	1984/118					
Feel Better/Uplift	Inner Circle, The	1991/134	Balancing Work & Family	Boss/Employee		Achieving Career Goals	Class Prejudice
Feel Better/Uplift, Laughing Release	**Irreconcilable Differences**	1984/112	Balancing Work & Family	Parent/Child Two-Career Couples	20s 28-54	Changing Careers Divorcing	Creative Expression Loss
Feel Better/Uplift, Laughing Release	**It Happened One Night**	1934/105		Parent/Child Lovers	20s	Moving Out/Separating Living Together/Moving In	Class Prejudice Entrapment
Feel Better/Uplift, Laughing Release, Crying Release	**It's a Wonderful Life**	1946/129	Realizing Dreams Balancing Work & Family	Multi-Generation Family		Mid-Life Crisis 30s & 40s	Entrapment
Feel Better/Uplift, Laughing Release	**Jerry Maguire**	1996/135	Balancing Work & Family	Single Parent Colleagues & Co-Workers	28-54	Courting Losing Job Achieving Career Goals	Creative Expression
Feel Better/Uplift, Crying Release, Violent Content	Jewel in the Crown, The	1984/700		Multi-Generation Family Lovers	20s 28-54 55-81		Racial Prejudice Class Prejudice

After-View Feelings Key: Feel Better/Uplift · Laughing Release · Crying Release · Violent Content · **Boldface** See description in Chapter 8

After-View Feeling	Movie Title	Date/ Run Time	Work & Prosperity	Relationships	Finding Love	Transitions	Overcoming Obstacles
	Jewel of the Nile, The	1985/104		Lovers	28-54	Courting	Adventure
	Joy Luck Club	1993/139		Parent/Child Multi-Generation Family	Teen Years 20s 28-54		Cultural Abilities Entrapment
	Karate Kid, The	1984/126	Realizing Dreams	Teacher/Student	Teen Years	Teen Years	Physical Abilities Creative Expression
	Kindergarten Cop	1990/111	Collaborating w/ Colleagues	Teacher/Student Parent/Child	28-54	Changing Careers	Loss Entrapment
	L.A. Confidential	1997/138	Collaborating w/ Colleagues	Colleagues & Co-Workers		Achieving Career Goals	Entrapment
	L.A. Story	1991/95		Breaking Old Patterns Lovers	28-54	Divorcing Moving Out/Separating	Entrapment
	La Bamba	1987/108	Realizing Dreams	Colleagues & Co-Workers	20s	Achieving Career Goals	Racial Prejudice Creative Expression
	Lady From Shanghai, The	1948/87	Collaborating w/ Colleagues		28-54		Entrapment
	Last Picture Show, The	1971/118	Destructuring Workplace	Lovers Siblings	Teen Years 28-54	Teen Years	Class Prejudice Entrapment
	Laura	1944/85		Lovers Parent/Child	20s		Loss
	Lawnmower Man, The	1992/108	Loving Your Work	Boss/Employee			Mental Abilities Creative Expression

After-View Feeling	Movie Title	Date/ Run Time	Work & Prosperity	Relationships	Finding Love	Transitions	Overcoming Obstacles
Feel Better/Uplift, Violent Content	Lawrence of Arabia	1962/216	Realizing Dreams Collaborating w/ Colleagues	Boss/Employee		Achieving Career Goals	War Cultural Abilities
Feel Better/Uplift	League of Their Own, A	1992/128	Realizing Dreams Collaborating w/ Colleagues	Colleagues & Co-Workers Boss/Employee		Achieving Career Goals	Sexual Prejudice Physical Abilities
Feel Better/Uplift	Lemon Sisters, The	1990/93	Realizing Dreams	Friendship Friends	Teen Years 28-54	Teen Years Mid-Life Crisis 30s & 40s	Creative Expression Entrapment
Feel Better/Uplift	Lianna	1983/110		Married Couples	28-54 Same Sex	Mid-Life Crisis 30s & 40s	Sexual Prejudice
Feel Better/Uplift, Laughing Release	**Liar, Liar**	1997/87	Balancing Work & Family	Divorced Couple Parent/Child Colleagues & Co-Workers		Achieving Career Goals	
Feel Better/Uplift	Little Romance, A	1979/110		Lovers Friends	Teen Years	Teen Years	Age Prejudice
Feel Better/Uplift, Crying Release	Little Women (1933) Little Women (1994)	1933/115 1994/118		Parent/Child Lovers	20s	Courting	Sexual Prejudice Creative Expression
Feel Better/Uplift	Live Nude Girls	1995/92		Friends	28-54	Marrying Courting	
Laughing Release	Living in Oblivion	1994/92	Collaborating w/ Colleagues Loving Your Work	Colleagues & Co-Workers		Achieving Career Goals	Creative Expression
Feel Better/Uplift	**Local Hero**	1983/111	Collaborating w/ Colleagues	Boss/Employee Colleagues & Co-Workers	28-54	Achieving Career Goals	Entrapment

After-View Feelings Key: Feel Better/Uplift Laughing Release Crying Release Violent Content **Boldface** See description in Chapter 8

After-View Feeling	Movie Title	Date/ Run Time	Work & Prosperity	Relationships	Finding Love	Transitions	Overcoming Obstacles
	Lone Star	1995/137	Loving Your Work	Parent/Child Lovers	28-54	Courting	Adventure
	Lonely Hearts (Australian)	1981/101		Lovers		Moving Out/Separating Mid-Life Crisis 30s & 40s	Entrapment
	Long Walk Home, The	1991/97	Balancing Work & Family	Boss/Employee Married Couples			Racial Prejudice Entrapment
	Lorenzo's Oil	1992/135		Parent/Child			Physical Abilities
	Losing Chase	1996/95		Married Couples Breaking Old Patterns Boss/Employee		Mid-Life Crisis 30s & 40s	Mental Abilities Loss
	Losing Isaiah	1994/108		Parent/Child Breaking Old Patterns		Becoming Parent	Racial Prejudice Loss
	Love Affair (1939)	1939/87		Lovers	28-54	Courting	Loss
	Love Affair (1994) *(See Sleepless in Seattle.)*	1994/108					
	Lucas	1985/99		Self-Esteem Lovers	Teen Years	Teen Years	Creative Expression Physical Abilities
	Mac	1993/121	Balancing Work & Family	Parent/Child		Achieving Career Goals	Creative Expression
	Madness of King George, The	1994/110		Multi-Generation Family Colleagues & Co-Workers		Achieving Career Goals	Entrapment

After-View Feeling	Movie Title	Date/ Run Time	Work & Prosperity	Relationships	Finding Love	Transitions	Overcoming Obstacles
Feel Better/Uplift	Magnificent Ambersons, The	1942/88	Realizing Dreams Destructuring Workplace	Multi-Generation Family			Loss
Feel Better/Uplift, Laughing Release	Major League	1989/107	Loving Your Work Collaborating w/ Colleagues	Colleagues & Co-Workers Boss/Employee	28-54	Achieving Career Goals	Creative Expression
Feel Better/Uplift, Laughing Release	**Making Mr. Right**	1987/95	Loving Your Work	Lovers Colleagues & Co-Workers	28-54		Creative Expression
Feel Better/Uplift, Violent Content	**Malcolm X**	1992/201	Realizing Dreams	Teacher/Student Leader/Follower	28-54	Achieving Career Goals	Racial Prejudice Entrapment
Feel Better/Uplift	**Mambo Kings, The**	1992/104	Realizing Dreams	Siblings Lovers	20s	Achieving Career Goals	Creative Expression
Feel Better/Uplift	Man Who Fell to Earth	1976/140		Lovers	28-54		Entrapment
Feel Better/Uplift	Manufacturing Consent	1993/166	Destructuring Workplace	Colleagues & Co-Workers		Achieving Career Goals	Cultural Abilities Creative Expression
Feel Better/Uplift, Violent Content	**Map of the Human Heart**	1993/126	Realizing Dreams	Lovers	Teen Years 28-54	Losing Mate	Physical Abilities Racial Prejudice Loss
Feel Better/Uplift	Married to It	1993/112	Balancing Work & Family	Lovers	28-54	Mid-Life Crisis 30s & 40s	Entrapment
Feel Better/Uplift	**Marva Collins Story, The**	1981/100	Loving Your Work	Teacher/Student		Pre-Teen Years Achieving Career Goals	Mental Abilities
Feel Better/Uplift, Crying Release	**Marvin's Room**	1996/98		Multi-Generation Family Elder Care Breaking Old Patterns			Physical Abilities

After-View Feelings Key: Feel Better/Uplift · Laughing Release · Crying Release · Violent Content **Boldface** See description in Chapter 8

After-View Feeling	Movie Title	Date/ Run Time	Work & Prosperity	Relationships	Finding Love	Transitions	Overcoming Obstacles
	Mask	1985/120		Parent/Child		Teen Years	Physical Abilities
	Melvin & Howard	1980/95	Realizing Dreams	Divorced Couples Friends	28-54	Changing Careers	Creative Expression Loss
	Michael	1996/105		Colleagues & Co-Workers Lovers	28-54		
	Mighty Aphrodite	1995/90		Married Couples Lovers		Becoming Parent	
	Mighty Quinn, The	1989/98	Balancing Work & Family	Divorced Couples Friends		Achieving Career Goals	Adventure Loss
	Miracle on 34th Street (1947)	1947/96	Realizing Dreams Balancing Work & Family	Single Parent Lovers	28-54		Age Prejudice Loss
	Miracle, The	1991/100		Parent/Child Friends		Teen Years	Loss Creative Expression
	Mississippi Masala	1992/118	Realizing Dreams	Parent/Child Lovers	20s	Moving Out/Separating	Racial Prejudice Cultural Abilities
	Month by the Lake, A	1995/91		Lovers	28-54	Courting	Age Prejudice
	Mother	1996/104		Parent/Child	28-54	Moving In	
	Mr. Blandings Builds His Dream House	1948/93	Balancing Work & Family	Married Couples Parent/Child		Living Together/Moving In	Creative Expression
	Mr. Holland's Opus	1995/142	Realizing Dreams	Married Couples Teacher/Student		Achieving Career Goals	Creative Expression

After-View Feeling	Movie Title	Date/ Run Time	Work & Prosperity	Relationships	Finding Love	Transitions	Overcoming Obstacles
Feel Better/Uplift, Laughing Release	**Mr. Mom**	1983/92	Destructuring Workplace	Two-Career Couples Parent/Child		Losing Job	Loss Entrapment
Feel Better/Uplift, Laughing Release	Mrs. Doubtfire	1993/125		Parent/Child Divorced Couples	28-54	Divorcing	Loss
Feel Better/Uplift, Laughing Release	**Much Ado About Nothing**	1993/111		Lovers	Teen Years 28-54	Courting	
Crying Release	Music Box	1989/123		Parent/Child Divorced Couples			Loss Entrapment
Feel Better/Uplift, Laughing Release	**My Cousin Vinny**	1992/119	Realizing Dreams Collaborating w/ Colleagues	Lovers Colleagues & Co-Workers	28-54	Changing Careers	Cultural Abilities
Feel Better/Uplift, Crying Release	My Family (Mi Familia)	1994/126		Multi-Generation Family		Achieving Career Goals	Cultural Abilities Racial Prejudice
Feel Better/Uplift, Laughing Release	My Favorite Year	1982/92		Colleagues & Co-Workers		Landing First Job	Creative Expression
Feel Better/Uplift	**My Left Foot**	1989/103	Realizing Dreams	Parent/Child		Achieving Career Goals	Physical Abilities Creative Expression
Crying Release	My Life	1993/114		Married Couples		Losing Mate	Loss
Feel Better/Uplift, Laughing Release	My Life as a Dog	1985/101		Parent/Child Siblings		Pre-Teen Years Moving Out/Separating	Loss
Feel Better/Uplift, Laughing Release	My Little Chickadee	1940/83	Collaborating w/ Colleagues Loving Your Work		28-54	Achieving Career Goals	Entrapment
Feel Better/Uplift	**Mystic Pizza**	1988/101	Realizing Dreams	Friends Lovers	Teen Years	Moving Out/Separating	Entrapment Creative Expression

After-View Feelings Key: Feel Better/Uplift Laughing Release Crying Release Violent Content **Boldface** See description in Chapter 8

After-View Feeling	Movie Title	Date/ Run Time	Work & Prosperity	Relationships	Finding Love	Transitions	Overcoming Obstacles
	Natural, The	1984/134	Realizing Dreams Team Work	Lovers Colleagues & Co-Workers	20s	Achieving Career Goals	Physical Abilities Entrapment
	Nell	1994/114		Colleagues & Co-Workers Friends			Physical Abilities
	Never Cry Wolf	1983/105	Loving Your Work	Boss/Employee		Achieving Career Goals	Adventure Creative Expression
	Night at the Opera, A	1935/92	Collaborating w/ Colleagues	Colleagues & Co-Workers			Class Prejudice
	Night We Never Met, The	1993/99	Realizing Dreams	Lovers	28-54	20s to 30s Passage Moving Out/Separating	Entrapment Creative Expression
	Nina Takes a Lover	1994/100		Married Couples	28-54	Living Together/Moving In	Entrapment
	Nine to Five	1980/111	Balancing Work & Family	Boss/Employee Friends		Achieving Career Goals	Entrapment Creative Expression
	Norma Rae	1979/114	Realizing Dreams	Colleagues & Co-Workers Boss/Employee		Achieving Career Goals	Entrapment
	Not Without My Daughter	1991/114		Divorced Couples	28-54	Divorcing	Entrapment
	Nothing in Common	1986/119	Balancing Work & Family	Parent/Child Elder Care		Achieving Career Goals	Entrapment Loss
	Now and Then	1995/97		Friends		Teen Years Becoming Parent 20s to 30s Passage	
	On Golden Pond	1981/109		Parent/Child Elder Care	55-81	After Retirement Mid-Life Crisis 30s & 40s	Loss

After-View Feeling	Movie Title	Date/ Run Time	Work & Prosperity	Relationships	Finding Love	Transitions	Overcoming Obstacles
Feel Better/Uplift, Violent Content	Once Were Warriors	1994/102		Married Couples Parent/Child		Moving Out/Separating	Entrapment
Feel Better/Uplift, Violent Content	One Against the Wind	1991/100	Collaborating w/ Colleagues	Colleagues & Co-Workers Boss/Employee		Changing Careers	War Creative Expression
Feel Better/Uplift, Laughing Release	One Flew Over the Cuckoo's Nest	1975/133		Self-Esteem Friends			Mental Abilities Entrapment
Feel Better/Uplift	**One Trick Pony**	1980/98	Loving Your Work	Colleagues & Co-Workers Married Couples	28-54	Achieving Career Goals Mid-Life Crisis 30s & 40s	Creative Expression Loss
Feel Better/Uplift, Laughing Release	Only You	1994/109		Lovers	Courting		
Crying Release	**Ordinary People**	1980/125		Parent/Child Self-Esteem Married Couples		Teen Years	Loss
Feel Better/Uplift	Paper, The	1994/112	Destructuring Workplace Balancing Work & Family	Colleagues & Co-Workers Boss/Employee	28-54	Achieving Career Goals Surviving Downsizing	Loss Creative Expression
Feel Better/Uplift, Laughing Release, Crying Release	**Parenthood**	1989/124	Balancing Work & Family	Working Parents Parent/Child Multi-Generation Family Divorced Couples	20s 28-54 55-81	Living Together/Moving In After Retirement Achieving Career Goals	Loss Entrapment
Feel Better/Uplift	**Paris Is Burning**	1991/78	Realizing Dreams	Friends			Racial Prejudice Sexual Prejudice Creative Expression
Feel Better/Uplift, Laughing Release	Pat and Mike	1952/95	Collaborating w/ Colleagues	Colleagues & Co-Workers Lovers	28-54	Changing Careers	Physical Abilities Sexual Prejudice

After-View Feelings Key: Feel Better/Uplift — Laughing Release — Crying Release — Violent Content — **Boldface** See description in Chapter 8

After-View Feeling	Movie Title	Date/ Run Time	Work & Prosperity	Relationships	Finding Love	Transitions	Overcoming Obstacles
	Personal Best	1982/126	Realizing Dreams	Lovers	College Years	Achieving Career Goals	Sexual Prejudice
	Persuasion	1995/104		Lovers	28-54	Courting	Class Prejudice
	Peter's Friends	1992/100	Realizing Dreams	Friends	28-54	Mid-Life Crisis 30s & 40s	Creative Expression Loss
	Phar Lap	1983/108	Realizing Dreams Love Work	Colleagues & Co-Workers		Achieving Career Goals	Creative Expression
	Phenomenon	1996/123		Lovers	28-54	Courting Losing Mate	Physical Abilities
	Philadelphia	1993/119	Collaborating w/ Colleagues	Boss/Employee Colleagues & Co-Workers	Same Sex	Losing Job	Physical Abilities Sexual Prejudice
	Philadelphia Story, The	1940/112		Divorced Couples Parent/Child	28-54	Divorcing	Loss Entrapment
	Piano, The	1993/121		Lovers Parent/Child	28-54	Living Together/Moving In	Sexual Prejudice Entrapment Creative Expression
	Planes, Trains & Automobiles	1987/93	Collaborating w/ Colleagues	Breaking Old Patterns Friends		Mid-Life Crisis 30s & 40s	Loss
	Playboys, The	1992/110		Lovers	20s Radical Age Differences	Moving Out/Separating	Sexual Prejudice Entrapment
	Player, The	1992/123	Collaborating w/ Colleagues Destructuring Workplace	Colleagues & Co-Workers Lovers	28-54	Achieving Career Goals Surviving Downsizing	Entrapment Creative Expression

After-View Feeling	Movie Title	Date/ Run Time	Work & Prosperity	Relationships	Finding Love	Transitions	Overcoming Obstacles
Feel Better/Uplift	Pontiac Moon	1994/108		Married Couples Parent/Child			Entrapment
Feel Better/Uplift, Crying Release	Powder	1995/111		Friends Teacher/Student		Teen Years	Mental Abilities
Feel Better/Uplift	Pretty Woman	1990/117		Lovers	Radical Age Differences	Changing Careers Living Together/Moving In	Class Prejudice
Feel Better/Uplift, Laughing Release	**Pride and Prejudice**	1995/300		Lovers	College Years	Courting	Class Prejudice
Feel Better/Uplift	Priest	1994/98	Loving Your Work	Colleagues & Co-Workers Lovers	28-54	Achieving Career Goals Courting	Sexual Prejudice
Feel Better/Uplift	Princess Bride	1987/98	Realizing Dreams	Lovers	20s	20s Moving Out/Separating	Adventure Entrapment
Feel Better/Uplift	Princess Caraboo	1994/96	Realizing Dreams			Changing Careers	Sexual Prejudice
Feel Better/Uplift, Laughing Release	Private Benjamin	1980/100	Collaborating w/ Colleagues		20s	Changing Careers 20s to 30s Passage	Sexual Prejudice
Feel Better/Uplift, Laughing Release	Private Parts	1997/108	Realizing Dreams	Parent/Child Boss/Employee		Achieving Career Goals	Creative Expression
Feel Better/Uplift, Laughing Release, Crying Release	**Queen of Hearts**	1989/112		Married Couples Colleagues & Co-Workers	20s 28-54 55-81	Marrying Moving Out/Separating	Entrapment
Feel Better/Uplift	Quiz Show	1994/133		Parent/Child Colleagues & Co-Workers		Changing Careers	Mental Abilities
Feel Better/Uplift, Violent Content	**Raiders of the Lost Ark**	1981/115	Loving Your Work	Teacher/Student		Achieving Career Goals	Adventure

After-View Feelings Key: Feel Better/Uplift · Laughing Release · Crying Release · Violent Content **Boldface** See description in Chapter 8

After-View Feeling	Movie Title	Date/ Run Time	Work & Prosperity	Relationships	Finding Love	Transitions	Overcoming Obstacles
	Rain Man	1988/140		Siblings		Moving Out/Separating	Mental Abilities
	Rambling Rose	1991/112		Teacher/Student Lovers	20s	Teen Years	Sexual Prejudice
	Razor's Edge, The (1946)	1946/146	Realizing Dreams	Lovers	28-54	Changing Careers	Creative Expression Adventure
	Razor's Edge, The (1984)	1984/128					
	Reality Bites	1994/99	Realizing Dreams	Boss/Employee Lovers	20s	20s Landing First Job	Creative Expression
	Rebecca	1940/130		Boss/Employee	Radical Age Differences	Living Together/Moving In	Loss Entrapment
	Regarding Henry	1991/107	Balancing Work & Family	Parent/Child	28-54	Changing Careers	Physical Abilities Entrapment
	Restoration	1994/118	Realizing Dreams	Lovers	28-54	Achieving Career Goals	Class Prejudice
	Resurrection	1980/103	Loving Your Work	Parent/Child Lovers	Radical Age Differences	Changing Careers	Physical Abilities Creative Expression
	Return of the Jedi	1983/133	Realizing Dreams	Parent/Child Colleagues & Co-Workers	20s	Achieving Career Goals	Adventure
	Right Stuff, The	1983/193	Loving Your Work Collaborating w/ Colleagues	Colleagues & Co-Workers	28-54	Achieving Career Goals	Adventure
	Risky Business	1983/96	Realizing Dreams	Colleagues & Co-Workers Parent/Child	Teen Years	Teen Years	Creative Expression Entrapment

After-View Feeling	Movie Title	Date/ Run Time	Work & Prosperity	Relationships	Finding Love	Transitions	Overcoming Obstacles
Crying Release	River Runs Through It, A	1992/123		Parent/Child Siblings	College Years	College Years Moving Out/Separating	Creative Expression Entrapment
Feel Better/Uplift	Rocketeer, The	1991/108	Realizing Dreams Collaborating w/ Colleagues	Lovers Colleagues & Co-Workers	20s	Achieving Career Goals	Adventure Creative Expression
Feel Better/Uplift, Violent Content	**Rocky**	1976/119	Realizing Dreams	Lovers Colleagues & Co-Workers	28-54	Achieving Career Goals	Physical Abilities
	Rocky II	1979/119					
	Rocky III	1982/99					
	Rocky IV	1985/104					
	Rocky V	1990/104					
Laughing Release	**Roger & Me**	1989/100	Destructuring Workplace	Boss/Employee		Losing Job	Loss
Feel Better/Uplift	Roman Holiday	1953/119		Lovers	20s	Moving Out/Separating	Entrapment Adventure
Feel Better/Uplift, Laughing Release	Romancing the Stone	1984/105	Loving Your Work	Lovers	28-54		Adventure
Feel Better/Uplift, Laughing Release	**Room with a View, A**	1986/117	Realizing Dreams	Lovers	20s	Marrying	Entrapment Class Prejudice
Feel Better/Uplift, Laughing Release	Roommates	1995/108		Multi-Generation Family Elder Care		After Retirement	Age Prejudice
Feel Better/Uplift, Crying Release, Violent Content	**Roots**	1977/570	Realizing Dreams	Multi-Generation Family Boss/Employee Breaking Old Patterns		Achieving Career Goals	Racial Prejudice Entrapment War

After-View Feelings Key: Feel Better/Uplift Laughing Release Crying Release Violent Content **Boldface** See description in Chapter 8

After-View Feeling	Movie Title	Date/ Run Time	Work & Prosperity	Relationships	Finding Love	Transitions	Overcoming Obstacles
	Rosalie Goes Shopping	1990/94	Balancing Work & Family	Working Parents		Changing Careers	Creative Expression
	Rose, The	1979/134	Balancing Work & Family	Two-Career Couples	20s	Achieving Career Goals	Creative Expression
	Ruby in Paradise	1993/115	Realizing Dreams	Lovers Boss/Employee	Teen Years	Teen Years Moving Out/Separating	Entrapment
	Rudy	1993/112	Realizing Dreams	Teacher/Student	College Years	College Years	Physical Abilities
	Ruthless People	1986/93	Realizing Dreams	Colleagues & Co-Workers	28-54	Changing Careers	Loss Entrapment
	Sabrina (1996)	1996/124	Realizing Dreams	Lovers	Radical Age Differences	Courting	Class Prejudice
	Sabrina (1954)	1954/113					
	Same Time, Next Year	1978/117		Lovers	20s 28-54	20s to 30s Passage Mid-Life Crisis 30s & 40s Mid-50s Passage	Entrapment Loss
	Scrooged	1988/101		Boss/Employee Lovers Breaking Old Patterns	28-54	Mid-Life Crisis 30s & 40s	Entrapment
	Search for Signs of Intelligent Life in the Universe, The	1991/120	Balancing Work & Family	Lovers Friends	28-54		Creative Expression
	Searchers, The	1956/119	Realizing Dreams	Multi-Generation Family		Moving Out/Separating	Loss
	Searching for Bobby Fisher	1993/110		Parent/Child		Pre-Teen Years	Mental Abilities

After-View Feeling	Movie Title	Date/ Run Time	Work & Prosperity	Relationships	Finding Love	Transitions	Overcoming Obstacles
Feel Better/Uplift, Laughing Release	Secret Life of Walter Mitty, The	1947/110		Lovers Parent/Child		Achieving Career Goals	Adventure
Feel Better/Uplift	**Secret of Roan Inish, The**	1994/102	Realizing Dreams	Siblings Parent/Child		Pre-Teen Years	Loss
Feel Better/Uplift, Crying Release	**Secrets and Lies**	1995/142		Parent/Child		Mid-Life Crisis 30s & 40s	Loss
Feel Better/Uplift, Laughing Release	**Sense and Sensibility**	1995/135		Siblings	20s	Courting	Entrapment
Feel Better/Uplift	**Sex, Lies, & Videotape**	1989/100		Friends Married Couples	28-54	20s to 30s Passage	Entrapment
Crying Release	**Shadowlands**	1993/130	Balancing Work & Family	Parent/Child Married Couples	28-54	Marrying	Loss
Feel Better/Uplift	Shall We Dance? (1937)	1937/116		Two-Career Couples	28-54	Marrying	Creative Expression
Feel Better/Uplift	Shawshank Redemption	1994/142	Realizing Dreams	Friends			Entrapment
Feel Better/Uplift, Laughing Release	She Done Him Wrong	1933/66	Loving Your Work	Lovers	28-54	Courting	Creative Expression
Feel Better/Uplift, Laughing Release	She's Gotta Have It	1986/84		Lovers	20s	Courting	Sexual Prejudice Entrapment
Feel Better/Uplift, Laughing Release	**She's the One**	1996/95		Multi-Generation Family Lovers Married Couples	20s 55-81	20s Mid-50s Passage Courting	Entrapment

After-View Feelings Key: Feel Better/Uplift Laughing Release Crying Release Violent Content **Boldface** See description in Chapter 8

After-View Feeling	Movie Title	Date/ Run Time	Work & Prosperity	Relationships	Finding Love	Transitions	Overcoming Obstacles
	Shine	1995/105	Realizing Dreams	Parent/Child Married Couples	28-54	Teen Years College Years Achieving Career Goals	Creative Expression Mental Abilities
	Singin' in the Rain	1952/102	Loving Your Work	Lovers	Radical Age Differences	Landing First Job Achieving Career Goals	Creative Expression
	Singles	1992/100		Friends Lovers	20s	20s	Age Prejudice
	Sister Act	1992/100	Collaborating w/ Colleagues	Colleagues & Co-Workers		Changing Careers	Creative Expression Entrapment
	Sister Act II: Back in the Habit	1993/106					
	Six Degrees of Separation	1993/112		Married Couples Friends		College Years	Racial Prejudice Class Prejudice
	Slap Shot	1977/122	Collaborating w/ Colleagues Balancing Work & Family	Boss/Employee Colleagues & Co-Workers Lovers	28-54	Achieving Career Goals	Creative Expression Loss
	Sleepless in Seattle	1993/104		Single Parent Lovers	28-54	Courting	Loss
	Small Wonders	1995/77	Loving Your Work	Teacher/Student Single Parent		Achieving Career Goals	Creative Expression
	Smoke	1995/112		Friends Parent/Child Lovers			Racial Prejudice Cultural Abilities Entrapment

After-View Feeling	Movie Title	Date/ Run Time	Work & Prosperity	Relationships	Finding Love	Transitions	Overcoming Obstacles
Feel Better/Uplift, Violent Content	**Sneakers**	1992/125	Collaborating w/ Colleagues	Colleagues & Co-Workers		Achieving Career Goals	Adventure Creative Expression Entrapment
Feel Better/Uplift, Laughing Release	**Soapdish**	1991/92	Collaborating w/ Colleagues Balancing Work & Family	Colleagues & Co-Workers Lovers	28-54	Achieving Career Goals	Age Prejudice Loss
Feel Better/Uplift, Laughing Release	**Some Like It Hot**	1959/119	Collaborating w/ Colleagues	Colleagues & Co-Workers Lovers	28-54	Courting	Sexual Prejudice Entrapment
Crying Release	**Some Mother's Son**	1997/111		Parent/Child Friends			War
Feel Better/Uplift	Soul Food	1997/115	Balancing Work & Family	Multi-Generation Family Siblings Married Couples			Entrapment
Crying Release	**Spitfire Grill, The**	1995/117		Boss/Employee Lovers	20s	Landing First Job	Class Prejudice
Feel Better/Uplift, Laughing Release	Splash	1984/111	Realizing Dreams	Lovers Siblings	20s		Loss
Feel Better/Uplift, Violent Content	Stakeout	1987/115	Collaborating w/ Colleagues	Colleagues & Co-Workers Lovers	28-54	Achieving Career Goals	Entrapment
Feel Better/Uplift	Stand and Deliver	1987/105	Realizing Dreams	Teacher/Student		Teen Years Achieving Career Goals	Racial Prejudice
Feel Better/Uplift	Stand By Me	1986/87		Friends		Pre-Teen Years	Loss

After-View Feelings Key: Feel Better/Uplift · Laughing Release · Crying Release · Violent Content · **Boldface** See description in Chapter 8

After-View Feeling	Movie Title	Date/ Run Time	Work & Prosperity	Relationships	Finding Love	Transitions	Overcoming Obstacles
	Star Is Born, A (1937)	1937/111	Balancing Work & Family	Two-Career Couples	Radical Age Differences	Losing Mate Achieving Career Goals	Loss Creative Expression
	Star Is Born, A (1954)	1954/154					
	Star Is Born, A (1976)	1976/140	Collaborating w/ Colleagues				
	Star Trek IV: The Voyage Home	1986/119	Realizing Dreams	Colleagues & Co-Workers		Achieving Career Goals	Loss Adventure
	Star Wars (1977)	1977/121		Parent/Child Colleagues & Co-Workers	20s		Adventure Physical Abilities
	Star Wars Episodes IV, V, & VI	1977/378				Losing Mate	
	Starman	1984/112		Lovers	28-54	Divorcing Courting	Loss Entrapment
	Starting Over	1979/106		Divorced Couples Lovers	28-54	Achieving Career Goals Divorcing	Loss
	State of the Union	1948/124			28-54	Teen Years Mid-Life Crisis 30s & 40s	Creative Expression
	Stealing Beauty	1996/118		Married Couples Lovers Friends	Teen Years	Marrying Losing Mate	Loss Creative Expression
	Steel Magnolias	1989/118		Multi-Generation Family Parent/Child	20s	Achieving Career Goals	Loss

After-View Feeling	Movie Title	Date/ Run Time	Work & Prosperity	Relationships	Finding Love	Transitions	Overcoming Obstacles
Feel Better/Uplift	Sting, The	1973/129	Collaborating w/ Colleagues	Colleagues & Co-Workers Friends		Achieving Career Goals Courting	Entrapment
Feel Better/Uplift, Laughing Release	**Strictly Ballroom**	1992/94	Realizing Dreams Loving Your Work	Parent/Child Lovers	20s	Achieving Career Goals Landing First Job	Creative Expression Entrapment
Feel Better/Uplift	Stunt Man, The	1980/129	Collaborating w/ Colleagues	Colleagues & Co-Workers Lovers	20s	Teen Years	Creative Expression Entrapment
Crying Release	Summer of '42	1971/102		Lovers	Radical Age Differences		War Loss
Feel Better/Uplift	Superman	1978/143	Team Work	Lovers	20s		Loss
	Superman II	1980/127					
	Superman III	1983/123					
	Superman IV	1987/90					
Feel Better/Uplift, Laughing Release	**Sure Thing, The**	1985/94		Lovers	College Years	College Years Courting	Entrapment
Feel Better/Uplift	Swing Time	1936/103		Lovers	28-54	Courting	Creative Expression
Feel Better/Uplift, Laughing Release	Swingers	1996/96		Friends Lovers	20s	Courting	
Feel Better/Uplift, Laughing Release	Taking Care of Business	1990/107	Collaborating w/ Colleagues	Breaking Old Patterns Colleagues & Co-Workers		Achieving Career Goals	Entrapment
Feel Better/Uplift, Laughing Release	Taking Off	1971/93		Multi-Generation Family	Teen Years	Teen Years Achieving Career Goals	Entrapment
Feel Better/Uplift	Tap	1989/110	Loving Your Work	Colleagues & Co-Workers Lovers	28-54	Achieving Career Goals 60s & 70s	Creative Expression

After-View Feelings Key: Feel Better/Uplift Laughing Release Crying Release Violent Content **Boldface** See description in Chapter 8

After-View Feeling	Movie Title	Date/ Run Time	Work & Prosperity	Relationships	Finding Love	Transitions	Overcoming Obstacles
	Terms of Endearment	1983/129		Parent/Child Lovers	20s 55-81 28-54	Courting Marrying Losing Mate	Loss Entrapment
	Texasville	1990/123	Balancing Work & Family	Lovers Married Couples	28-54 Teen Years	Mid-Life Crisis 30s & 40s	Entrapment Class Prejudice
	35 Up (See *25 Up.*)	1992/127	Realizing Dreams	Lovers Married Couples Parent/Child	Teen Years 20s 28-54	Courting Marrying Achieving Career Goals	Class Prejudice Creative Expression
	This Is Spinal Tap	1984/82	Loving Your Work	Colleagues & Co-Workers		Achieving Career Goals	Creative Expression
	Thousand Pieces of Gold	1991/105	Realizing Dreams	Lovers Colleagues & Co-Workers	28-54	Achieving Career Goals Courting	Racial Prejudice Sexual Prejudice
	3 Men and a Baby	1987/102	Balancing Work & Family	Single Parent Lovers	28-54	Becoming Parent	Sexual Prejudice
	3 Men and a Little Lady	1990/100	Balancing Work & Family	Lovers Single Parent	28-54	Courting	Sexual Prejudice
	Three Days of the Condor	1975/117	Destructuring Workplace	Colleagues & Co-Workers		Losing Job	Entrapment Adventure
	Three of Hearts	1993/97		Lovers	28-54	Changing Careers Courting	Loss
	Tin Cup	1996/133	Realizing Dreams	Lovers Colleagues & Co-Workers	28-54	Achieving Career Goals	Creative Expression
	To Die For	1995/107	Realizing Dreams	Married Couples Colleagues & Co-Workers		Achieving Career Goals	Creative Expression

After-View Feeling	Movie Title	Date/ Run Time	Work & Prosperity	Relationships	Finding Love	Transitions	Overcoming Obstacles
Feel Better/Uplift, Crying Release	To Gillian on Her 37th Birthday	1996/92		Married Couples Parent/Child		Losing Mate Teen Years	Loss
Feel Better/Uplift	To Kill a Mockingbird	1962/129	Balancing Work & Family	Parent/Child Colleagues & Co-Workers		Achieving Career Goals	Racial Prejudice
Feel Better/Uplift, Laughing Release	**Tootsie**	1982/110	Realizing Dreams	Breaking Old Patterns Lovers	28-54	Achieving Career Goals Courting	Sexual Prejudice Creative Expression
Feel Better/Uplift	Top Hat	1935/99		Lovers	28-54	Courting	Creative Expression
Feel Better/Uplift, Violent Content	**Town Like Alice, A**	1985/301	Realizing Dreams	Lovers Husband/Wife	20s 28-54	Courting	Class Prejudice War Loss
Feel Better/Uplift, Laughing Release	**Toy Story**	1995/84		Colleagues & Co-Workers		Living Together/Moving In	Entrapment
Feel Better/Uplift	Trading Places	1983/116	Loving Your Work	Colleagues & Co-Workers	20s	Landing First Job	Racial Prejudice Loss
Feel Better/Uplift, Laughing Release	**Truly, Madly, Deeply**	1991/89		Breaking Old Patterns Lovers	28-54	Losing Mate	Loss
Feel Better/Uplift, Laughing Release	**Truth About Cats and Dogs, The**	1996/97		Lovers Friends	20s	Courting	Entrapment
Feel Better/Uplift	Tucker: A Man and His Dream	1988/111	Collaborating w/ Colleagues	Colleagues & Co-Workers		Achieving Career Goals	Creative Expression
Feel Better/Uplift, Laughing Release	**Tune in Tomorrow**	1990/90	Loving Your Work Collaborating w/ Colleagues	Boss/Employee Married Couples	Radical Age Differences	Marrying Achieving Career Goals	Creative Expression

After-View Feelings Key: Feel Better/Uplift · Laughing Release · Crying Release · Violent Content · **Boldface** See description in Chapter 8

After-View Feeling	Movie Title	Date/ Run Time	Work & Prosperity	Relationships	Finding Love	Transitions	Overcoming Obstacles
	28 Up (See *35 Up.*)	1985/261	Realizing Dreams	Parent/Child Lovers Married Couples	Teen Years 20s 28-54	Achieving Career Goals Courting Marrying	Class Prejudice Creative Expression
	Twins	1988/112		Siblings Lovers	28-54		Loss
	Two for the Road	1967/112	Balancing Work & Family	Colleagues & Co-Workers	College Years 20s 28-54	Courting Living Together/Moving In Marrying	Loss Entrapment
	2001: a Space Odyssey **2010**	1968/141 1984/114	Collaborating w/ Colleagues	Colleagues & Co-Workers Boss/Employee		Achieving Career Goals	Adventure Entrapment
	Ulee's Gold	1997/111		Parent/Child Multi-Generation Family		Mid-50s Passage	Loss
	Unbearable Lightness of Being	1988/171	Balancing Work & Family	Lovers	20s 28-54	Courting Living Together/Moving In Marrying	War Entrapment Loss
	Uncle Buck	1989/100		Single Parent	28-54	Mid-Life Crisis 30s & 40s Changing Careers	Entrapment
	Unexpected Family, An	1996/93		Parent/Child Lovers		Becoming Parent	Entrapment
	Unstrung Heroes	1995/93		Parent/Child Married Couples		Pre-Teen Years Losing Mate	Loss
	Untamed Heart	1993/102		Lovers	20s	Losing Mate	Physical Abilities Loss

After-View Feeling	Movie Title	Date/ Run Time	Work & Prosperity	Relationships	Finding Love	Transitions	Overcoming Obstacles
Feel Better/Uplift	**Used People**	1992/115		Lovers Multi-Generation Family Breaking Old Patterns	55-81	Losing Mate Courting	Loss Age Prejudice
Feel Better/Uplift	Valmont	1989/137		Lovers	Radical Age Differences 28-54	Teen Years Marrying	Entrapment
Feel Better/Uplift, Laughing Release	Very Brady Sequel, A	1996/90	Collaborating w/ Colleagues Loving Your Work	Siblings Parent/Child Lovers	Teen Years	Courting Teen Years	
Feel Better/Uplift	**Visions of Light**	1992/95	Realizing Dreams	Colleagues & Co-Workers		Achieving Career Goals	Creative Expression
Feel Better/Uplift, Laughing Release	**Waiting for Guffman**	1996/84		Colleagues & Co-Workers		Achieving Career Goals	Creative Expression
Feel Better/Uplift	Waiting to Exhale	1995/120		Lovers Married Couples Friends	28-54	Divorcing Courting	Entrapment
Feel Better/Uplift	Walk in the Clouds	1995/103		Lovers	College Years	Courting	Class Prejudice
Feel Better/Uplift, Laughing Release	Walking and Talking	1996/86		Lovers Friends	28-54	Courting Marrying	Entrapment
Feel Better/Uplift, Crying Release	Waterdance, The	1992/106	Balancing Work & Family	Lovers Friends	28-54		Physical Abilities
Feel Better/Uplift, Crying Release	Way We Were, The	1973/118		Breaking Old Patterns Lovers	College Years 20s	Courting Marrying	Class Prejudice Entrapment
Feel Better/Uplift, Laughing Release	**Wedding Banquet, The**	1993/111		Lovers Parent/Child	28-54	Courting	Sexual Prejudice Entrapment

After-View Feelings Key: Feel Better/Uplift · Laughing Release · Crying Release · Violent Content · **Boldface** See description in Chapter 8

After-View Feeling	Movie Title	Date/ Run Time	Work & Prosperity	Relationships	Finding Love	Transitions	Overcoming Obstacles
	Welcome Home, Roxy Carmichael	1990/98		Parent/Child		Teen Years	Loss
	Welcome to the Dollhouse	1995/87		Parent/Child Teacher/Student Siblings		Pre-Teen Years	
	What's Eating Gilbert Grape?	1993/118		Parent/Child Siblings		Living Together/Moving In	Entrapment
	When a Man Loves a Woman	1994/126		Married Couples		Marrying	Physical Abilities
	When Harry Met Sally	1989/96	Balancing Work & Family	Lovers Friends	College Years 28-54	Courting	Loss
	Where's Poppa?	1970/82	Loving Your Work	Elder Care Lovers	28-54	Mid-Life Crisis 30s & 40s	Entrapment
	Who Framed Roger Rabbit?	1988/103		Lovers	28-54	Achieving Career Goals Losing Mate	Loss
	Widow's Peak	1994/101		Multi-Generation Family Friends	28-54	Losing Mate	Loss
	Woman of the Year	1942/112	Loving Your Work	Two-Career Couples	28-54	Living Together/Moving In Achieving Career Goals	Creative Expression
	Wonderful, Horrible Life of Leni Riefenstahl, The	1993/182	Realizing Dreams Changing Careers	Colleagues & Co-Workers		After Retirement	Creative Expression

After-View Feeling	Movie Title	Date/ Run Time	Work & Prosperity	Relationships	Finding Love	Transitions	Overcoming Obstacles
Feel Better/Uplift, Laughing Release	**Working Girl**	1988/115		Boss/Employee Lovers	28-54	Late 20s to 30s Passage 20s to 30s Passage Changing Careers	Class Prejudice Entrapment
Crying Release	**Wuthering Heights (1939)**	1939/103	Loving Your Work	Lovers	Teen Years	Moving Out/Separating	Class Prejudice
Feel Better/Uplift, Violent Content	**Year of Living Dangerously, The**	1983/114	Loving Your Work	Lovers Colleagues & Co-Workers	28-54	Achieving Career Goals	War Entrapment
Feel Better/Uplift	Year of the Comet	1992/89		Lovers Boss/Employee	28-54	Achieving Career Goals	Adventure
Feel Better/Uplift	You Were Never Lovelier	1942/97		Parent/Child Lovers	Radical Age Differences	Marrying	Creative Expression

After-View Feelings Key: Feel Better/Uplift · Laughing Release · Crying Release · Violent Content · **Boldface** See description in Chapter 8

Life's Changes Cross-Index

All 501 movies are sorted by after-view feeling, and by life change category.

After-View Feeling Index

Feel Better

Adam's Rib
Airplane
Aladdin
All the President's Men
Amadeus
American Graffiti
American President
Angels and Insects
Annie Hall
Apollo 13
Associate, The
Atlantic City
Austin Powers
Avalon
Babe
Baby Boom
Back to School
Back to the Future
Backbeat
Bad and the Beautiful, The
Bagdad Cafe
Ballad of Little Jo, The
Barbarians at the Gate
Barcelona
Batteries Not Included
Beautiful Dreamers
Beautiful Girls
Beauty and the Beast
Before Sunrise
Being There
Benny & Joon
Big
Big Chill, The
Big Easy, The
Big Night
Big Picture, The
Birdcage, The
Blazing Saddles
Bodyguard, The
Boys On the Side
Breaker Morant
Breaking Away
Breaking In
Brideshead Revisited
Brief History in Time, A
Broadcast News
Bronco Billy
Brother From Another Planet, The
Brothers McMullen, The
Buddy Holly Story, The
Bull Durham
Bullets Over Broadway
Butch Cassidy and the Sundance Kid
Bye Bye Blues
Bye Bye, Love
Can't Buy Me Love
Casablanca
Celluloid Closet, The
Cemetery Club
Chances Are
Chaplin
Charade
Chariots of Fire
Children of a Lesser God
Circle of Friends
Citizen Kane
City Slickers
Clara's Heart
Clerks
Cliffhanger
Close Encounters of a Third Kind
Clueless
Coal Miner's Daughter, The
Cocoon
Cold Comfort Farm
Cold Sassy Tree
Conrack
Contact
Cool Runnings
Corrina, Corrina
Cousin Bobby
Cousins
"Crocodile" Dundee
Crossing Delancy
Cutting Edge, The
Dances with Wolves
Dangerous Liaisons
Dangerous Minds
Dave
Dead Again
Dead Poets Society
Deep Cover
Desk Set
Desperately Seeking Susan
Devil in a Blue Dress
Diary of a Hit Man
Diary of a Mad Housewife
Diner
Dirty Dancing
Dominick and Eugene
Don Juan deMarco
Down and Out in Beverly Hills
Dr. Strangelove
Dragon: the Bruce Lee Story
Driving Miss Daisy
E.T.–The Extra Terrestrial
Earth Girls Are Easy
Ed Wood
Ed's Next Move
Educating Rita
El Norte
Electric Horseman
Emerald Forest, The
Emma
Empire Strikes Back
Enchanted April
English Patient, The
Excalibur
Fabulous Baker Boys, The
Fame
Far and Away
Father of the Bride
Ferris Bueller's Day Off
Field of Dreams
Finnegan Begin Again
Firm, The
First Wives Club, The
Fish Called Wanda, A
Fisher King, The
Five Easy Pieces
Five Heartbeats, The
Flashdance
Flirting with Disaster
For the Boys
Forever Young
Forrest Gump
Four Seasons, The
Four Weddings and a Funeral
Frankie Starlight
French Lieutenant's Woman, The
Freshman, The
Fried Green Tomatoes
Full Monty, The
Gaby, A True Story
Gay Divorcee
Gentleman's Agreement
George of the Jungle
Get Shorty
Ghost
Ghost and Mrs. Muir, The
Ghostbusters
Giant
Godfather Trilogy, The
Gods Must Be Crazy, The
Gone with the Wind
Good Man in Africa, A
Good Morning Vietnam
Goodbye, Columbus
Gorillas in the Mist
Grace of My Heart
Graduate, The
Grass Harp, The
Great Santini, The
Green Card
Grey Fox, The
Groundhog Day

Feel Better *(cont'd)*

Grumpy Old Men
Happy Together
Hard Day's Night
Harold and Maude
Harvey
Hear My Song
Heart Like a Wheel
Hearts of Darkness
Heaven Can Wait
His Girl Friday
Holiday
Hollywood Shuffle
Home of Our Own, A
Honey, I Shrunk the Kids
Hoop Dreams
Hope and Glory
House Party
How to Make an American Quilt
I Love You to Death
I Was a Male War Bride
I've Heard the Mermaids Singing
Impromptu
In Love with an Older Woman
In the Line of Fire
In the Mood
Incredibly True Adventure of Two Girls in Love
Indiana Jones Trilogy
Inner Circle, The
Irreconcilable Differences
It Happened One Night
It's a Wonderful Life
Jerry Maguire
Jewel in the Crown, The
Karate Kid, The
Kindergarten Cop
L.A. Confidential
L.A. Story
La Bamba
Lady From Shanghai, The
Last Picture Show, The
Laura
Lawnmower Man, The
Lawrence of Arabia
League of Their Own, A
Lemon Sisters, The
Liar, Liar
Lianna
Little Romance, A
Little Women
Live Nude Girls
Local Hero
Lone Star
Lonely Hearts
Long Walk Home, The
Lorenzo's Oil
Losing Chase
Love Affair (1994)
Lucas
Mac
Madness of King George, The
Magnificent Ambersons, The
Major League
Making Mr. Right
Malcolm X
Mambo Kings, The
Man Who Fell to Earth
Manufacturing Consent
Map of the Human Heart
Married to It
Marva Collins Story, The
Marvin's Room
Mask
Melvin & Howard
Michael
Mighty Aphrodite
Mighty Quinn, The
Miracle on 34th Street
Miracle, The
Mississippi Masala
Month By the Lake, A
Mother
Mr. Blandings Builds His Dream House
Mr. Holland's Opus
Mr. Mom
Mrs. Doubtfire
Much Ado About Nothing
My Cousin Vinny
My Family (Mi Familia)
My Favorite Year
My Left Foot
My Life as a Dog
My Little Chickadee
Mystic Pizza
Natural, The
Nell
Never Cry Wolf
Night at the Opera, A
Night We Never Met, The
Nina Takes a Lover
Nine to Five
Norma Rae
Not Without My Daughter
Nothing in Common
Now and Then
On Golden Pond
Once Were Warriors
One Against the Wind
One Flew over the Cuckoo's Nest
One Trick Pony
Only You
Paper, The
Parenthood
Paris is Burning
Pat and Mike
Personal Best
Persuasion
Peter's Friends
Phar Lap
Phenomenon
Philadelphia Story, The
Piano, The
Planes, Trains & Automobiles
Playboys, The
Pontiac Moon
Powder
Pretty Woman
Pride and Prejudice
Priest
Princess Bride
Princess Caraboo
Priscilla, Queen of the Desert
Private Benjamin
Private Parts
Queen of Hearts
Quiz Show
Raiders of the Lost Ark
Rain Man
Rambling Rose
Razor's Edge, The
Reality Bites
Rebecca
Regarding Henry
Restoration
Resurrection
Return of the Jedi
Right Stuff, The
Risky Business
Rocketeer, The
Rocky
Roman Holiday
Romancing the Stone
Room with a View, A
Roommates
Roots
Rosalie Goes Shopping
Ruby in Paradise
Rudy
Ruthless People
Sabrina
Same Time, Next Year
Scrooged
Search for Signs of Intelligent Life in the Universe, The
Searchers, The
Searching for Bobby Fisher
Secret Life of Walter Mitty, The
Secret of Roan Inish, The
Secrets and Lies
Sense and Sensibility
Sex, Lies, & Videotape
Shall We Dance?
Shawshank Redemption
She Done Him Wrong
She's Gotta Have It
She's the One
Shine
Singin' in the Rain
Singles
Sister Act

Six Degrees of Separation
Slap Shot
Sleepless in Seattle
Small Wonders
Smoke
Sneakers
Soapdish
Some Like It Hot
Soul Food
Splash
Stakeout
Stand and Deliver
Stand By Me
Star Trek IV: The Voyage Home
Star Wars Trilogy
Starting Over
State of the Union
Stealing Beauty
Sting, The
Strictly Ballroom
Superman
Sure Thing, The
Swing Time
Swingers
Taking Care of Business
Taking off
Tap
Terms of Endearment
Texasville
35 Up
This Is Spinal Tap
Thousand Pieces of Gold
3 Men and a Baby
3 Men and a Little Lady
Three Days of the Condor
Three of Hearts
Tin Cup
To Gillian On Her 37th Birthday
To Kill a Mockingbird
Tootsie
Top Hat
Town Like Alice, A
Toy Story
Trading Places
Truly, Madly, Deeply
Truth About Cats and Dogs, The
Tucker: A Man and His Dream
Tune in Tomorrow
28 Up
2010
Twins
Two for the Road
2001: A Space Odyssey
Ulee's Gold
Uncle Buck
Unexpected Family, An
Used People
Valmont
Very Brady Sequel, A
Visions of Light
Waiting for Guffman
Waiting to Exhale
Walk in the Clouds
Walking and Talking
Waterdance, The
Way We Were, The
Wedding Banquet, The
Welcome Home, Roxy Carmichael
What's Eating Gilbert Grape?
When Harry Met Sally
Where's Poppa?
Who Framed Roger Rabbit?
Widow's Peak
Woman of the Year
Wonderful, Horrible Life of Leni Riefenstahl, The
Working Girl
Year of Living Dangerously, The
Year of the Comet
You Were Never Lovelier

Laughing Release

Adam's Rib
Airplane!
Aladdin
Annie Hall
Associate, The
Austin Powers
Babe
Back to School
Back to the Future
Barbarians at the Gate
Barcelona
Beautiful Girls
Beverly Hills Cop
Big
Big Night
Big Picture, The
Birdcage, The
Blazing Saddles
Breaking Away
Brother From Another Planet, The
Brothers McMullen, The
Bull Durham
Bullets Over Broadway
Bye Bye, Love
Can't Buy Me Love
City Slickers
Clerks
Clueless
Cocoon
Cold Comfort Farm
Cool Runnings
Corrina, Corrina
"Crocodile" Dundee
Dave
Desk Set
Desperately Seeking Susan
Diner
Down and Out in Beverly Hills
Dr. Strangelove
Earth Girls Are Easy
Ed Wood
Ed's Next Move
Emma
Enchanted April
Fargo
Father of the Bride
Finnegan Begin Again
First Wives Club, The
Fish Called Wanda, A
Flirting with Disaster
Forrest Gump
Four Weddings and a Funeral
Freshman, The
Fried Green Tomatoes
Full Monty, The
Gaby, A True Story
George of the Jungle
Get Shorty
Ghostbusters
Gods Must Be Crazy, The
Good Morning Vietnam
Goodbye, Columbus
Graduate, The
Groundhog Day
Grumpy Old Men
Harvey
Hear My Song
His Girl Friday
Hollywood Shuffle
Home for the Holidays
Honey, I Shrunk the Kids
In & Out
Incredibly True Adventure of Two Girls in Love
Irreconcilable Differences
It Happened One Night
It's a Wonderful Life
Jerry Maguire
L.A. Story
Liar, Liar
Living in Oblivion
Lonely Hearts
Lucas
Madness of King George, The
Major League
Making Mr. Right
Melvin & Howard
Mighty Aphrodite
Mother
Mr. Blandings Builds His Dream House
Mr. Mom
Mrs. Doubtfire
Much Ado About Nothing
My Cousin Vinny
My Favorite Year
My Life as a Dog
Little Chickadee

Laughing Release *(cont'd)*

One Flew over the Cuckoo's Nest
Only You
Parenthood
Pat and Mike
Peter's Friends
Planes, Trains & Automobiles
Player, The
Pride and Prejudice
Priscilla, Queen of the Desert
Private Benjamin
Private Parts
Queen of Hearts
Roger & Me
Romancing the Stone
Room with a View, A
Roommates
Rosalie Goes Shopping
Ruthless People
Same Time, Next Year
Scrooged
Search for Signs of Intelligent Life in the Universe, The
Secret Life of Walter Mitty, The
Sense and Sensibility
She Done Him Wrong
She's Gotta Have It
She's the One
Shine
Sister Act
Slap Shot
Soapdish
Some Like It Hot
Splash
State of the Union
Strictly Ballroom
Sure Thing, The
Swingers
Taking Care of Business
Taking off
Terms of Endearment
This Is Spinal Tap
3 Men and a Baby
To Die For
Tootsie
Toy Story
Truly, Madly, Deeply
Truth About Cats and Dogs, The
Tune in Tomorrow
Twins
Two for the Road
Uncle Buck
Very Brady Sequel, A
Waiting for Guffman
Walking and Talking
Wedding Banquet, The
When Harry Met Sally
Where's Poppa?
Who Framed Roger Rabbit?
Widow's Peak
Woman of the Year
Working Girl

Crying Release

Affair to Remember, An
Avalon
Baby Boom
Backbeat
Beaches
Boys On the Side
Bridges of Madison County
Clara's Heart
Color Purple, The
Cry, The Beloved Country
Cure, The
Dances with Wolves
Dark Victory
Dead Poets Society
Dirty Dozen
Doctor Zhivago
Dominick and Eugene
English Patient, The
Forever Young
Gone with the Wind
Goodbye, Mr. Chips
Gorillas in the Mist
Grass Harp, The
Great Santini, The
Heart Like a Wheel
Home of Our Own, A
In Love with an Older Woman
It's a Wonderful Life
Jewel in the Crown, The
Joy Luck Club
Little Women
Lorenzo's Oil
Losing Isaiah
Love Affair
Marvin's Room
Mr. Holland's Opus
Music Box
My Family (Mi Familia)
My Life
Not Without My Daughter
On Golden Pond
Ordinary People
Parenthood
Phar Lap
Phenomenon
Philadelphia
Powder
Queen of Hearts
River Runs Through It, A
Roots
Rose, The
Secrets and Lies
Shadowlands
Sleepless in Seattle
Some Mother's Son
Spitfire Grill, The
Star is Born, A
Starman
Steel Magnolias
Summer of '42
Terms of Endearment
To Gillian On Her 37th Birthday
Two for the Road
Unbearable Lightness of Being
Unexpected Family, An
Unstrung Heroes
Untamed Heart
Waterdance, The
Way We Were, The
Welcome to the Dollhouse
When a Man Loves a Woman
Where's Poppa?
Wuthering Heights

Violent Content

Angels and Insects
Apocalypse Now
Beverly Hills Cop
Big Easy, The
Blazing Saddles
Bodyguard, The
Boys On the Side
Bullets Over Broadway
Casablanca
Cliffhanger
Close Encounters of a Third Kind
Color Purple, The
"Crocodile" Dundee
Dances with Wolves
Dead Again
Deep Cover
Devil in a Blue Dress
Diary of a Hit Man
Dirty Dozen
Doctor Zhivago
Dominick and Eugene
Dr. Strangelove
Dragon: the Bruce Lee Story
El Norte
Empire Strikes Back
Excalibur
Far and Away
Fargo
Fat Man and Little Boy
Firm, The
Ghost
Godfather Trilogy, The
Gone with the Wind
Good Man in Africa, A
Good Morning Vietnam
Great Santini, The
Grey Fox, The
In the Line of Fire

Indiana Jones Trilogy
Jewel in the Crown, The
Kindergarten Cop
L.A. Confidential
Lady From Shanghai, The
Lawnmower Man, The
Lawrence of Arabia
Lone Star
Malcolm X
Map of the Human Heart
Mighty Quinn, The
Natural, The
Once Were Warriors
One Against the Wind
Piano, The
Player, The
Priscilla, Queen of the Desert
Raiders of the Lost Ark
Return of the Jedi
Rocky
Scrooged
Searchers, The
Sneakers
Stakeout
Star Wars Trilogy
Three Days of the Condor
Three of Hearts
Town Like Alice, A
Ulee's Gold
Who Framed Roger Rabbit?
Year of Living Dangerously, The

Work & Prosperity

Loving Your Work

All the President's Men
Angels and Insects
Austin Powers
Big Night
Brief History in Time, A
Celluloid Closet, The
Citizen Kane
Cliffhanger
Cold Sassy Tree
Conrack
"Crocodile" Dundee
Cutting Edge, The
Dangerous Minds
Deep Cover
Dirty Dancing
Ed Wood
Gentleman's Agreement
Goodbye, Mr. Chips
Gorillas in the Mist
Grace of My Heart
Hearts of Darkness
Impromptu
In the Line of Fire
Indiana Jones Trilogy
Lawnmower Man, The
Living in Oblivion
Lone Star
Major League
Making Mr. Right
Marva Collins Story, The
My Little Chickadee
Never Cry Wolf
One Trick Pony
Priest
Raiders of the Lost Ark
Resurrection
Right Stuff, The
Romancing the Stone
She Done Him Wrong
Singin' in the Rain
Small Wonders
Strictly Ballroom
Tap
This Is Spinal Tap
Trading Places
Tune in Tomorrow
Visions of Light
Who Framed Roger Rabbit?
Wonderful, Horrible Life of Leni Riefenstahl, The
Year of Living Dangerously, The
Year of the Comet

Realizing Dreams

Aladdin
Amadeus
Apollo 13
Associate, The
Avalon
Babe
Back to the Future
Backbeat
Bagdad Cafe
Ballad of Little Jo, The
Barbarians at the Gate
Beaches
Beautiful Dreamers
Beautiful Girls
Big
Big Chill, The
Big Night
Big Picture, The
Breaking Away
Bronco Billy
Buddy Holly Story, The
Bull Durham
Can't Buy Me Love
Chariots of Fire
City Slickers
Coal Miner's Daughter, The
Cocoon
Cold Sassy Tree
Color Purple, The
Contact
Cool Runnings
Cousin Bobby
Dead Poets Society
Diary of a Hit Man
Dirty Dancing
Doctor Zhivago
Dragon: the Bruce Lee Story
Educating Rita
El Norte
Electric Horseman
Empire Strikes Back
Excalibur
Fame
Far and Away
Ferris Bueller's Day Off
Field of Dreams
Fisher King, The
Five Heartbeats, The
Flashdance
For the Boys
Get Shorty
Giant
Godfather Trilogy, The
Gone with the Wind
Green Card
Hear My Song
Heart Like a Wheel
Holiday
Hollywood Shuffle
Hoop Dreams
I've Heard the Mermaids Singing
It's a Wonderful Life
Karate Kid, The
La Bamba
Lawrence of Arabia
League of Their Own, A
Lemon Sisters, The
Magnificent Ambersons, The
Malcolm X
Mambo Kings, The
Map of the Human Heart
Melvin & Howard
Miracle on 34th Street
Mississippi Masala
Mr. Holland's Opus
My Cousin Vinny
My Left Foot
Mystic Pizza
Natural, The
Night We Never Met, The
Norma Rae
Paris is Burning
Personal Best
Peter's Friends
Phar Lap
Princess Bride
Private Parts
Razor's Edge, The
Reality Bites
Restoration
Return of the Jedi
Risky Business
Rocketeer, The
Rocky
Room with a View, A
Roots

Realizing Dreams (cont'd)

Ruby in Paradise
Rudy
Ruthless People
Sabrina
Search for Signs of Intelligent Life in the Universe, The
Secret Life of Walter Mitty, The
Shine
Splash
Stand and Deliver
Star Wars Trilogy
Strictly Ballroom
35 Up
Thousand Pieces of Gold
Tin Cup
To Die For
Tootsie
Town Like Alice, A
Tucker: A Man and His Dream
28 Up
Waiting for Guffman
Working Girl

Balancing Work & Family

Adam's Rib
American President
Baby Boom
Bodyguard, The
Broadcast News
Bye Bye Blues
Chaplin
Cousins
Dave
Dominick and Eugene
Down and Out in Beverly Hills
Godfather Trilogy, The
Gorillas in the Mist
Grace of My Heart
Great Santini, The
Heart Like a Wheel
His Girl Friday
Honey, I Shrunk the Kids
Inner Circle, The
Irreconcilable Differences
It's a Wonderful Life
Jerry Maguire
Liar, Liar
Long Walk Home, The
Mac
Married to It
Mighty Quinn, The
Miracle on 34th Street
Mr. Blandings Builds His Dream House
Nine to Five
Nothing in Common
Paper, The
Parenthood
Regarding Henry
Rosalie Goes Shopping
Rose, The
Scrooged
Shadowlands
Slap Shot
Soapdish
Soul Food
Star is Born, A
Texasville
3 Men and a Baby
3 Men and a Little Lady
To Kill a Mockingbird
Two for the Road
Uncle Buck
Way We Were, The
Where's Poppa?

Collaborating w/ Colleagues

Airplane!
All the President's Men
Associate, The
Atlantic City
Babe
Backbeat
Bad and the Beautiful, The
Being There
Beverly Hills Cop
Big Easy, The
Big Picture, The
Blazing Saddles
Breaker Morant
Breaking In
Bull Durham
Bullets Over Broadway
Butch Cassidy and the Sundance Kid
Casablanca
Celluloid Closet, The
Chaplin
Chariots of Fire
Citizen Kane
Clerks
Close Encounters of a Third Kind
Cocoon
Cool Runnings
Cutting Edge, The
Dances with Wolves
Dave
Dead Again
Deep Cover
Devil in a Blue Dress
Dirty Dozen
Dr. Strangelove
Driving Miss Daisy
E.T.–The Extra Terrestrial
Excalibur
Fabulous Baker Boys,The
Fargo
Fat Man and Little Boy
Firm, The
Fish Called Wanda, A
Five Heartbeats, The
For the Boys
Freshman, The
Fried Green Tomatoes
Full Monty, The
Ghostbusters
Good Man in Africa, A
Grey Fox, The
Groundhog Day
Hard Day's Night
Hearts of Darkness
Kindergarden Cop
L.A. Confidential
Lady From Shanghai, The
Lawrence of Arabia
League of Their Own, A
Living in Oblivion
Local Hero
Major League
My Cousin Vinny
My Little Chickadee
Night at the Opera, A
One Against the Wind
Pat and Mike
Philadelphia
Player, The
Private Benjamin
Right Stuff, The
Rocketeer, The
Sister Act
Slap Shot
Sneakers
Soapdish
Some Like It Hot
Stakeout
Star Trek IV: The Voyage Home
Sting, The
Stunt Man, The
Taking Care of Business
Tucker: A Man and His Dream
Tune in Tomorrow
2010
2001: A Space Odyssey
Visions of Light

Destructuring Workplace

Adam's Rib
Broadcast News
Desk Set
Dr. Strangelove
Full Monty, The
Last Picture Show, The
Magnificent Ambersons, The
Manufacturing Consent
Mr. Mom
Nine to Five
Paper, The
Player, The
Roger & Me
Three Days of the Condor

Relationships

Lovers

Affair to Remember, An
Airplane!
Aladdin
American Graffiti
American President
Angels and Insects
Annie Hall
Atlantic City
Austin Powers
Baby Boom
Back to School
Back to the Future
Ballad of Little Jo, The
Barcelona
Beautiful Girls
Beauty and the Beast
Before Sunrise
Benny & Joon
Big
Big Chill, The
Big Easy, The
Big Picture, The
Birdcage, The
Bodyguard, The
Boys On the Side
Brideshead Revisited
Bridges of Madison County
Broadcast News
Brother From Another Planet, The
Brothers McMullen, The
Bull Durham
Butch Cassidy and the Sundance Kid
Can't Buy Me Love
Casablanca
Cemetery Club
Chances Are
Chaplin
Charade
Children of a Lesser God
Circle of Friends
Cold Comfort Farm
Cold Sassy Tree
Contact
Corrina, Corrina
Cousins
"Crocodile" Dundee
Crossing Delancy
Cutting Edge, The
Dances with Wolves
Dangerous Liaisons
Dark Victory
Dave
Dead Again
Desk Set
Desperately Seeking Susan
Diner
Dirty Dancing
Doctor Zhivago
Dominick and Eugene
Don Juan deMarco
Earth Girls Are Easy
Ed's Next Move
Electric Horseman
English Patient, The
Excalibur
Fabulous Baker Boys, The
Far and Away
Ferris Bueller's Day Off
Finnegan Begin Again
Fish Called Wanda, A
Fisher King, The
Five Easy Pieces
Flashdance
Forever Young
Forrest Gump
Four Seasons, The
Four Weddings and a Funeral
Frankie Starlight
French Lieutenant's Woman, The
Freshman, The
Gaby, A True Story
Gay Divorcee
George of the Jungle
Get Shorty
Ghost and Mrs. Muir, The
Gone with the Wind
Good Morning Vietnam
Goodbye, Columbus
Gorillas in the Mist
Graduate, The
Grass Harp, The
Grey Fox, The
Groundhog Day
Happy Together
Harold and Maude
Hear My Song
Holiday
Home for the Holidays
House Party
How to Make an American Quilt
Impromptu
In Love with an Older Woman
In & Out
In the Line of Fire
Incredibly True Adventure of Two Girls in Love
It Happened One Night
Jewel in the Crown, The
L.A. Story
Last Picture Show, The
Laura
Little Romance, A
Little Women
Lone Star
Lonely Hearts
Love Affair
Lucas
Making Mr. Right
Mambo Kings, The
Man Who Fell to Earth
Map of the Human Heart
Married to It
Michael
Mighty Aphrodite
Miracle on 34th Street
Mississippi Masala
Month By the Lake, A
Much Ado About Nothing
My Cousin Vinny
Mystic Pizza
Natural, The
Night We Never Met, The
Only You
Pat and Mike
Personal Best
Persuasion
Phenomenon
Piano, The
Playboys, The
Player, The
Pretty Woman
Pride and Prejudice
Priest
Princess Bride
Rambling Rose
Razor's Edge, The
Reality Bites
Restoration
Resurrection
Rocketeer, The
Rocky
Roman Holiday
Romancing the Stone
Room with a View, A
Ruby in Paradise
Sabrina
Same Time, Next Year
Scrooged
Search for Signs of Intelligent Life in the Universe, The
Secret Life of Walter Mitty, The
She Done Him Wrong
She's Gotta Have It
She's the One
Singin' in the Rain
Singles
Slap Shot
Sleepless in Seattle
Smoke
Soapdish
Some Like It Hot
Spitfire Grill, The
Splash
Stakeout
Starman
Starting Over
Stealing Beauty
Strictly Ballroom
Stunt Man, The
Summer of '42

Lovers *(cont'd.)*

Superman
Sure Thing, The
Swing Time
Swingers
Tap
Terms of Endearment
Texasville
35 Up
Thousand Pieces of Gold
3 Men and a Baby
3 Men and a Little Lady
Three of Hearts
Tin Cup
Tootsie
Top Hat
Town Like Alice, A
Truly, Madly, Deeply
Truth About Cats and Dogs, The
28 Up
Twins
Unbearable Lightness of Being
Unexpected Family, An
Untamed Heart
Used People
Valmont
Very Brady Sequel, A
Waiting to Exhale
Walk in the Clouds
Walking and Talking
Waterdance, The
Way We Were, The
Wedding Banquet, The
When Harry Met Sally
Where's Poppa?
Who Framed Roger Rabbit?
Working Girl
Wuthering Heights
Year of Living Dangerously, The
Year of the Comet
You Were Never Lovelier

Married Couples

Angels and Insects
Birdcage, The
Brothers McMullen, The
Dead Again
Diary of a Mad Housewife
Don Juan deMarco
Enchanted April
Father of the Bride
Flirting with Disaster
Four Seasons, The
Full Monty, The
Green Card
Grumpy Old Men
Honey, I Shrunk the Kids
Lianna
Long Walk Home, The
Losing Chase
Mighty Aphrodite
Mr. Blandings Builds His Dream House
Mr. Holland's Opus
My Life
Nina Takes a Lover
Once Were Warriors
One Trick Pony
Ordinary People
Private Parts
Sex, Lies, & Videotape
Shadowlands
She's the One
Shine
Six Degrees of Separation
Soul Food
Stealing Beauty
Texasville
35 Up
To Die For
To Gillian On Her 37th Birthday
Tune in Tomorrow
28 Up
Unstrung Heroes
Waiting to Exhale
When a Man Loves a Woman

Two-Career Couples

Adam's Rib
Big Chill, The
For the Boys
Gorillas in the Mist
Grace of My Heart
Grey Fox, The
Heart Like a Wheel
Irreconcilable Differences
Mr. Mom
Mrs. Doubtfire
Rose, The
Shall We Dance?
Singin' in the Rain
Star is Born, A
A Starting Over
State of the Union
Woman of the Year

Divorced Couples

Bye Bye, Love
Clara's Heart
First Wives Club, The
Four Seasons, The
His Girl Friday
Liar, Liar
Melvin & Howard
Mighty Quinn, The
Mrs. Doubtfire
Music Box
Not Without My Daughter
Parenthood
Philadelphia Story, The
Starting Over

Parent/Child

Aladdin
Amadeus
Baby Boom
Back to School
Back to the Future
Beauty and the Beast
Birdcage, The
Breaking Away
Bye Bye Blues
Bye Bye, Love
Chances Are
Clueless
Corrina, Corrina
Cry, The Beloved Country
Dead Poets Society
Dirty Dancing
Emerald Forest, The
Emma
Empire Strikes Back
Father of the Bride
Field of Dreams
Five Easy Pieces
Flirting with Disaster
Forrest Gump
Frankie Starlight
Gaby, A True Story
Get On the Bus
Gods Must Be Crazy, The
Graduate, The
Great Santini, The
Grumpy Old Men
Heart Like a Wheel
Home of Our Own, A
Honey, I Shrunk the Kids
I Love You to Death
In & Out
Incredibly True Adventure of Two Girls in Love
Indiana Jones Trilogy
Irreconcilable Differences
It Happened One Night
Jerry Maguire
Joy Luck Club
Kindergarten Cop
Laura
Liar, Liar
Little Women
Lone Star
Lorenzo's Oil
Losing Isaiah
Mac
Mask
Miracle on 34th Street
Miracle, The
Mississippi Masala
Mr. Blandings Builds His Dream House
Mr. Mom
Mrs. Doubtfire
Music Box
My Left Foot
My Life as a Dog
Nothing in Common

On Golden Pond
Once Were Warriors
Ordinary People
Parenthood
Philadelphia Story, The
Piano, The
Private Benjamin
Queen of Hearts
Quiz Show
Regarding Henry
Resurrection
Return of the Jedi
Risky Business
River Runs Through It, A
Rosalie Goes Shopping
Secret Life of Walter Mitty, The
Secret of Roan Inish, The
Secrets and Lies
Shadowlands
Shine
Sleepless in Seattle
Small Wonders
Smoke
Some Mother's Son
Star Wars Trilogy
Steel Magnolias
Strictly Ballroom
Terms of Endearment
35 Up
3 Men and a Baby
3 Men and a Little Lady
To Gillian On Her 37th Birthday
To Kill a Mockingbird
28 Up
Ulee's Gold
Uncle Buck
Unexpected Family, An
Unstrung Heroes
Very Brady Sequel, A
Wedding Banquet, The
Welcome Home, Roxy Carmichael
Welcome to the Dollhouse
What's Eating Gilbert Grape?
You Were Never Lovelier

Working Parents

Breaking Away
Parenthood
Rosalie Goes Shopping

Single Parent

Baby Boom
Bye Bye Blues
Bye Bye, Love
Home of Our Own, A
Jerry Maguire
Miracle on 34th Street
Sleepless in Seattle
Small Wonders
3 Men and a Baby
3 Men and a Little Lady
Uncle Buck

Multi-Generation Family

Avalon
Brideshead Revisited
Cocoon
Cold Comfort Farm
Cold Sassy Tree
Color Purple, The
Cousin Bobby
Crossing Delancy
Driving Miss Daisy
Field of Dreams
Giant
Godfather Trilogy, The
Gone with the Wind
Grass Harp, The
Grumpy Old Men
Home for the Holidays
Hope and Glory
It's a Wonderful Life
Jewel in the Crown, The
Joy Luck Club
Last Picture Show, The
Madness of King George, The
Magnificent Ambersons, The
Marvin's Room
My Family (Mi Familia)
Parenthood
Philadelphia
Queen of Hearts
Roommates
Roots
Searchers, The
She's the One
Soul Food
Steel Magnolias
Taking off
Terms of Endearment
Ulee's Gold
Used People
Wedding Banquet, The
Widow's Peak

Siblings

Beautiful Dreamers
Benny & Joon
Big Night
Brothers McMullen, The
Dominick and Eugene.
El Norte
Grass Harp, The
Harvey
Holiday
Home for the Holidays
Last Picture Show, The
Mambo Kings, The
My Life as a Dog
Rain Man
River Runs Through It, A
Secret of Roan Inish, The
Sense and Sensibility
Soul Food
Splash
Twins
Very Brady Sequel, A
Welcome to the Dollhouse
What's Eating Gilbert Grape?

Elder Care

Driving Miss Daisy
Finnegan Begin Again
Fried Green Tomatoes
Marvin's Room
Nothing in Common
On Golden Pond
Roommates
Where's Poppa?

Friends

American Graffiti
Backbeat
Beaches
Beautiful Dreamers
Beautiful Girls
Big
Big Chill, The
Boys On the Side
Breaking Away
Brideshead Revisited
Butch Cassidy and the Sundance Kid
Can't Buy Me Love
Casablanca
Cemetery Club
Circle of Friends
Class of '44
Color Purple, The
Cure, The
Desperately Seeking Susan
Diner
Down and Out in Beverly Hills
Driving Miss Daisy
E.T.–The Extra Terrestrial
Emma
Enchanted April
Four Weddings and a Funeral
Fried Green Tomatoes
Gentleman's Agreement
Ghost and Mrs. Muir, The
Ghostbusters
Great Santini, The
Grumpy Old Men
Hard Day's Night
Harvey
House Party
Lemon Sisters, The
Little Romance, A
Live Nude Girls
Melvin & Howard
Mighty Quinn, The
Miracle, The
Mystic Pizza

Friends *(cont'd)*

Nell
Nine to Five
Now and Then
One Flew over the Cuckoo's Nest
Paris is Burning
Peter's Friends
Planes, Trains & Automobiles
Powder
Search for Signs of Intelligent Life in the Universe, The
Sex, Lies, & Videotape
Singles
Six Degrees of Separation
Smoke
Some Mother's Son
Stand By Me
Stealing Beauty
Sting, The
Swingers
Truth About Cats and Dogs, The
Waiting to Exhale
Walking and Talking
Waterdance, The
When Harry Met Sally
Widow's Peak

Colleagues & Co-Workers

Airplane!
All the President's Men
Amadeus
Apocalypse Now
Apollo 13
Associate, The
Babe
Bad and the Beautiful, The
Barbarians at the Gate
Beverly Hills Cop
Big Easy, The
Big Picture, The
Blazing Saddles
Breaking In
Brief History in Time, A
Broadcast News
Bronco Billy
Brother From Another Planet, The
Buddy Holly Story, The
Bull Durham
Bullets Over Broadway
Butch Cassidy and the Sundance Kid
Bye Bye Blues
Casablanca
Celluloid Closet, The
Chariots of Fire
Cliffhanger
Close Encounters of a Third Kind
Cocoon
Contact
Cool Runnings
Cutting Edge, The
Dances with Wolves
Dangerous Liaisons
Dave
Deep Cover
Desk Set
Devil in a Blue Dress
Diary of a Hit Man
Dirty Dozen
Doctor Zhivago
Dr. Strangelove
Ed Wood
Empire Strikes Back
English Patient, The
Excalibur
Fabulous Baker Boys, The
Fame
Fargo
Fat Man and Little Boy
Fish Called Wanda, A
Five Heartbeats, The
Flashdance
For the Boys
Full Monty, The
Gentleman's Agreement
Get On the Bus
Get Shorty
Ghost
Ghostbusters
Good Man in Africa, A
Gorillas in the Mist
Groundhog Day
Hard Day's Night
Hear My Song
Hearts of Darkness
Heaven Can Wait
Hollywood Shuffle
Jerry Maguire
L.A. Confidential
La Bamba
League of Their Own, A
Liar, Liar
Living in Oblivion
Local Hero
Madness of King George, The
Major League
Making Mr. Right
Manufacturing Consent
Michael
My Cousin Vinny
My Favorite Year
Natural, The
Nell
Night at the Opera, A
Norma Rae
One Against the Wind
One Trick Pony
Paper, The
Pat and Mike
Phar Lap
Philadelphia
Player, The
Priest
Private Parts
Quiz Show
Return of the Jedi
Right Stuff, The
Risky Business
Rocketeer, The
Rocky
Ruthless People
Sister Act
Slap Shot
Sneakers
Soapdish
Some Like It Hot
Stakeout
Star Trek IV: The Voyage Home
Star Wars Trilogy
Sting, The
Stunt Man, The
Taking Care of Business
Tap
This Is Spinal Tap
Thousand Pieces of Gold
Three Days of the Condor
Tin Cup
To Die For
To Kill a Mockingbird
Toy Story
Trading Places
Tucker: A Man and His Dream
2010
2001: A Space Odyssey
Visions of Light
Waiting for Guffman
Wonderful, Horrible Life of Leni Riefenstahl, The
Year of Living Dangerously, The

Teacher/Student

Children of a Lesser God
Clara's Heart
Conrack
Dangerous Minds
Dead Poets Society
Don Juan deMarco
Educating Rita
Excalibur
Fame
Ferris Bueller's Day Off
Goodbye, Mr. Chips
Hoop Dreams
Indiana Jones Trilogy
Karate Kid, The
Kindergarten Cop
Malcolm X
Marva Collins Story, The
Mr. Holland's Opus
Powder
Raiders of the Lost Ark
Rambling Rose
Rudy

Small Wonders
Stand and Deliver
Welcome to the Dollhouse

Boss/Employee

All the President's Men
Associate, The
Babe
Baby Boom
Bagdad Cafe
Big
Bodyguard, The
Breaker Morant
Celluloid Closet, The
Citizen Kane
Clerks
"Crocodile" Dundee
Driving Miss Daisy
Fat Man and Little Boy
Firm, The
Freshman, The
Good Man in Africa, A
Good Morning Vietnam
I've Heard the Mermaids Singing
Inner Circle, The
Lawnmower Man, The
Lawrence of Arabia
League of Their Own, A
Local Hero
Long Walk Home, The
Losing Chase
Major League
Never Cry Wolf
Nine to Five
Norma Rae
One Against the Wind
Paper, The
Philadelphia
Private Benjamin
Reality Bites
Rebecca
Roger & Me
Roots
Ruby in Paradise
Scrooged
Slap Shot
Spitfire Grill, The
Tune in Tomorrow
2001: A Space Odyssey
Working Girl
Year of the Comet

Leader/Follower

Apocalypse Now
Being There
Blazing Saddles
Dr. Strangelove
Malcolm X

Self-Esteem

Back to the Future
Can't Buy Me Love
Color Purple, The
Diary of a Mad Housewife
Enchanted April
Fried Green Tomatoes
Harold and Maude
Hoop Dreams
Lucas
One Flew over the Cuckoo's Nest
Ordinary People

Breaking Old Patterns

Airplane!
Annie Hall
Ballad of Little Jo, The
Beaches
Casablanca
Cemetery Club
City Slickers
Close Encounters of a Third Kind
Clueless
Coal Miner's Daughter, The
Cry, The Beloved Country
Dead Again
Diary of a Hit Man
Down and Out in Beverly Hills
Earth Girls Are Easy
Electric Horseman
Emerald Forest, The
Finnegan Begin Again
Fisher King, The
Four Weddings and a Funeral
French Lieutenant's Woman, The
Full Monty, The
Get On the Bus
Great Santini, The
Groundhog Day
In Love with an Older Woman
L.A. Story
Losing Chase
Losing Isaiah
Marvin's Room
Planes, Trains & Automobiles
Roots
Scrooged
Taking Care of Business
Tootsie
Truly, Madly, Deeply
Used People
Way We Were, The

Finding Love

Teen Years

Aladdin
American Graffiti
Back to the Future
Breaking Away
Can't Buy Me Love
Clueless
Coal Miner's Daughter, The
Dirty Dancing
Fame
Ferris Bueller's Day off
Gaby, A True Story
Hope and Glory
House Party
Incredibly True Adventure of Two Girls in Love
Joy Luck Club
Karate Kid, The
Last Picture Show, The
Lemon Sisters, The
Little Romance, A
Lucas
Map of the Human Heart
Much Ado About Nothing
Mystic Pizza
Rambling Rose
Risky Business
Ruby in Paradise
Stealing Beauty
Taking off
Texasville
35 Up
28 Up
Very Brady Sequel, A
Wuthering Heights

College Years

Before Sunrise
Brideshead Revisited
Class of '44
Goodbye, Columbus
Graduate, The
Happy Together
Personal Best
Pride and Prejudice
River Runs Through It, A
Rudy
Sure Thing, The
Two for the Road
Walk in the Clouds
Way We Were, The
When Harry Met Sally

20s

Austin Powers
Barcelona
Beauty and the Beast
Benny & Joon
Big Picture, The
Birdcage, The
Boys On the Side
Brothers McMullen, The
Chances Are
Chaplin
Children of a Lesser God
Circle of Friends
Clerks

20s *(cont'd)*

Coal Miner's Daughter, The
Cold Comfort Farm
Cutting Edge, The
Desperately Seeking Susan
Diner
Dominick and Eugene
Don Juan deMarco
Dragon: the Bruce Lee Story
Earth Girls Are Easy
Ed's Next Move
Emma
Empire Strikes Back
Excalibur
Far and Away
Father of the Bride
Firm, The
Five Easy Pieces
Forever Young
Freshman, The
George of the Jungle
Giant
Godfather Trilogy, The
Gone with the Wind
Good Morning Vietnam
Grace of My Heart
Hard Day's Night
Holiday
Hollywood Shuffle
How to Make an American Quilt
I Was a Male War Bride
Irreconcilable Differences
It Happened One Night
Jewel in the Crown, The
Joy Luck Club
La Bamba
Laura
Little Women
Mambo Kings, The
Mississippi Masala
Natural, The
Parenthood
Playboys, The
Princess Bride
Private Benjamin
Queen of Hearts
Rambling Rose
Reality Bites
Return of the Jedi
Rocketeer, The
Roman Holiday
Room with a View, A
Rose, The
Sabrina
Same Time, Next Year
Sense and Sensibility
She's Gotta Have It
She's the One
Singles
Spitfire Grill, The
Splash
Star Wars Trilogy
Steel Magnolias
Strictly Ballroom
Stunt Man, The
Superman
Swingers
Terms of Endearment
35 Up
Town Like Alice, A
Trading Places
Truth About Cats and Dogs, The
28 Up
Two for the Road
Unbearable Lightness of Being
Untamed Heart
Way We Were, The

28-54

Affair to Remember, An
Airplane!
American President
Annie Hall
Atlantic City
Austin Powers
Baby Boom
Back to School
Bagdad Cafe
Ballad of Little Jo, The
Beautiful Girls
Big Chill, The
Big Easy, The
Birdcage, The
Bodyguard, The
Boys On the Side
Brideshead Revisited
Bridges of Madison County
Broadcast News
Brother From Another Planet, The
Bull Durham
Butch Cassidy and the Sundance Kid
Bye Bye, Love
Casablanca
Chaplin
Charade
Coal Miner's Daughter, The
Color Purple, The
Contact
Corrina, Corrina
Cousins
"Crocodile" Dundee
Crossing Delancy
Dances with Wolves
Dangerous Liaisons
Dark Victory
Dave
Dead Again
Desk Set
Diary of a Hit Man
Diary of a Mad Housewife
Doctor Zhivago
Educating Rita
Electric Horseman
Enchanted April
English Patient, The
Fabulous Baker Boys, The
Field of Dreams
First Wives Club, The
Fish Called Wanda, A
Fisher King, The
Four Seasons, The
Four Weddings and a Funeral
Frankie Starlight
French Lieutenant's Woman, The
Fried Green Tomatoes
Gay Divorcee
Ghost
Ghost and Mrs. Muir, The
Giant
Godfather Trilogy, The
Gorillas in the Mist
Grace of My Heart
Green Card
Groundhog Day
Hear My Song
Heart Like a Wheel
Heaven Can Wait
His Girl Friday
I Love You to Death
Impromptu
In & Out
Irreconcilable Differences
Jerry Maguire
Jewel in the Crown, The
Joy Luck Club
Kindergarten Cop
L.A. Story
Lady From Shanghai, The
Last Picture Show, The
Lemon Sisters, The
Lianna
Live Nude Girls
Lone Star
Lonely Hearts
Love Affair
Major League
Making Mr. Right
Malcolm X
Man Who Fell to Earth
Map of the Human Heart
Married to It
Melvin & Howard
Michael
Miracle on 34th Street
Month By the Lake, A
Mrs. Doubtfire
Much Ado About Nothing
My Cousin Vinny
My Little Chickadee
Night We Never Met, The
Nina Takes a Lover

Not Without My Daughter
One Trick Pony
Paper, The
Parenthood
Pat and Mike
Persuasion
Peter's Friends
Phenomenon
Philadelphia Story, The
Piano, The
Player, The
Priest
Queen of Hearts
Razor's Edge, The
Regarding Henry
Restoration
Right Stuff, The
Rocky
Romancing the Stone
Ruthless People
Same Time, Next Year
Scrooged
Search for Signs of Intelligent Life in the Universe, The
Sex, Lies, & Videotape
Shadowlands
Shall We Dance?
She Done Him Wrong
Shine
Slap Shot
Sleepless in Seattle
Soapdish
Some Like It Hot
Stakeout
Starman
Starting Over
State of the Union
Swing Time
Tap
Terms of Endearment
Texasville
35 Up
Thousand Pieces of Gold
3 Men and a Baby
3 Men and a Little Lady
Three of Hearts
Tin Cup
Tootsie
Top Hat
Town Like Alice, A
Truly, Madly, Deeply
28 Up
Twins
Two for the Road
Unbearable Lightness of Being
Uncle Buck
Valmont
Waiting to Exhale
Walking and Talking
Waterdance, The
Wedding Banquet, The
When Harry Met Sally
Where's Poppa?
Who Framed Roger Rabbit?
Widow's Peak
Woman of the Year
Working Girl
Year of Living Dangerously, The
Year of the Comet

55-81

Batteries Not Included
Cemetery Club
Chaplin
Cocoon
Don Juan deMarco
Giant
Godfather Trilogy, The
Grass Harp, The
Grey Fox, The
Grumpy Old Men
Jewel in the Crown, The
On Golden Pond
Parenthood
Queen of Hearts
She's the One
Terms of Endearment
Used People

Radical Age Difference

Big
Bull Durham
Chances Are
Cold Sassy Tree
Dangerous Liaisons
Finnegan Begin Again
Flashdance
Harold and Maude
In Love with an Older Woman
In the Line of Fire
In the Mood
Playboys, The
Pretty Woman
Rebecca
Resurrection
Sabrina
Singin' in the Rain
Star is Born, A
Summer of '42
Tune in Tomorrow
Valmont
You Were Never Lovelier

Same Sex

Boys On the Side
Brideshead Revisited
Lianna
Priscilla, Queen of the Desert

Transitions

Pre-Teen Years

Cure, The
E.T.–The Extra Terrestrial
Frankie Starlight
Hope and Glory
Marva Collins Story, The
My Life as a Dog
Secret of Roan Inish, The
Stand By Me
Unstrung Heroes
Welcome to the Dollhouse

Teen Years

Aladdin
American Graffiti
Back to the Future
Beaches
Breaking Away
Can't Buy Me Love
Clara's Heart
Clueless
Color Purple, The
Dangerous Liaisons
Dangerous Minds
Dead Poets Society
Dirty Dancing
Fame
Ferris Bueller's Day Off
Great Santini, The
Home of Our Own, A
Hoop Dreams
House Party
Incredibly True Adventure of Two Girls in Love
Karate Kid, The
Last Picture Show, The
Lemon Sisters, The
Little Romance, A
Lucas
Mask
Miracle, The
Now and Then
Ordinary People
Powder
Rambling Rose
Risky Business
Ruby in Paradise
Shine
Stand and Deliver
Stealing Beauty
Summer of '42
Taking off
To Gillian On Her 37th Birthday
Valmont
Very Brady Sequel, A
Welcome Home, Roxy Carmichael

College Years

Back to School
Before Sunrise
Brideshead Revisited
Chariots of Fire
Class of '44

College Years *(cont'd)*

Diner
Freshman, The
Graduate, The
Happy Together
Hoop Dreams
River Runs Through It, A
Rudy
Shine
Six Degrees of Separation
Sure Thing, The

20s

Apocalypse Now
Back to the Future
City Slickers II: The Legend of Curly's Gold
Class of '44
Cousin Bobby
"Crocodile" Dundee
Cry, The Beloved Country
Fargo
Forrest Gump
Get On the Bus
Ghostbusters II
Heaven Can Wait (1943)
Here Comes Mr. Jordan
Home for the Holidays
Jewel of the Nile, The
Marvin's Room
Michael
Mother
Nell
Night at the Opera, A
Only You
Pontiac Moon
Princess Caraboo
Priscilla, Queen of the Desert
Razor's Edge, The
Sabrina
Search for Signs of Intelligent Life in the Universe, The
Searching for Bobby Fisher
Shawshank Redemption
Singles
Smoke
Some Mother's Son
Soul Food
Stakeout
Superman

20s to 30s Passage

Amadeus
Annie Hall
Avalon
Beautiful Girls
Beverly Hills Cop
Big Easy, The
Broadcast News
Desperately Seeking Susan
Dominick and Eugene
Dragon: the Bruce Lee Story
Earth Girls Are Easy
Five Easy Pieces
I've Heard the Mermaids Singing
Night We Never Met, The
Now and Then
Private Benjamin
Same Time, Next Year
Sex, Lies, & Videotape
She's the One
Working Girl

Mid-Life Crisis 30s & 40s

Adam's Rib
Avalon
Baby Boom
Bagdad Cafe
Beaches
Big Chill, The
Brideshead Revisited
Butch Cassidy and the Sundance Kid
City Slickers
Dangerous Liaisons
Dark Victory
Diary of a Hit Man
Diary of a Mad Housewife
Down and Out in Beverly Hills
Fabulous Baker Boys, The
Field of Dreams
Fisher King, The
Fried Green Tomatoes
It's a Wonderful Life
Lemon Sisters, The
Lianna
Lonely Hearts
Losing Chase
Married to It
On Golden Pond
One Trick Pony
Peter's Friends
Planes, Trains & Automobiles
Same Time, Next Year
Scrooged
Secrets and Lies
Stealing Beauty
Texasville
Uncle Buck
Where's Poppa?

Mid-50s Passage

Back to School
Educating Rita
Same Time, Next Year
Ulee's Gold

After Retirement

Avalon
Batteries Not Included
Cocoon
Don Juan deMarco
Driving Miss Daisy
Grumpy Old Men
On Golden Pond
Parenthood
Roommates
Wonderful, Horrible Life of Leni Riefenstahl, The

Courting

Affair to Remember, An
American President
Angels and Insects
Annie Hall
Barcelona
Birdcage, The
Bridges of Madison County
Brothers McMullen, The
Bull Durham
Bye Bye, Love
Can't Buy Me Love
Circle of Friends
Clueless
Corrina, Corrina
Cousins
Crossing Delancy
Don Juan deMarco
Ed's Next Move
Emma
English Patient, The
Four Seasons, The
Frankie Starlight
George of the Jungle
Grass Harp, The
Groundhog Day
Grumpy Old Men
His Girl Friday
Jerry Maguire
Little Women
Live Nude Girls
Lone Star
Love Affair
Month By the Lake, A
Much Ado About Nothing
Only You
Persuasion
Phenomenon
Pride and Prejudice
Priest
Sabrina
Sense and Sensibility
She Done Him Wrong
She's Gotta Have It
She's the One
Sleepless in Seattle
Some Like It Hot
Starting Over
Strictly Ballroom
Sure Thing, The
Swing Time
Swingers
Terms of Endearment

35 Up
Thousand Pieces of Gold
3 Men and a Little Lady
Three of Hearts
Tootsie
Top Hat
Town Like Alice, A
Truth About Cats and Dogs, The
28 Up
Two for the Road
Unbearable Lightness of Being
Used People
Very Brady Sequel, A
Waiting to Exhale
Walk in the Clouds
Walking and Talking
Way We Were, The
Wedding Banquet, The
When Harry Met Sally

Living Together/ Moving In

Annie Hall
Beauty and the Beast
Birdcage, The
Boys On the Side
Brothers McMullen, The
Cold Comfort Farm
Cold Sassy Tree
Fisher King, The
Happy Together
In Love with an Older Woman
It Happened One Night
Mr. Blandings Builds His Dream House
Nina Takes a Lover
Parenthood
Piano, The
Pretty Woman
Rebecca
Toy Story
Two for the Road
Unbearable Lightness of Being
What's Eating Gilbert Grape?
Woman of the Year

Marrying

Cold Sassy Tree
Color Purple, The
Father of the Bride
Four Weddings and a Funeral
Goodbye, Columbus
Grace of My Heart
Green Card
How to Make an American Quilt
I Was a Male War Bride
In & Out
In the Mood
Live Nude Girls
Queen of Hearts
Room with a View, A
Shadowlands
Shall We Dance?
Steel Magnolias
Terms of Endearment
35 Up
Tune in Tomorrow
28 Up
Two for the Road
Unbearable Lightness of Being
Valmont
Walking and Talking
Way We Were, The
When a Man Loves a Woman
You Were Never Lovelier

Divorcing

Bye Bye, Love
Diary of a Hit Man
First Wives Club, The
Four Seasons, The
Gay Divorcee
Irreconcilable Differences
L.A. Story
Mrs. Doubtfire
Not Without My Daughter
Philadelphia Story, The
Starting Over
State of the Union
Waiting to Exhale

Moving Out/ Separating

Aladdin
American Graffiti
Bagdad Cafe
Benny & Joon
Cousins
Desperately Seeking Susan
Diner
Dominick and Eugene
El Norte
Far and Away
Father of the Bride
First Wives Club, The
French Lieutenant's Woman, The
Gods Must Be Crazy, The
Graduate, The
Grass Harp, The
Harvey
It Happened One Night
L.A. Story
Lonely Hearts
Mississippi Masala
My Life as a Dog
Mystic Pizza
Night We Never Met, The
Once Were Warriors
Playboys, The
Princess Bride
Queen of Hearts
Rain Man
River Runs Through It, A
Roman Holiday
Ruby in Paradise
Searchers, The
Wuthering Heights

Losing Mate

Airplane!
Bye Bye Blues
Cemetery Club
Chances Are
Charade
Corrina, Corrina
Dead Again
Forever Young
I Love You to Death
Map of the Human Heart
My Life
Phenomenon
Star is Born, A
Starman
Steel Magnolias
Terms of Endearment
To Gillian On Her 37th Birthday
Truly, Madly, Deeply
Unstrung Heroes
Untamed Heart
Used People
Who Framed Roger Rabbit?
Widow's Peak

Becoming Parent

Baby Boom
Flirting with Disaster
Losing Isaiah
Mighty Aphrodite
Now and Then
3 Men and a Baby
Unexpected Family, An

Landing First Job

Backbeat
Big Picture, The
Breaking In
Buddy Holly Story, The
Bull Durham
Bullets Over Broadway
Bye Bye Blues
Clerks
Conrack
Fabulous Baker Boys, The
Fame
Far and Away
Firm, The
Freshman, The
My Favorite Year
Reality Bites
Singin' in the Rain
Spitfire Grill, The
Stunt Man, The
Trading Places

Achieving Career Goals

All the President's Men
Angels and Insects
Apollo 13
Associate, The
Atlantic City
Austin Powers
Babe
Bad and the Beautiful, The
Barbarians at the Gate
Beautiful Dreamers
Big Night
Brief History in Time, A
Bronco Billy
Celluloid Closet, The
Chaplin
Citizen Kane
Cliffhanger
Coal Miner's Daughter, The
Contact
Cousin Bobby
Ed Wood
Empire Strikes Back
Fat Man and Little Boy
Fish Called Wanda, A
Five Heartbeats, The
Flashdance
For the Boys
Frankie Starlight
Ghostbusters
Giant
Godfather Trilogy, The
Gone with the Wind
Good Man in Africa, A
Goodbye, Mr. Chips
Gorillas in the Mist
Grace of My Heart
Hard Day's Night
Hear My Song
Heart Like a Wheel
Hearts of Darkness
His Girl Friday
Hollywood Shuffle
Honey, I Shrunk the Kids
I've Heard the Mermaids Singing
Impromptu
In the Line of Fire
Indiana Jones Trilogy
Inner Circle, The
Jerry Maguire
L.A. Confidential
La Bamba
Lawrence of Arabia
League of Their Own, A
Liar, Liar
Living in Oblivion
Local Hero
Mac
Madness of King George, The
Major League
Malcolm X
Mambo Kings, The
Manufacturing Consent
Marva Collins Story, The
Mighty Quinn, The
Mr. Holland's Opus
My Family (Mi Familia)
My Left Foot
My Little Chickadee
Natural, The
Never Cry Wolf
Nine to Five
Norma Rae
Nothing in Common
One Trick Pony
Paper, The
Parenthood
Personal Best
Phar Lap
Player, The
Priest
Private Parts
Raiders of the Lost Ark
Restoration
Return of the Jedi
Right Stuff, The
Rocketeer, The
Rocky
Roots
Rose, The
Secret Life of Walter Mitty, The
Shine
Singin' in the Rain
Slap Shot
Small Wonders
Sneakers
Soapdish
Stakeout
Stand and Deliver
Star is Born, A
Star Wars Trilogy
State of the Union
Sting, The
Strictly Ballroom
Stunt Man, The
Taking Care of Business
Taking off
Tap
35 Up
This Is Spinal Tap
Thousand Pieces of Gold
Tin Cup
To Die For
To Kill a Mockingbird
Tootsie
Tucker: A Man and His Dream
Tune in Tomorrow
2010
Visions of Light
Waiting for Guffman
Who Framed Roger Rabbit?
Woman of the Year
Year of Living Dangerously, The
Year of the Comet

Changing Careers

Baby Boom
Ballad of Little Jo, The
Beautiful Dreamers
Beauty and the Beast
Being There
Big
Blazing Saddles
Bodyguard, The
Brief History in Time, A
Brother From Another Planet, The
Casablanca
Chances Are
Children of a Lesser God
Close Encounters of a Third Kind
Color Purple, The
Cool Runnings
"Crocodile" Dundee
Cutting Edge, The
Dances with Wolves
Dave
Dead Again
Deep Cover
Desk Set
Dirty Dozen
Doctor Zhivago
Down and Out in Beverly Hills
Dr. Strangelove
Dragon: the Bruce Lee Story
E.T.–The Extra Terrestrial
Earth Girls Are Easy
El Norte
Electric Horseman
Emerald Forest, The
Enchanted April
Excalibur
Field of Dreams
Finnegan Begin Again
Five Easy Pieces
Forever Young
Fried Green Tomatoes
Gaby, A True Story
Gentleman's Agreement
Get Shorty
Ghost
Ghost and Mrs. Muir, The
Gods Must Be Crazy, The
Good Morning Vietnam
Grey Fox, The
Groundhog Day
Harold and Maude
Harvey
Heaven Can Wait
Holiday
Irreconcilable Differences
Jewel in the Crown, The
Joy Luck Club
Kindergarten Cop

Lady From Shanghai, The
Laura
Lawnmower Man, The
Local Hero
Long Walk Home, The
Lorenzo's Oil
Magnificent Ambersons, The
Making Mr. Right
Man Who Fell to Earth
Map of the Human Heart
Mask
Melvin & Howard
Miracle on 34th Street
Mrs. Doubtfire
Music Box
My Cousin Vinny
Never Cry Wolf
Not Without My Daughter
One Against the Wind
One Flew over the Cuckoo's Nest
Paris is Burning
Pat and Mike
Piano, The
Pretty Woman
Private Benjamin
Quiz Show
Razor's Edge, The
Rebecca
Regarding Henry
Resurrection
Romancing the Stone
Rosalie Goes Shopping
Ruthless People
Sister Act
Some Like It Hot
Splash
Star Trek IV: The Voyage Home
Starman
Superman
Three of Hearts
Truly, Madly, Deeply
Twins
2001: A Space Odyssey
Uncle Buck
Waterdance, The
Working Girl
Year of Living Dangerously, The

Losing Job

Airplane!
Breaker Morant
Bull Durham
Bye Bye Blues
Cemetery Club
Chances Are
Charade
Corrina, Corrina
Dead Again
Devil in a Blue Dress
Forever Young
Full Monty, The
I Love You to Death
Jerry Maguire
Map of the Human Heart
Mr. Mom
My Life
Phenomenon
Philadelphia
Roger & Me
Star is Born, A
Starman
Steel Magnolias
Terms of Endearment
Three Days of the Condor
To Gillian On Her 37th Birthday
Truly, Madly, Deeply
Unstrung Heroes
Untamed Heart
Used People
Who Framed Roger Rabbit?
Widow's Peak

Surviving Downsizing

Desk Set
Full Monty, The
Paper, The
Player, The

Overcoming Obstacles

Sexual Prejudice

Adam's Rib
Associate, The
Baby Boom
Ballad of Little Jo, The
Big Easy, The
Birdcage, The
Broadcast News
Bye Bye Blues
Celluloid Closet, The
Coal Miner's Daughter, The
Cold Sassy Tree
Color Purple, The
Desk Set
Diary of a Mad Housewife
Diner
Enchanted April
Fargo
French Lieutenant's Woman, The
Gone with the Wind
Heart Like a Wheel
His Girl Friday
Home for the Holidays
I Was a Male War Bride
Impromptu
In & Out
Incredibly True Adventure of Two Girls in Love
League of Their Own, A
Lianna
Little Women
Paris is Burning
Pat and Mike
Personal Best
Philadelphia
Piano, The
Playboys, The
Priest
Private Benjamin
Rambling Rose
She's Gotta Have It
Some Like It Hot
Thousand Pieces of Gold
3 Men and a Baby
3 Men and a Little Lady
Tootsie
Wedding Banquet, The

Racial Prejudice

Brother From Another Planet, The
Corrina, Corrina
Cry, The Beloved Country
Dances with Wolves
Devil in a Blue Dress
Dragon: the Bruce Lee Story
Driving Miss Daisy
El Norte
Five Heartbeats, The
Fried Green Tomatoes
Gentleman's Agreement
Get On the Bus
Great Santini, The
Hollywood Shuffle
Jewel in the Crown, The
La Bamba
Long Walk Home, The
Losing Isaiah
Malcolm X
Map of the Human Heart
Mississippi Masala
My Family (Mi Familia)
Paris is Burning
Roots
Six Degrees of Separation
Smoke
Stand and Deliver
Thousand Pieces of Gold
To Kill a Mockingbird
Trading Places

Class Prejudice

Aladdin
Breaker Morant
Breaking Away
Brideshead Revisited
Can't Buy Me Love
Chariots of Fire
"Crocodile" Dundee

Class Prejudice *(cont'd)*

Crossing Delancy
Cutting Edge, The
Dirty Dancing
Down and Out in Beverly Hills
Educating Rita
Emma
Far and Away
Flashdance
Giant
Godfather Trilogy, The
Goodbye, Columbus
Holiday
Hoop Dreams
Inner Circle, The
It Happened One Night
Jewel in the Crown, The
Last Picture Show, The
Night at the Opera, A
Persuasion
Pretty Woman
Pride and Prejudice
Restoration
Room with a View, A
Sabrina
Six Degrees of Separation
Spitfire Grill, The
Texasville
35 Up
Town Like Alice, A
28 Up
Walk in the Clouds
Way We Were, The
Working Girl
Wuthering Heights

Age Prejudice

Back to School
Cocoon
Driving Miss Daisy
Finnegan Begin Again
Grey Fox, The
In the Line of Fire
In the Mood
Little Romance, A
Miracle on 34th Street
Month By the Lake, A
Roommates
Singles
Soapdish
Used People

Physical Abilities

Babe
Beauty and the Beast
Big
Brief History in Time, A
Children of a Lesser God
Cocoon
Cool Runnings
Dark Victory
Dirty Dancing
Dragon: the Bruce Lee Story
Frankie Starlight
Gaby, A True Story
Ghost
Karate Kid, The
League of Their Own, A
Lorenzo's Oil
Lucas
Map of the Human Heart
Marvin's Room
Mask
My Left Foot
Natural, The
Nell
Pat and Mike
Phenomenon
Philadelphia
Regarding Henry
Resurrection
Rocky
Rudy
Star Wars Trilogy
Untamed Heart
Waterdance, The
When a Man Loves a Woman

Mental Abilities

Beautiful Dreamers
Being There
Benny & Joon
Dominick and Eugene
Forrest Gump
Harvey
Lawnmower Man, The
Losing Chase
Marva Collins Story, The
One Flew over the Cuckoo's Nest
Powder
Quiz Show
Rain Man
Shine

Cultural Abilities

Avalon
Barcelona
Breaker Morant
Close Encounters of a Third Kind
Dangerous Minds
E.T.–The Extra Terrestrial
Earth Girls Are Easy
Emerald Forest, The
Godfather Trilogy, The
Gods Must Be Crazy, The
Good Morning Vietnam
Groundhog Day
Joy Luck Club
Lawrence of Arabia
Manufacturing Consent
Mississippi Masala
My Cousin Vinny
My Family (Mi Familia)
Smoke

Loss

Affair to Remember, An
American Graffiti
Beaches
Beverly Hills Cop
Big Chill, The
Boys On the Side
Casablanca
Cemetery Club
Chances Are
Clara's Heart
Color Purple, The
Corrina, Corrina
Cure, The
Dead Again
Desk Set
Diner
Doctor Zhivago
Emerald Forest, The
Father of the Bride
First Wives Club, The
Flirting with Disaster
Forever Young
Four Seasons, The
Full Monty, The
Gay Divorcee
Ghost
Ghost and Mrs. Muir, The
Gone with the Wind
Gorillas in the Mist
Grumpy Old Men
Heart Like a Wheel
Heaven Can Wait
Irreconcilable Differences
Kindergarten Cop
Laura
Losing Chase
Losing Isaiah
Love Affair
Magnificent Ambersons, The
Map of the Human Heart
Melvin & Howard
Mighty Quinn, The
Miracle on 34th Street
Miracle, The
Mr. Mom
Mrs. Doubtfire
Music Box
My Life
My Life as a Dog
Nothing in Common
On Golden Pond
One Trick Pony
Ordinary People
Paper, The
Parenthood
Peter's Friends
Philadelphia Story, The
Planes, Trains & Automobiles
Rebecca
Roger & Me
Ruthless People
Same Time, Next Year
Searchers, The
Secret of Roan Inish, The
Secrets and Lies
Shadowlands
Slap Shot

Sleepless in Seattle
Soapdish
Splash
Stand By Me
Star is Born, A
Star Trek IV: The Voyage Home
Starman
Starting Over
Stealing Beauty
Steel Magnolias
Summer of '42
Superman
Terms of Endearment
Three of Hearts
To Gillian On Her 37th Birthday
Town Like Alice, A
Trading Places
Truly, Madly, Deeply
2010
Twins
Two for the Road
Ulee's Gold
Unbearable Lightness of Being
Unstrung Heroes
Untamed Heart
Used People
Welcome Home Roxy Carmichael
When Harry Met Sally
Who Framed Roger Rabbit?
Widow's Peak

Entrapment

Aladdin
American President
Angels and Insects
Annie Hall
Back to the Future
Bagdad Cafe
Batteries Not Included
Beautiful Girls
Beauty and the Beast
Bodyguard, The
Breaking In
Bridges of Madison County
Brother From Another Planet, The
Brothers McMullen, The
Butch Cassidy and the Sundance Kid
Circle of Friends
Clerks
Cold Comfort Farm
Cold Sassy Tree
Color Purple, The
Cousins
Dangerous Liaisons
Dead Poets Society
Deep Cover
Desperately Seeking Susan
Diary of a Hit Man
Diary of a Mad Housewife
Dirty Dozen
Don Juan deMarco
Electric Horseman
Enchanted April
Far and Away
Ferris Bueller's Day Off
Field of Dreams
Finnegan Begin Again
Firm, The
Fisher King, The
Five Easy Pieces
Four Seasons, The
Four Weddings and a Funeral
French Lieutenant's Woman, The
Freshman, The
Fried Green Tomatoes
Gentleman's Agreement
Godfather Trilogy, The
Good Man in Africa, A
Graduate, The
Grass Harp, The
Great Santini, The
Grey Fox, The
Harold and Maude
Holiday
Home for the Holidays
Home of Our Own, A
How to Make an American Quilt
I Love You to Death
In Love with an Older Woman
It Happened One Night
It's a Wonderful Life
Joy Luck Club
Kindergarten Cop
L.A. Confidential
L.A. Story
Lady From Shanghai, The
Last Picture Show, The
Lemon Sisters, The
Local Hero
Lonely Hearts
Long Walk Home, The
Madness of King George, The
Malcolm X
Man Who Fell to Earth
Married to It
Mr. Mom
Music Box
My Little Chickadee
Mystic Pizza
Natural, The
Night We Never Met, The
Nina Takes a Lover
Nine to Five
Norma Rae
Not Without My Daughter
Nothing in Common
Once Were Warriors
One Flew over the Cuckoo's Nest
Parenthood
Philadelphia Story, The
Piano, The
Playboys, The
Player, The
Princess Bride
Queen of Hearts
Rebecca
Regarding Henry
Risky Business
River Runs Through It, A
Roman Holiday
Room with a View, A
Roots
Ruby in Paradise
Ruthless People
Same Time, Next Year
Scrooged
Sense and Sensibility
Sex, Lies, & Videotape
She's Gotta Have It
She's the One
Sister Act
Smoke
Sneakers
Some Like It Hot
Soul Food
Stakeout
Starman
Sting, The
Strictly Ballroom
Stunt Man, The
Sure Thing, The
Taking Care of Business
Taking off
Terms of Endearment
Texasville
Three Days of the Condor
Toy Story
Truth About Cats and Dogs, The
Two for the Road
2001: A Space Odyssey
Unbearable Lightness of Being
Uncle Buck
Unexpected Family, An
Valmont
Waiting to Exhale
Walking and Talking
Way We Were, The
Wedding Banquet, The
What's Eating Gilbert Grape?
Where's Poppa?
Working Girl
Year of Living Dangerously, The

Creative Expression

Amadeus
Backbeat
Bad and the Beautiful, The
Barbarians at the Gate
Big Night

Creative Expression *(cont'd)*

Big Picture, The
Bronco Billy
Buddy Holly Story, The
Bullets Over Broadway
Bye Bye Blues
Celluloid Closet, The
Chaplin
Citizen Kane
Coal Miner's Daughter, The
Conrack
Cutting Edge, The
Dead Poets Society
Ed Wood
Fabulous Baker Boys, The
Fame
Five Heartbeats, The
Flashdance
For the Boys
Get Shorty
Goodbye, Mr. Chips
Grace of My Heart
Green Card
Happy Together
Hard Day's Night
Hear My Song
Hearts of Darkness
His Girl Friday
Hollywood Shuffle
Honey, I Shrunk the Kids
I've Heard the Mermaids Singing
Impromptu
In Love with an Older Woman
Irreconcilable Differences
Jerry Maguire
Karate Kid, The
La Bamba
Lawnmower Man, The
Lemon Sisters, The
Little Women
Living in Oblivion
Lucas
Mac
Major League
Making Mr. Right
Mambo Kings, The
Manufacturing Consent
Melvin & Howard
Miracle, The
Mr. Blandings Builds His Dream House
Mr. Holland's Opus
My Favorite Year
My Left Foot
Mystic Pizza
Never Cry Wolf
Night We Never Met, The
Nine to Five
One Against the Wind
One Trick Pony
Paper, The
Paris is Burning
Peter's Friends
Phar Lap
Piano, The
Player, The
Private Parts
Razor's Edge, The
Reality Bites
Resurrection
Risky Business
River Runs Through It, A
Rocketeer, The
Rosalie Goes Shopping
Rose, The
Search for Signs of Intelligent Life in the Universe, The
Shall We Dance?
She Done Him Wrong
Shine
Singin' in the Rain
Sister Act
Slap Shot
Small Wonders
Sneakers
Star is Born, A
State of the Union
Stealing Beauty
Strictly Ballroom
Stunt Man, The
Swing Time
Tap
35 Up
This Is Spinal Tap
Tin Cup
To Die For
Tootsie
Top Hat
Tucker: A Man and His Dream
Tune in Tomorrow
28 Up
Visions of Light
Waiting for Guffman
Woman of the Year
Wonderful, Horrible Life of Leni Riefenstahl, The
You Were Never Lovelier

War

Apocalypse Now
Breaker Morant
Bye Bye Blues
Casablanca
Dirty Dozen
Doctor Zhivago
Dr. Strangelove
El Norte
English Patient, The
Fat Man and Little Boy
Gone with the Wind
Good Morning Vietnam
Hope and Glory
I Was a Male War Bride
Lawrence of Arabia
One Against the Wind
Roots
Some Mother's Son
Summer of '42
Town Like Alice, A
Unbearable Lightness of Being
Year of Living Dangerously, The

Adventure

Airplane!
All the President's Men
Apollo 13
Austin Powers
Before Sunrise
Big
Big Easy, The
Blazing Saddles
Bull Durham
Butch Cassidy and the Sundance Kid
Charade
City Slickers
Cliffhanger
Contact
Cool Runnings
"Crocodile" Dundee
Dave
Deep Cover
Desperately Seeking Susan
El Norte
Empire Strikes Back
Enchanted April
Excalibur
Field of Dreams
Fish Called Wanda, A
Ghostbusters
Gods Must Be Crazy, The
Gorillas in the Mist
House Party
Indiana Jones Trilogy
Lone Star
Mighty Quinn, The
Never Cry Wolf
Princess Bride
Raiders of the Lost Ark
Razor's Edge, The
Return of the Jedi
Right Stuff, The
Rocketeer, The
Roman Holiday
Romancing the Stone
Secret Life of Walter Mitty, The
Sneakers
Star Trek IV: The Voyage Home
Star Wars Trilogy
Three Days of the Condor
2001: A Space Odyssey
Year of the Comet

CHAPTER 8

Movie Descriptions

How to Read the Listings

This chapter gives you plot outlines of movies available on video. Each outline is presented in the format shown below.

Title

***Release date** and **run time** in minutes*

Director and cast

***After-View Feeling** These icons tell you how you'll feel when you've finished watching the film*

Feel Better/Uplift

Laughing Release

Crying Release

This icon indicates Violent Content.

Plot Outline

***Life Changes** explored in the film (see page 71 for the complete list)*

Boys on the Side

1995/120

D: *Herbert Ross.* **Cast:** *Whoopi Goldberg, Mary-Louise Parker, Drew Barrymore.*

This is a touching examination of the complexities of female friendship amidst the quest for true love. An unlikely trio—an uptight HIV-positive real estate agent, a gay black piano player, and her young pregnant druggie friend—set off on a cross-country drive and end up as bickering, but supportive housemates in Tucson, waiting out the gradual demise of their ill friend.

Relationships	Friends Lovers
Finding Love	20s 28 to 54 Same Sex
Transitions	Living Together/ Moving In
Overcoming Obstacles	Loss

Adam's Rib

1950/101

D: *George Cukor.* **Cast:** *Spencer Tracy, Katharine Hepburn, Judy Holliday, Tom Ewell, David Wayne.*

Possibly the best of the Hepburn-Tracy movies, this classic telling of the battle of the sexes details the challenge of separating work from relationships. It's a comical losing battle for husband Tracy and wife Hepburn as opposing lawyers. Superb screenplay by husband-and-wife writers Garson Kanin and Ruth Gordon spins witty, sophisticated repartee, still fresh today. An annual must-see for two-career couples.

Work & Prosperity	Balancing Work & Family Destructuring Workplace
Relationships	Two-Career Couples
Transitions	Balancing Work & Family Mid-Life Crisis 30s & 40s
Overcoming Obstacles	Sexual Prejudice

Adventures of Priscilla, Queen of the Desert, The

1994/102

D: *Stephan Elliott.* **Cast:** *Terence Stamp, Hugo Weaving, Guy Pearce.*

This hilarious Australian musical comedy offers up the quirky adventure of two drag queens and a transsexual taking their '60s girl-group act to the outback in a garish bus named Priscilla. Between the laughs, there are sensitive portrayals of each man's struggles as an artist and a non-conformist. The widowed transsexual seeks renewal with a new man. One of the female impersonators wants to establish a connection with his son, who is being raised by his mother. The other entertains fantasies of starring with the Swedish rock group ABBA.

Work & Prosperity	Collaborating w/ Colleagues
Finding Love	Same Sex
Overcoming Obstacles	Sexual Prejudice

Affair to Remember, An

1957/115

See *Sleepless in Seattle*.

Airplane!

1980/88

D: *Jim Abrahams, Jerry Zucker.* **Cast:** *Robert Hays, Julie Hagerty, Lloyd Bridges, Peter Graves, Leslie Nielsen.*

This was the first fast-paced feature of the Zucker-Abrahams-Zucker team, here sending up a gag-a-minute parody of disaster films. For people who feel like their lives are a disaster, this is the perfect laughing release movie because the situations are so stupid and surreal, you just gotta laugh, chortle, guffaw, chuckle, groan, and everything in between. Jilted ex-pilot Hays tries to regain his nerve and his flight attendant girlfriend, by taking control of a plane whose passengers experience food poisoning. If only we could find this kind of humor in our own life challenges. Same writers/directors went on to do the 1982 *Airplane II: The Sequel* (85m.), which wasn't as side-splitting, and the *Naked Gun* series.

Work & Prosperity	Balance Collaborating w/ Colleagues
Relationships	Colleagues & Co-Workers Lovers Breaking Old Patterns
Finding Love	28-54
Transitions	Losing Mate
Overcoming Obstacles	Adventure

Airplane II: The Sequel

1982/85

See *Airplane*!

Aladdin

1992/90

D: *Ron Clements, John Musker.* **Cast:** *Robin Williams.*

Robin Williams' improvised comedic riffs find a natural home (as the genie's voice) in this classic Arab fairy tale. In this film, teens rebel against parental control to realize their dreams, despite overwhelming odds. This must be seen more than once to catch all of the genie's rapid-fire one-liners and exhilarating impersonations.

Work & Prosperity	Realizing Dreams
Relationships	Parent/Child Lovers
Finding Love	Teen Years
Transitions	Teen Years Moving Out/Separating
Overcoming Obstacles	Class Prejudice Entrapment

All the President's Men

1976/135

D: *Alan J. Pakula.* **Cast:** *Robert Redford, Dustin Hoffman, Jack Warden, Martin Balsam, Jason Robards.*

There has never been a more realistic film portrayal of investigative journalism than this true story of two young *Washington Post* reporters taking on the Nixon presidency. As with other seemingly "glamorous" occupations, good reporting involves a mixture of luck, blind alleys, dogged attention to detail, and occasional truths in a repetitious cycle. Viewers experience the range of emotions that grip *Post* staff as the pursuit heats up—the elation, the daily grind, the courage, and the doubts.

Work & Prosperity	Collaborating w/ Colleagues Loving Your Work
Relationships	Colleagues & Co-Workers Boss/Employee
Transitions	20s Achieving Career Goals
Overcoming Obstacles	Adventure

Amadeus

1984/158

D: *Milos Forman.* **Cast:** *F. Murray Abraham Tom Hulce, Elizabeth Berridge, Simon Callow.*

Shot in Prague, this film is a lush visual and musical meditation on the nature of genius and the envy it engenders in those who can only aspire to it. Told from rival court composer Salieri's perspective, the story centers on Mozart's relationships with his controlling, disapproving father, his loving and harebrained wife, and the jealous Salieri, who blocks his official recognition. Mozart is a hardworking, wacky, fun-loving man-child pushing the envelope of musical expression while struggling to break free from his father and obtain accolades for his own work. Mozart's death at 35 precluded his wishes, but his music continues to deliver joy to our souls.

Work & Prosperity	Realizing Dreams
Relationships	Colleagues & Co-Workers Parent/Child
Transitions	20s to 30s Passage
Overcoming Obstacles	Creative Expression

American Graffiti
1973/112

D: *George Lucas.* **Cast:** *Richard Dreyfuss, Ron Howard, Paul LeMat, Cindy Williams, Mackenzie Phillips.*

This film takes a look at the baby boomers' innocent times before the Kennedy assassination and the Vietnam War, when choices seemed simple for a group of friends celebrating high school graduation with an all-night party in Northern California. George Lucas' autobiographical tale evokes a strong sense of the early 1960s with a musical score of hits disc jockeyed by the voice of Wolfman Jack. A nighttime shoot heightens the sense of exhilaration and exhaustion at this teen rite of passage.

Relationships	Friends Lovers
Finding Love	Teen Years
Transitions	Teen Years Moving Out/Separating
Overcoming Obstacles	Loss

American President
1995/120

D: *Rob Reiner.* **Cast:** *Michael Douglas, Annette Benning.*

This polished, witty story of a liberal, widowed chief executive trying to date a lobbyist provides a pleasant mixture of romantic comedy and political satire. It's fun to see the lengths to which one of the most powerful men in the world has to go with his skeptical daughter, presidential advisors, and the press to have a rendezvous with his new crush.

Work & Prosperity	Balancing Work & Family
Relationships	Lovers
Finding Love	28-54
Transitions	Courting
Overcoming Obstacles	Entrapment

Annie Hall
1977/95

D: *Woody Allen.* **Cast:** *Woody Allen, Diane Keaton, Tony Roberts.*

Allen's comedy is predicated on his over-intellectualized denial that he is the creator, rather than the victim, of his life's choices. In this film, he picks a romantic partner who matches his New York angst, but is all wrong in every other respect. His fear of entrapment and refusal to break his old pattern ultimately encages him in an even more fearful place of loneliness. This is a funny and sad look at the truth of making a relationship work: You have to start with the right partner.

Relationships	Breaking Old Patterns Lovers
Finding Love	28-54
Transitions	20s to 30s Passage Courting
Overcoming Obstacles	Entrapment

Apocalypse Now
1979/150

See *Hearts of Darkness.*

Austin Powers
1997/88

D: *Jay Roach.* **Cast:** *Mike Myers, Elizabeth Hurley, Michael York.*

A wonderful spoof of the Bond movies and the fashion-challenged '60s presents a swinging '60s spy, Austin Powers, pursuing the elusive Dr. Evil (both played by Myers). Both are caught in a time warp and deposited into the '90s, woefully clueless. The contrast between the morality of two eras is a very funny illustration of the differences in the times and the generations. Try this one with a vintage Bond movie for an entertaining double bill.

Work & Prosperity	Loving Your Work
Relationships	Lovers
Finding Love	20's 28-54
Transitions	Achieving Career Goals
Overcoming Obstacles	Adventure

Avalon

1990/126

D: *Barry Levinson.* **Cast:** *Armin Mueller-Stahl, Elizabeth Perkins, Joan Plowright, Aidan Quinn.*

Based on the true saga of director Levinson's Russian immigrant family, this tender, amusing, and heart-wrenching film looks at three generations pursuing their dreams, dealing with life's transitions, and overcoming obstacles in their own unique way. It contrasts the close-knit generation that arrived in Baltimore full of hope to the next one, as the extended family structure cracks apart after World War II with the move to the isolating suburbs.

Work & Prosperity	Realizing Dreams
Relationships	Multi-Generation Family
Transitions	Mid-Life Crisis 30s & 40s After Retirement 20s to 30s Passage
Overcoming Obstacles	Cultural Abilities

Babe

1995/85

D: *Chris Noonan.* **Cast:** *James Cromwell, Magda Szubanski.*

Based on a children's book, this delightful tale of a young pig named Babe who aspires to be a sheepdog reveals some wise lessons for the child in us all. First, seek and accept love where you find it: Babe is adopted by a female sheepdog after Babe's mother goes to hog heaven. Second, express your talents in your own way: Ignoring the terrorist tactics of dogs, Babe learns to herd with the sheep's cooperation. Third, take risks and challenge the accepted order of things, despite ridicule: Owner Farmer Hoggett enters Babe in a sheepdog herding contest because there is no rule limiting the competition to dogs.

Work & Prosperity	Realizing Dreams Collaborating w/ Colleagues
Relationships	Boss/Employee Colleagues & Co-Workers
Transitions	Achieving Career Goals
Overcoming Obstacles	Physical Abilities

Baby Boom

1987/103

D: *Charles Shyer.* **Cast:** *Diane Keaton, Sam Shepard, Harold Ramis, Sam Wanamaker, James Spader.*

This film charts a woman's emotional highs and lows as she makes the transition from a high-powered corporate job to self-employment. Diane Keaton plays a woman who seeks power in a traditionally male fashion. Her quest is to become a partner in her Manhattan management consulting firm. Unexpectedly, she inherits a baby girl (a bit of a plot stretch). Her investment banker boyfriend leaves her. She then buys her dream house in Vermont, which turns out to be the house from hell. It's amusing to watch her go through her three phases of the void—reacting and resisting, reluctantly acting, and then creating a completely new way of life. She ends up having something that is much better than her initial idea. She gets to have power in a woman's way—her own business, balance of work and family, and a loving relationship with the local veterinarian, played by Sam Shepard. Some ambitious working moms use this movie as a crying release.

Work & Prosperity	Balancing Work & Family
Relationships	Single Parent Lovers Boss/Employee
Finding Love	28-54
Transitions	Changing Careers Becoming Parent Mid-Life Crisis 30s & 40s
Overcoming Obstacles	Sexual Prejudice

Back to School

1986/94

D: *Alan Metter.* **Cast:** *Rodney Dangerfield, Sally Kellerman, Burt Young, Keith Gordon.*

This is about a self-made millionaire (Dangerfield) who enrolls in his beloved-but-wimpy son's college as a student to show the boy the ropes to success. His hilarious "buy the best" approach has him remodeling his dorm room and consulting with experts like Kurt Vonnegut, Jr. on his own writing. Along the way, he falls for a sexy English teacher. Like film comedic greats W. C. Fields and Groucho Marx, Dangerfield holds underneath his loud exterior the poignancy of a man who cannot fulfill his need for respect. So he laughs to mask his pain.

Relationships	Parent/Child Lovers
Finding Love	28-54
Transitions	Mid-50s Passage College Years
Overcoming Obstacles	Age Prejudice

Back to the Future

1985/116

D: *Robert Zemeckis.* **Cast:** *Michael J. Fox, Christopher Lloyd, Lea Thompson, Crispin Glover.*

This story's premise—smart kid (Fox) in middle-class suburb redefines reality for his parents (Thompson and Glover)—presents the ultimate optimistic solution to everyone's problems. Travel back in time and straighten out your parents' problems in their formative teenage years. Watching this movie several times sustains a tremendous uplifting feeling because of the zany comic effect of the time shifts between the 50s and the 80s and the expansive humanistic possibilities of transforming the present. Which of your parents' dreams and hopes did they never get to realize? What would your own life be like if they could have made their dreams come true? The 1989 *Part II* (107m.) and 1990 *Part III* (118m.) sequels continue the story of the McFly family and Doc in the future and the past, but not with quite the same charm and wit as the original.

Work & Prosperity	Realizing Dreams
Relationships	Parent/Child Self-Esteem Lovers
Finding Love	Teen Years
Transitions	Teen Years
Overcoming Obstacles	Entrapment

Back to the Future, Part II

1989/107

See *Back to the Future.*

Back to the Future, Part III

1990/118

See *Back to the Future.*

Backbeat
1993/100

D: *Iain Softley.* **Cast:** *Stephen Dorff, Sheryl Lee, Ian Hart.*

This intriguing examination of young ambition and artistic choices follows John Lennon, his pal Stu Sutcliffe, and their band to Germany, where they feud, play, and experiment with the sound and visual look of the soon-to-be infamous Beatles. The story focuses on Stu, an unenthusiastic stage performer torn between friendship and his love of painting. The authentic re-creation of the early 1960s mood heightens this well-acted English drama.

Work & Prosperity	Realizing Dreams Collaborating w/ Colleagues
Relationships	Friends
Transitions	20s Landing First Job
Overcoming Obstacles	Creative Expression

Bad and the Beautiful, The
1952/118

D: *Vincente Minnelli.* **Cast:** *Kirk Douglas, Lana Turner, Dick Powell, Gloria Grahame, Barry Sullivan.*

This superb yarn tells how an ambitious Hollywood producer collaborates with another producer, an actress, and a writer through good times and bad. The film offers compelling examples of the first three stages of how to achieve career goals.

Work & Prosperity	Collaborating w/ Colleagues
Relationships	Colleagues & Co-Workers
Transitions	Achieving Career Goals
Overcoming Obstacles	Creative Expression

Bagdad Cafe
1988/91

D: *Percy Adlon.* **Cast:** *Marianne Sägebrecht, CCH Pounder, Jack Palance.*

This is a lilting tale of an overweight, uptight German matron, who is abandoned by her husband while they are on a vacation, in the U.S., and how she adjusts to a new life at a Mojave Desert truck stop. Told with an insightful European eye for the little details of everyday American life, the gradual relaxation of this lady is contrasted with the laid-back black woman proprietor and her family, employees, and tenants, who unsuspectingly fall under the Teutonic spell of cleanliness and magic.

Work & Prosperity	Realizing Dreams
Relationships	Boss/Employee
Finding Love	28-54
Transitions	Mid-Life Crisis 30s & 40s Moving Out/Separating
Overcoming Obstacles	Entrapment

Ballad of Little Jo, The
1993/120

D: *Maggie Greenwald.* **Cast:** *Suzy Amis, Bo Hopkins, Ian McKellen, David Chung.*

This is an engaging tale of a pioneer woman, posing as a man, who becomes a sheep rancher and learns to love her new-found freedom. Inspired by a woman who left the East in 1866 disgraced by a child born out of wedlock, this film takes an honest look at the stifling sexual prejudices of the Victorian West, and the courage and consequences of defying them. The visual feast of Montana scenery and a lush score enhance a superbly-acted script.

Work & Prosperity	Realizing Dreams
Relationships	Breaking Old Patterns Lovers

Finding Love	28-54
Transitions	Changing Careers
Overcoming Obstacles	Sexual Prejudice

Barcelona

1994/102

D: *Whit Stillman.* **Cast:** *Taylor Nichols, Chris Eigeman, Tuska Bergen, Mira Sorvino.*

Set in anti-American Barcelona after Franco's downfall, this quirky romance is about two bickering cousins, a salesman and a U.S. Naval officer, who court sexually aggressive Spanish women. The salesman can't get rid of his unwelcome relative, who operates in an oblivious cloud of arrogant naïveté. Part of the fun is the foreign blindness that makes this military jerk attractive to the opposite sex in Spain but an impossible nerd at home. The writer/director hits exactly the right period tone and manner.

Relationships	Lovers
Finding Love	20s
Transitions	Courting
Overcoming Obstacles	Cultural Abilities

Batteries Not Included

1987/106

D: *Matthew Robbins.* **Cast:** *Hume Cronyn, Jessica Tandy.*

This is a whimsical fantasy about New York tenement residents being terrorized by thugs hired by an evil land developer to evict them. There seems to be no hope until a tiny fleet of aliens shows up to help. Solid performances by Cronyn and Tandy help deliver a strong sense of renewed faith in life.

Relationships	Married Couples
Finding Love	55-81
Transitions	After Retirement
Overcoming Obstacles	Entrapment

Beaches

1988/123

D: *Garry Marshall.* **Cast:** *Bette Midler, Barbara Hershey.*

Make sure the tissue box is full before you watch this tale of a 30-year friendship between two women—one rich and pampered, the other poor and stagestruck. An excellent vehicle to showcase Midler's talent, it traces the shifting tides of friendship and fortunes at each stage—the teens, the 20s, and midlife.

Work & Prosperity	Realizing Dreams
Relationships	Friends Breaking Old Patterns
Transitions	Mid-Life Crisis 30s & 40s 20s Teen Years
Overcoming Obstacles	Loss

Beautiful Dreamers

1992/108

D: *John Kent Harrison.* **Cast:** *Rip Torn, Colm Feore.*

Based on a true story, this film details a friendship between poet Walt Whitman and a Canadian physician who runs an asylum for the mentally ill. Whitman is concerned about who will care for his retarded brother after his death. Sparked by their mutual outrage at the Victorian treatment practices, they join forces and "mainstream" inmates into a local intermural sports program, to the chagrin of the town leaders.

Work & Prosperity	Realizing Dreams
Relationships	Siblings Friends

After-View Feelings Key:

Feel Better/Uplift   Laughing Release   Crying Release   Violent Content

Transitions	Achieving Career Goals
Overcoming Obstacles	Mental Abilities

Beautiful Girls
1996/110

D: *Ted Demme.* **Cast:** *Timothy Hutton, Matt Dillon, Michael Rapaport, Rosie O'Donnell, Uma Thurman.*

This charming ensemble film lays out the amusing challenges of men and the women who love them, all of whom are making the jump-shift passage from their immature 20s to their adult-oriented 30s. In their 20s, they have been focusing on what they did not want—committed relationships. Now they must "grow up" and make long-term choices. For the men, it's time to seek power, such as giving up lounge piano playing to sell office equipment. O'Donnell shines as the cynic who tells it like it is.

Work & Prosperity	Realizing Dreams
Relationships	Lovers Friends
Finding Love	28-54
Transitions	20s to 30s Passage
Overcoming Obstacles	Entrapment

Beauty and the Beast
1991/84

D: *Kirk Wise, Gary Trousdale.* **Cast:** *Paige O'Hara, Robby Benson, Rex Everhart, Richard White, Angela Lansbury.*

This charming animated musical recasts the classic fairy tale with an independent, educated beauty who refuses to be intimidated by the crotchety beast. A splendid cast of endearing characters, such as teapots and candelabras, drawn in a lively style, enrich the upbeat score. Based on its all-round excellence, it garnered the first Oscar nomination for an animated feature.

Relationships	Parent/Child Lovers
Finding Love	20s
Transitions	Living Together/Moving In
Overcoming Obstacles	Physical Abilities Entrapment

Before Sunrise
1995/101

D: *Richard Linklater.* **Cast:** *Julie Delpy, Ethan Hawke.*

On a train bound for Paris, a chance encounter between a beautiful, determined French Sorbonne student and a floundering American, jilted, unfolds into an overnight romance in Vienna. This film is filled with charm, tenderness, and the bittersweet knowledge that this is all there will ever be to their relationship. The intelligent script, honest acting by Delpy and Hawke, and Viennese scenery hold your attention and might just ignite your own memories of youthful possibilities gone by.

Relationships	Lovers
Finding Love	College Years
Transitions	College Years
Overcoming Obstacles	Adventure

Being There
1979/130

D: *Hal Ashby.* **Cast:** *Peter Sellers, Shirley MacLaine.*

In this adaptation of Jerzy Kosinski's satiric novel, Peter Sellers is marvelous as a simple, dim-witted estate gardener whose knowledge of life comes from television. When his rich employer dies, Sellers is forced into the real world, dressed in his boss' fancy clothes and armed with his trusty remote control. He falls into high political circles and is regarded as a fresh sage, spouting gardening and TV truisms. This much-awarded film is a tribute to Hal Ashby's ability to play every scene for its innate honesty.

Work & Prosperity	Collaborating w/ Colleagues
Relationships	Leader/Follower
Transitions	Changing Careers
Overcoming Obstacles	Mental Abilities

Benny & Joon

1993/98

D: *Jeremiah S. Chechik.* **Cast:** *Johnny Depp, Mary Stuart Masterson, Aidan Quinn.*

This is a fascinating study of love and madness and letting go, made beguiling by Depp's superb tributes to Chaplin and Keaton, and accented by a charming score. A brother (Quinn) supports his schizophrenic sister Joon, who is relatively calm unless she forgets her medication. A poker game loss brings the dyslexic Benny (Depp) to live in their spare bedroom. As the couple slip into love, Joon's brother is unable to release her to live a life of her own, uncertain as that may be. This film creates an air of hope that lingers days later, despite the downbeat topic.

Relationships	Siblings Lovers
Finding Love	20s
Transitions	Moving Out/Separating
Overcoming Obstacles	Mental Abilities

Beverly Hills Cop

1984/105

D: *Martin Brest.* **Cast:** *Eddie Murphy, Judge Reinhold.*

A slapstick Eddie Murphy action vehicle spins out the premise of a smooth-talking Detroit cop seeking the killer of a close friend in tony Beverly Hills. While learning the ropes of affluence, Eddie is pursued by the murderer and suspicious local police in a story with more plot twists than most pretzels.

Work & Prosperity	Collaborating w/ Colleagues
Relationships	Colleagues & Co-Workers
Transitions	20s to 30s Passage
Overcoming Obstacles	Loss

Big

1988/102

D: *Penny Marshall.* **Cast:** *Tom Hanks, Elizabeth Perkins, Robert Loggia, Jared Rushton.*

In this film a 12-year-old boy's wish to be big enough to pass an amusement park height requirement is granted. He is transformed into a 30-year-old who must learn to do such adult things as making a living. In one of Tom Hanks' finest roles, he's totally credible as a kid trapped in an executive's body, and his genuine love of toys puts him way ahead of the other toy company executives who have forgotten how to play. It's a wise and funny example of how easy it is to get what you want by focusing on the quality (big) and why it's important to consider carefully what you're asking for before making the request. This film has fun demonstrating the risks and problems of not taking each growth step in its proper order.

Work & Prosperity	Realizing Dreams
Relationships	Lovers Boss/Employee Friends
Finding Love	Radical Age Differences
Transitions	Changing Careers
Overcoming Obstacles	Physical Abilities Adventure

After-View Feelings Key:

Feel Better/Uplift   Laughing Release   Crying Release   Violent Content

Big Chill, The

1983/108

D: *Lawrence Kasdan.* **Cast:** *Tom Berenger, Glenn Close, Jeff Goldblum, William Hurt, Kevin Kline, Mary Kay Place.*

This is a beautiful ode to the mid-30s attitude adjustment needed to cope with increasing age and affluence. Heightened by a nostalgic 1960s score of mostly Motown hits, seven 1960s radicals reunite to mourn the suicide of a friend who never lived up to his great promise. Playing "You Can't Always Get What You Want" at his funeral, they recall their own youthful dreams before immersing themselves in the Yuppie lifestyle their success has brought them. Transitions are never neat, but the process of releasing the yearnings of a college-aged self and embracing the hopes of adulthood has never been shown in a more entertaining way.

Work & Prosperity	Realizing Dreams
Relationships	Lovers Friends Two-Career Couples
Finding Love	28-54
Transitions	Mid-Life Crisis 30s & 40s
Overcoming Obstacles	Loss

Big Easy, The

1987/106

D: *Jim McBride.* **Cast:** *Dennis Quaid, Ellen Barkin, Ned Beatty.*

Like its namesake city New Orleans, this captivating thriller is filled with fascinating characters who are at turns colorful, romantic, steamy, delicious, mysterious, dank, and decaying. Set to a throbbing Cajun music score, it is also an irresistible yet all-wrong romance between a decent cop on the take and an uptight investigating D.A., who join forces to solve a web of Mafia-style killings.

Work & Prosperity	Collaborating w/ Colleagues
Relationships	Lovers Colleagues & Co-Workers
Finding Love	28-54
Transitions	20s to 30s Passage
Overcoming Obstacles	Sexual Prejudice Adventure

Big Night

1995/109

D: *Stanley Tucci, Campbell Scott.* **Cast:** *Tony Shalhoub, Stanley Tucci, Ian Holm, Minnie Driver, Campbell Scott.*

Set in the 1950s, this delightful food film about two Italian brothers with a failing New Jersey restaurant will whet your appetite and warm your heart. Caught between the chef brother's non-commercial perfectionism and the younger brother's desire to Americanize for success, they plan a last-ditch special feast in honor of jazz trumpeter Louis Prima.

Work & Prosperity	Realizing Dreams Loving Your Work
Relationships	Siblings
Transitions	Achieving Career Goals
Overcoming Obstacles	Creative Expression

Big Picture, The

1989/95

D: *Christopher Guest.* **Cast:** *Kevin Bacon, Jennifer Jason Leigh, Martin Short, Michael McKean.*

This movie is a satirical take on the Hollywood picture-making system told through the experiences of an award-winning student filmmaker (Bacon). He is seduced by all the trappings of feature pictures and fame, including the beautiful women and the Porsche with car phone, and then dropped summarily by the studio. Reduced to being a bicycle messenger, he tries to convince his architect girlfriend to take him back. This feel-good film demonstrates the perils of too much, too soon. It shows how important it is for ambitious people to have a loving relationship to anchor them as they ride the emotional roller coaster of getting what they think they want.

Work & Prosperity	Realizing Dreams Collaborating w/ Colleagues
Relationships	Lovers Colleagues & Co-Workers
Finding Love	20s
Transitions	20s Landing First Job
Overcoming Obstacles	Creative Expression

Blazing Saddles

1974/90

D: *Mel Brooks, Alan Uger.* **Cast:** *Cleavon Little, Harvey Korman, Madeline Kahn, Gene Wilder.*

This wacky spoof of Westerns, written by a team of the best comedy writers of the 1970s, has fun with every cliche of the genre. This film offers a rollicking good time as it bounces along with sight gags and goofball characters, led by Little as Black Bart, a convict offered a reprieve if he will clean up a violent town as the sheriff. The job's previous holders are all six feet under.

Work & Prosperity	Collaborating w/ Colleagues
Relationships	Colleagues & Co-Workers Leader/Follower
Transitions	Changing Careers
Overcoming Obstacles	Adventure

Bodyguard, The

1992 /130

D: *Mick Jackson.* **Cast:** *Kevin Costner, Whitney Houston.*

An unlikely romance unfolds between a pampered pop singer diva and her reluctant bodyguard, a former Secret Service Security adviser. Houston does well in her movie debut, although it is no stretch from her real life fame, entourage, and celebrity trappings. Costner, in a Steve McQueen haircut, plays a tightly wound technician still blaming himself for Ronald Reagan's assassination attempt, even though it was his day off. The music helps elevate this tale of the longing we all have to be loved and to feel safe.

Work & Prosperity	Balancing Work & Family
Relationships	Lovers Boss/Employee
Finding Love	28-54
Transitions	Changing Careers
Overcoming Obstacles	Entrapment

Boys on the Side

1995/120

D: *Herbert Ross.* **Cast:** *Whoopi Goldberg, Mary-Louise Parker, Drew Barrymore.*

This is a touching examination of the complexities of female friendship amidst the quest for true love. An unlikely trio—an uptight HIV-positive real estate agent, a gay black piano player, and her young pregnant druggie friend—set off on a cross-country drive and end up as bickering, but supportive, housemates in Tucson, waiting out the gradual demise of their ill friend.

Relationships	Friends Lovers
Finding Love	Same Sex 28-54 20s

Transitions Living Together/Moving In
Overcoming Obstacles Loss

Breaker Morant

1980/107

D: *Bruce Beresford.* **Cast:** *Edward Woodward, Jack Thompson, John Waters, Bryan Brown.*

Based on a true story, this riveting courtroom drama shows the perils of being a second class citizen in an arrogant political organization trying to save face. In this case, three Australian soldiers in the Boer War are tried by the British on trumped-up charges for the murder of some prisoners. Actually, they were just following orders. Much awarded, this film initiated the Australian cinema renaissance.

Work & Prosperity Collaborating w/ Colleagues
Relationships Boss/Employee
Transitions Losing Job
Overcoming Obstacles Class Prejudice, Cultural Abilities, War

Breaking Away

1979/100

D: *Peter Yates.* **Cast:** *Dennis Christopher, Dennis Quaid, Paul Dooley, Barbara Barrie.*

This is a charming, uplifting coming-of-age story about four working class boys trying to figure what to do with their lives after high school. The tale is told with the fresh, tender acuity of the Yugoslavian-born writer's observation of American life in Bloomington, Indiana. One boy (Christopher), a romantic at heart, starts out on a quest to race bicycles against the Italians and ends up going to college. All the steps to making your dreams come true are here—setting up the challenge, the loss of innocence, overcoming the obstacles, letting go of the dream, getting what you want, and having it turn out much better than you could imagine. Dooley is very amusing as Christopher's befuddled used car dealer father. Barrie is sweet as his romantic co-conspirator mother.

Work & Prosperity Realizing Dreams
Relationships Friends, Working Parents
Finding Love Teen Years
Transitions Teen Years
Overcoming Obstacles Class Prejudice

Brideshead Revisited

1981/540

D: *Charles Sturridge, Michael Lindsay-Hogg.* **Cast:** *Jeremy Irons, Anthony Andrews, Diana Quick, Laurence Olivier, Claire Bloom.*

Perfect for viewing over several long winter nights, this adaptation of Evelyn Waugh's novel about English upper-class decadence is an insightful examination of how a person changes his or her definition of success and status from college age to mid-life. Irons is a genteel college man who is beguiled by the wealthy Marchmain family. He struggles to maintain his integrity and identity through a love affair in college with the Marchmain brother and another in mid-life with the sister. Superb British production values impart a true sense of the Edwardian and post-World War I periods.

Relationships Lovers, Friends, Multi-Generation Family
Finding Love 28-54, College Years, Same Sex
Transitions College Years, Mid-Life Crisis 30s & 40s
Overcoming Obstacles Class Prejudice

Bridges of Madison County, The 1995/135

D: *Clint Eastwood.* **Cast:** *Meryl Streep, Clint Eastwood.*

Set in the late 1960s, Robert Waller's bestselling older-adult romance novel is turned into an even better screen fantasy guaranteed to open up the tear ducts of anyone who has remorse about not following his or her heart. Alone for a few days, a 40-something Iowa farm homemaker and mother has a passionate affair "that happens only once in many lifetimes." Her lover, a 50-something *National Geographic* photographer, begs her to come with him, but she chooses to stay and remember. He leaves with his freedom and regrets that he has been denied the one thing in life he wants most—her loving presence. Jazz afficionado Eastwood selects the perfect slow ballads to support the mood of sexual tension, giddiness, and impending melancholy.

Relationships	Lovers
Finding Love	28-54
Transitions	Courting
Overcoming Obstacles	Entrapment

Brief History of Time, A 1992/85

D: *Errol Morris.* **Cast:** *Stephen Hawking.*

An inspiring documentary about British physicist Stephen Hawking, author of the best-selling book *A Brief History of Time*, shows how his brilliant mind has triumphed over a body debilitated by Lou Gehrig's disease. Ironically, his increasing physical disability focused his attention on his scientific explorations. The film is filled with interviews with Hawking's family, friends, and colleagues. Hawking narrates the film about his scientific theories in an eery, computer-generated voice with an American-English accent.

Work & Prosperity	Loving Your Work
Relationships	Colleagues & Co-Workers
Transitions	Achieving Career Goals
Overcoming Obstacles	Physical Abilities

Broadcast News 1987/125

D: *James L. Brooks.* **Cast:** *William Hurt, Albert Brooks, Holly Hunter, Lois Chiles, Joan Cusack.*

This film about a three-way workplace romance in a TV newsroom shows the stresses of layoffs, workaholism, and a lack of balance between work and a personal life. A TV news producer (Hunter) and two reporters (Brooks and Hurt) dance around their emotional feelings about each other through the haze of workaholism. A good look at how choosing career success over a love relationship can be difficult for women charting new territory in a man's world.

Work & Prosperity	Destructuring Workplace Balancing Work & Family
Relationships	Lovers Colleagues & Co-Workers
Finding Love	28-54
Transitions	20s to 30s Passage
Overcoming Obstacles	Sexual Prejudice

Brother From Another Planet, The 1984/109

D: *John Sayles.* **Cast:** *Joe Morton, Dee Dee Bridgewater, Ren Woods.*

This wry tale is about a telepathic black alien who can't speak and looks human except for three big toes, and how he escapes his home planet to wind up in Harlem, pursued by two alien bounty hunters. In one amusing scene after another, this mute mirror of our strange culture listens while people tell him what he thinks and acts as if they are right. Like the great silent comedians, Joe Morton is excellent as the lead who is surprised that he is black and that it makes a difference on this planet.

Relationships	Lovers Colleagues & Co-Workers
Finding Love	28-54
Transitions	Changing Careers
Overcoming Obstacles	Racial Prejudice

Brothers McMullen, The
1994/98

D: *Edward Burns.* **Cast:** *Edward Burns, Jack Mulcahy, Mike McGlone.*

This charming romantic comedy about three Irish-American brothers in their 20s seeking love shows a funny, Long Island, lower-class slice of life about honesty, sibling rivalry, and Catholic guilt. The oldest brother struggles with infidelity in his marriage, the middle one professes confirmed bachelorhood, and the youngest—engaged to a Jewish woman—mixes hopeless romanticism with religious angst. The brothers' primary bond is their mutual hatred of their late alcoholic father.

Relationships	Siblings Married Couples Lovers
Finding Love	20s
Transitions	Courting Living Together/Moving In
Overcoming Obstacles	Entrapment

Buddy Holly Story, The
1978/113

D: *Steve Rash.* **Cast:** *Gary Busey, Don Stroud, Charles Martin Smith.*

This is a completely credible acting and musical performance by Busey as R&B genius Buddy Holly, whose brief life left an uplifting musical legacy that still sounds fresh today. Holly's life has all the soap opera elements needed to keep a good plot moving: edgy talent, driving ambition, meteoric rise to fame, young marriage, and tragic airplane crash. Enjoy his tunes such as "That'll Be the Day," "Oh, Boy," "It's So Easy," "Well All Right," "Chantilly Lace," and "Peggy Sue."

Work & Prosperity	Realizing Dreams
Relationships	Colleagues & Co-Workers
Transitions	20s Landing First Job
Overcoming Obstacles	Creative Expression

Bull Durham
1988/108

D: *Ron Shelton.* **Cast:** *Kevin Costner, Susan Sarandon, Tim Robbins, Trey Wilson, Robert Wuhl.*

Annie Savoy (Sarandon) is on a quest to find a young baseball player for the season claiming "There's never been a ballplayer who slept with me who didn't have the best year of his career." But this season the ballplayer she really wants, Crash Davis (Costner), a catcher hanging on to break a league record before retiring, refuses to play her game. She ends up with a cocky young pitcher, Ebby Calvin "Nuke" LaLoosh (Robbins), whom Crash is supposed to "mature" for the major leagues. This hilarious, literate sex and baseball comedy offers lots of surprises, sharp commentary on baseball, and a driving R&B musical score to punctuate the witty dialogue.

Work & Prosperity	Realizing Dreams Collaborating w/ Colleagues
Relationships	Lovers Colleagues & Co-Workers
Finding Love	28-54 Radical Age Differences
Transitions	Landing First Job Losing Job Courting
Overcoming Obstacles	Adventure

Bullets Over Broadway
1995/95

D: *Woody Allen.* **Cast:** *John Cusack, Jennifer Tilly, Chazz Palminteri, Dianne Wiest, Tracey Ullman.*

This is a witty, wise tale of the difficulties created when a struggling playwright has his first play produced by a gangster, as a vehicle for the gangster's ambitious, untalented girlfriend. The fun begins when the writer starts heeding script development advice from her bodyguard, an illiterate mob hit man with a natural sense of the dramatic. Set in the 1920s, this film is filled with wonderful parodies of New York theatrical types.

Work & Prosperity	Collaborating w/ Colleagues
Relationships	Colleagues & Co-Workers
Transitions	Landing First Job
Overcoming Obstacles	Creative Expression

Bye Bye, Love
1994/107

D: *Sam Weisman.* **Cast:** *Matthew Modine, Randy Quaid, Paul Reiser, Rob Reiner, Janeane Garofalo.*

This is a funny, wistful look at three divorced dads living, loving their children, and seeking better relationships than what they had in their first marriages. The fathers are caught in the weekly seesaw of trading kids with the ex-spouses at McDonalds, The movie contrasts how one man still loves his ex, another hates his, and the third enjoys all women.

Relationships	Divorced Couples Parent/Child Single Parent
Finding Love	28-54
Transitions	Divorcing Courting

Can't Buy Me Love
1987/94

D: *Steve Rash.* **Cast:** *Amanda Peterson, Patrick Dempsey.*

This is a story of a geeky lawn boy's quest to be accepted by the in-crowd at his Tucson high school. He decides to buy a dress for one of the head cheerleaders in exchange for her spending time with him. The ploy works for a while, but he's not prepared for the emotional feelings that arise. His transformation—from nerd to popular man-about-campus to social outcast ultimately finding self-acceptance—is fun to watch. It holds wisdom for kids of any age about the importance of pleasing oneself before pleasing others.

Work & Prosperity	Realizing Dreams
Relationships	Lovers Friends Self-Esteem
Finding Love	Teen Years
Transitions	Teen Years Courting
Overcoming Obstacles	Class Prejudice

Casablanca
1942/102

D: *Michael Curtiz.* **Cast:** *Humphrey Bogart, Ingrid Bergman, Paul Henreid, Claude Rains, Sydney Greenstreet.*

This film represents the best of what the Hollywood studio system can do when the right team of actors, director, writers, and cinematographer is pulled together to inspire Americans to support the war effort. It's the story of how American Rick (Bogart) makes the transition from noncommitment in his relationship with Ilsa (Bergman) and to the World War II war effort, to releasing Ilsa to her husband and joining the fight against the Nazis. Early 1940s Casablanca is a place where everyone is in transition and making choices about which side to take in the war. Some of the dialogue is laughable by 1990s standards and fun to see with an audience. Still, it clearly shows Rick's emotional path of healing, setting aside his own needs, and, in the end, acting unselfishly for a greater cause.

Work & Prosperity	Collaborating w/ Colleagues
Relationships	Lovers Colleagues & Co-Workers Breaking Old Patterns Friends
Finding Love	28-54
Transitions	Changing Careers
Overcoming Obstacles	War Loss

Cemetery Club, The

1992/107

D: *Bill Duke.* **Cast:** *Ellen Burstyn, Olympia Dukakis, Diane Ladd, Danny Aiello, Lainie Kazan.*

Based on a stageplay, this amusing, touching film demonstrates that single life and the dating experience can be disconcerting at any age, especially for three long-married, recently widowed Jewish friends in their 60s. They visit the cemetery together and reminisce until two decide to let go of the past and seek new relationships. When one falls head over heels in love, the others are surprised at first, and then slip into jealousy and disapproval.

Relationships	Breaking Old Patterns Lovers Friends
Finding Love	55-81
Transitions	Losing Mate 60s & 70s
Overcoming Obstacles	Loss

Chances Are

1989/108

D: *Emile Ardolino.* **Cast:** *Cybill Shepherd, Robert Downey, Jr., Ryan O' Neal, Mary Stuart Masterson.*

This is a wonderful, witty, ironic, convincing tale about a widow and her late husband who reincarnates as their daughter's Yale boyfriend. The fun begins when he returns home and starts to remember, torn by his feelings for both women.

Relationships	Lovers Parent/Child
Finding Love	Radical Age Differences 20s
Transitions	Losing Mate
Overcoming Obstacles	Loss

Chariots of Fire

1981/123

D: *Hugh Hudson.* **Cast:** *Ben Cross, Ian Charleson, Nigel Havers, Ian Holm.*

A rousing score and beautiful photography sustain a deeply moving film about two runners whose superb athletic ability diffuses class prejudice long enough for British society toallow them begrudgingly to participate in the 1924 Olympic Games. This inspiring underdog story of an immigrant Jew and a Calvinist Scot achieving dignity in their own right leaves you feeling uplifted and ready to tackle your most difficult challenges.

Work & Prosperity	Realizing Dreams Collaborating w/ Colleagues
Relationships	Colleagues & Co-Workers
Transitions	College Years
Overcoming Obstacles	Class Prejudice

Circle of Friends

1994/96

D: *Pat O'Connor.* **Cast:** *Chris O'donnell, Minnie Driver, Geraldine O'Rawe, Saffron Burrows, Colin Firth.*

Based on a Maeve Binchy novel, this touching Irish coming-of-age tale focuses on three girlfriends resolving their childhood Catholicism with their heart and newly discovered hormones, as they navigate the passage into womanhood at a Dublin university. The whole range of emotions are here to be enjoyed as they court their men—the funny but embarrassing moments, the release of adolescent disappointments, and the small and large triumphs.

Relationships	Lovers Friends
Finding Love	20's College Years
Transitions	Courting

City Slickers

1991/114

D: *Ron Underwood.* **Cast:** *Billy Crystal, Bruno Kirby, Patricia Wettig, Helen Slater, Jack Palance.*

Here's a riotous look at three middle-aged New Yorkers taking their mid-life crisis to a "wild" West dude ranch, where they play out their anxieties on unsuspecting cattle. Palance steals the show as the wise old cowhand who has no time for neurotic city ways.

Work & Prosperity	Realizing Dreams
Relationships	Breaking Old Patterns
Finding Love	Radical Age Differences
Transitions	Mid-Life Crisis 30s & 40s
Overcoming Obstacles	Adventure

City Slickers II

1994/116

See *City Slickers*

Clerks

1994/92

D: *Kevin Smith.* **Cast:** *Brian O' Halloran, Jeff Anderson.*

This is a wickedly funny depiction of one day in the life of two aimless young New Jersey men working as clerks in adjacent convenience and video stores. Shot in black and white, the film highlights the sense of exploitation, frustration, confusion, rebellion, and drifting of a long day filled with a riotous parade of rude customers, offensive buddies, and old and new girlfriends.

Work & Prosperity	Collaborating w/ Colleagues
Relationships	Boss/Employee
Finding Love	20s
Transitions	Landing First Job
Overcoming Obstacles	Entrapment

Clueless

1995/113

D: *Amy Heckerling.* **Cast:** *Alicia Silverstone, Stacey Dash, Paul Rudd, Brittany Murphy, Donald A. Faison.*

A sharp satire on our materialistic culture is told through the teenage adventures of Cher, a nouveau rich spoiled brat who can't resist making over a lost soul classmate at Beverly Hills High. Only her skeptical stepbrother can call her bluff, but he eventually succumbs to her charm, as well. See Jane Austen's "Emma" for the English Regency-period version of this plot.

Relationships	Parent/Child Breaking Old Patterns

Finding Love	Teen Years
Transitions	Teen Years Courting

Cocoon

1985/115

D: *Ron Howard.* **Cast:** *Wilford Brimley, Jessica Tandy, Brian Dennehy, Hume Cronyn, Don Ameche.*

This sweet telling of the quest for everlasting life is based on the upbeat premise that technologically advanced aliens from outer space might be as silly and unpredictable as we humans are. Three friends (Brimley, Cronyn, and Ameche) in a Florida retirement home start sneaking dips in a nearby mansion's swimming pool, which has a bottom covered with large mossy rocks. Surprisingly, they start feeling incredibly youthful. The alien owner (Dennehy) is reawakening the rocks/cocoons left behind 10,000 years ago. And, it works on humans, too. Dennehy tells the trio not to tell anyone about it, but their transformation creates havoc in their relationships with their spouses and grandchildren.

Work & Prosperity	Collaborating w/ Colleagues Realizing Dreams
Relationships	Colleagues & Co-Workers Multi-Generation Family
Finding Love	55-81
Transitions	After Retirement
Overcoming Obstacles	Age Prejudice Physical Abilities

Cold Sassy Tree

1989/97

D: *Joan Tewkesbury.* **Cast:** *Faye Dunaway, Richard Widmark, Frances Fisher, Neil Patrick Harris.*

This multigenerational tale of Southern life, work, and love at the turn of the 20th century is told by the grandson. It details his grandfather's quest for love the second time around and his girlfriend's quest for respect in her work and her reluctance to receive his love. Tenderly acted by Richard Widmark and Faye Dunaway, with smart period sets, it evokes the mood of a time when automobiles were brand new and things seemed simpler, but in many ways were more restrictive.

Work & Prosperity	Loving Your Work Realizing Dreams
Relationships	Lovers Multi-Generation Family
Finding Love	Radical Age Differences
Transitions	Living Together/Moving In Marrying
Overcoming Obstacles	Sexual Prejudice Entrapment

Color Purple, The

1985/155

D: *Steven Spielberg.* **Cast:** *Danny Glover, Whoopi Goldberg, Margaret Avery, Oprah Winfrey, Willard Pugh.*

Based on Alice Walker's novel, this is a deep, brutal, yet lyrical telling of an uneducated, unattractive black woman's quest for self-esteem over four decades. Despite all odds, the heroine transforms from the mute, naive teen wife of an explosive, hard-hearted man into a confident, smiling middle-aged woman who knows her strengths. Outstanding performances all around are heightened by the authentic period look and swinging sound of the juke joint South from 1909 to 1947.

Work & Prosperity	Realizing Dreams
Relationships	Self-Esteem Friends Multi-Generation Family
Finding Love	28-54
Transitions	Teen Years Marrying
Overcoming Obstacles	Sexual Prejudice Entrapment Loss

Cool Runnings

1993/98

D: *Jon Turteltaub.* **Cast:** *Leon, Doug E. Doug, Rawle D. Lewis, Malik Yoba, John Candy.*

Based on the true story of the Jamaican bobsled team which participated in the 1988 Calgary Winter Olympics, this movie takes the feel-good effect to its highest height. A second-generation Olympic track contender is disqualified from the summer Olympics. In a wonderful example of how to turn a crisis into an opportunity, he puts together a bobsled team for the winter games with a reluctant coach (John Candy). No matter how you feel before you see it, you'll feel great afterward. You'll laugh a lot and be fired up to continue to tackle your own dreams with a new dedication and an elevated understanding of what it really takes to make them happen.

Work & Prosperity	Realizing Dreams Collaborating w/ Colleagues
Relationships	Colleagues & Co-Workers
Transitions	Changing Careers
Overcoming Obstacles	Physical Abilities Adventure

Corrina, Corrina

1994/115

D: *Jessie Nelson.* **Cast:** *Whoopi Goldberg, Ray Liotta.*

Set to the cool tunes of 1950s jazz classics like Louis Armstrong's "You Go to My Head," a black musicologist, working as a housekeeper, draws out a grieving little white girl, who has refused to speak since her mother's death. A romance unfolds with the music jingle-writing father, to the daughter's delight, over interracial objections by both families. A rare and moving examination of loss, grieving, and healing, told from the child's perspective.

Relationships	Parent/Child Lovers
Finding Love	28-54
Transitions	Courting Losing Mate
Overcoming Obstacles	Loss Racial Prejudice

Crossing Delancey

1988/97

D: *Joan Micklin Silver.* **Cast:** *Amy Irving, Reizl Bozyk, Peter Riegert, Jeroen Krabbé, Sylvia Miles.*

Based on the play, this is a pleasing story of a Manhattan Jewish bookworm in her 30s learning to find love through her heart, not her head. Her intellectually perfect life starts to unravel when her grandmother, concerned about her spinsterhood, hires a Lower East Side matchmaker, who offers up a big-hearted heir to a pickle store.

Relationships	Lovers
Finding Love	28-54
Transitions	Courting
Overcoming Obstacles	Class Prejudice

Cry, The Beloved Country 1995/109

D: *Darrell James Roodt.* **Cast:** *James Earl Jones, Richard Harris, Charles S. Dutton.*

This sad film, based on Alan Paton's classic South African novel, ultimately inspires us to keep our faith despite difficult circumstances. Jones stuns us with his portrayal of a spiritual black preacher and father of a son who murders a white civil rights advocate. He desperately clings to his principles despite living in a world totally corrupted by racial hate.

Relationships	Parent/Child Breaking Old Patterns
Overcoming Obstacles	Racial Prejudice

Dances with Wolves 1990/181

D: *Kevin Costner.* **Cast:** *Kevin Costner, Mary McDonnell, Graham Green.*

Overshadowed by sad historical realities, this gorgeous epic is an ode to understanding between Native Americans and whites. It follows a Union officer stranded on the prairie as he comes to know and appreciate a local tribe of Lakota Sioux. A tender love story gradually unfolds between the soldier (Costner) and a captured/adopted white translator (McDonnell).

Work & Prosperity	Collaborating w/ Colleagues
Relationships	Lovers Colleagues & Co-Workers
Finding Love	28-54
Transitions	Changing Careers
Overcoming Obstacles	Racial Prejudice

Dave 1993/110

D: *Ivan Reitman.* **Cast:** *Kevin Kline, Sigourney Weaver, Frank Langella.*

This is a refreshing, upbeat tale of ordinary nice guy Dave Kovic, a Presidential look-alike who is thrust into permanently posing as the chief of state, since the real prez has been felled by a debilitating stroke. Trouble begins when Dave starts to enjoy his new job and makes some decisions, such as bringing in his CPA to help balance the federal budget. With intelligent tenderness, a romance between the lonely President's wife and Dave blossoms as White House intrigue to dethrone him escalates.

Work & Prosperity	Collaborating w/ Colleagues Balancing Work & Family
Relationships	Lovers Colleagues & Co-Workers
Finding Love	28-54
Transitions	Changing Careers
Overcoming Obstacles	Adventure

Dead Again 1991/107

D: *Kenneth Branagh.* **Cast:** *Kenneth Branagh, Emma Thompson, Andy Garcia, Derek Jacobi.*

In a cinematic grand opera fashioned in homage to Hitchcock and Welles, this lush romantic thriller about love, murder, and reincarnation spins an intriguing tale of past-life sins bleeding through time to disrupt the present. In the 1940s, a composer is accused of murdering his lovely wife. In the present day, an amnesiac searches for her lost memory for the source of her nightmares with the aid of a hypnotist and a skeptical detective.

Work & Prosperity	Collaborating w/ Colleagues
Relationships	Breaking Old Patterns Lovers Married Couples

Finding Love	28-54
Transitions	Losing Mate
Overcoming Obstacles	Loss

Deep Cover

1992/112

D: *Bill Duke.* **Cast:** *Laurence Fishburne, Jeff Goldblum, Victoria Dillard, Charles Martin Smith.*

Masquerading as a thriller, this is a powerful morality tale about a cop who goes undercover and dislikes being involved with big-time cocaine dealers. In deep cover, he must re-examine the foundation of his good guy image created when, as a child, he witnessed his father's murder.

Work & Prosperity	Loving Your Work Collaborating w/ Colleagues
Relationships	Colleagues & Co-Workers
Transitions	Changing Careers
Overcoming Obstacles	Adventure Entrapment

Desperately Seeking Susan

1985/103

D: *Susan Seidelman.* **Cast:** *Rosanna Arquette, Madonna, Aidan Quinn.*

In this screwball comedy of mistaken identity, a bored young New Jersey housewife seeks adventure by responding to a classified ad seeking Susan, and quickly joins an exciting world filled with kooky punk New York City characters. With more plot reverses than it takes to get out of a tight parking spot, this cheerful film caroms along and invites you in on the fun.

Relationships	Lovers Friends
Finding Love	20s
Transitions	20s to 30s Passage Moving Out/Separating
Overcoming Obstacles	Entrapment Adventure

Diary of a Mad Housewife

1970/95

D: *Frank Perry.* **Cast:** *Carrie Snodgrass, Richard Benjamin, Frank Langella.*

Told from the suffering wife's perspective, this is a bemused meditation on the emotional pitfalls of a New York City marriage focused on material perfection. How the wife has gotten herself into this heartless relationship with an insensitive, whining, social climber seems perplexing at first, until she repeats her pattern in a love affair with a writer who turns out to be equally cruel. After all, it's her story to tell as she wishes.

Relationships	Self-Esteem Married Couples
Finding Love	28-54
Transitions	Mid-Life Crisis 30s & 40s
Overcoming Obstacles	Sexual Prejudice Entrapment

Diner

1982/110

D: *Barry Levinson.* **Cast:** *Steve Guttenberg, Daniel Stern, Mickey Rourke, Kevin Bacon, Tim Daly.*

Diner is an episodic college coming-of-age story about a group of Baltimore buddies in their early 20s who are on a reluctant quest for love despite their fear of the opposite sex. The women in their lives try to accommodate and mold themselves to fit into their men's world, but what they really want is to be loved as people, not objects. Shot in black and white with a nostalgic R&B score of the late 1950s, it has a fine ensemble cast and humorously evokes the confusion and frustration created by trying to conform to the simplistic sexual stereotypes of the time.

Relationships	Lovers Friends
Finding Love	20s
Transitions	College Years Moving Out/Separating
Overcoming Obstacles	Loss Sexual Prejudice

Dirty Dancing

1987/100

D: *Emile Ardolino.* **Cast:** *Jennifer Grey, Patrick Swayze, Jerry Orbach, Cynthia Rhodes, Jack Weston.*

This is an energetic 1960s R&B ballet about the coming of age of a protected Jewish high school girl (Grey) and her summer romance with a lower-class gentile dancer (Swayze) at a Catskills resort. Like a good 1930s dance movie, this movie integrates elegant numbers by professional dancers Swayze and Rhodes with a nostalgic music score and sweet, if predictable, scenes of amateur-dancer Grey being coached for a big show by Swayze.

Work & Prosperity	Realizing Dreams Loving Your Work
Relationships	Parent/Child Lovers
Finding Love	Teen Years
Transitions	Teen Years
Overcoming Obstacles	Class Prejudice Physical Abilities

Dominick and Eugene

1988/111

D: *Robert M. Young.* **Cast:** *Tom Hulce, Ray Liotta, Jamie Lee Curtis.*

This is a moving story, honestly told and brilliantly acted, of a slightly retarded brother, Dominick (Hulce), who works as a garbage man to put his intern brother Eugene (Liotta) through medical school. Their loving and carefully supportive relationship is jeopardized when Eugene considers transferring to a California school. Told from Dominick's perspective, it is a glimpse into a unique, innocent world where memories of darker times are overshadowed by a dream of meeting Hulk Hogan.

Work & Prosperity	Balancing Work & Family
Relationships	Siblings Lovers
Finding Love	20s
Transitions	Moving Out/Separating 20s to 30s Passage
Overcoming Obstacles	Mental Abilities

Don Juan deMarco

1995/92

D: *Jeremy Leven.* **Cast:** *Marlon Brando, Johnny Depp, Faye Dunaway.*

This is a thoroughly charming tale of the power of romance to heal pain. An imaginative young man posing as the world's greatest lover enchants a psychiatrist who is trying to cure him in the few weeks before he retires. Transfixed, the doctor begins to enliven his comfortable marriage, to the surprised delight of his wife.

Relationships	Married Couples Lovers Teacher/Student
Finding Love	55-81 20s

Transitions	After Retirement Courting
Overcoming Obstacles	Entrapment

Dr. Strangelove
1964/93

D: *Stanley Kubrick.* **Cast:** *Peter Sellers, George C. Scott, Sterling Hayden.*

This is a timeless satire on the blind stupidity and dire consequences of ego-driven decisions made by large, hierarchical organizations, such as the military and the government. A protest against Cold War brinksmanship, this film captures the frustrations of well-meaning individuals caught in a fail-safe system gone amuck. Sellers showcases his versatile, comic talent as three characters: the U.S. President negotiating to avert a nuclear war; the crippled, maniacal, ex-Nazi war room advisor, Dr. Strangelove; and a British group captain trying to do his duty.

Work & Prosperity	Collaborating w/ Colleagues
Relationships	Colleagues & Co-Workers Leader/Follower
Overcoming Obstacles	War

Dragon: The Bruce Lee Story
1993/119

D: *Rob Cohen.* **Cast:** *Jason Scott Lee, Lauren Holly, Robert Wagner, Michael Learned, Nancy Kwan.*

Based on Bruce Lee's wife's autobiography, *Bruce Lee: The Man Only I Knew,* this film demonstrates the sheer power and joy of doing what you love. It also shows how Mr. Lee's big dream of changing the way Westerners perceive Asians is realized in small steps. First, he writes a book about martial arts while rebuilding his body after a debilitating accident. Then, he founds the first martial arts school for Westerners. Next, he plays a masked character in the Batman television show. And finally, he stars in Hong Kong movies that still hold broad appeal in the West. Unfortunately, Bruce Lee died in his 30s before he could see the fruits of his dream. But a new movie genre, martial arts, is carried on by Steven Seagal and Jean-Claude Van Damme. Lee is the only Asian star, to date, to become well-known in the U.S.

Work & Prosperity	Realizing Dreams
Relationships	Married Couples
Finding Love	20s
Transitions	20s to 30s Passage Changing Careers
Overcoming Obstacles	Racial Prejudice Physical Abilities

Ed Wood
1994/127

D: *Tim Burton.* **Cast:** *Johnny Depp, Martin Landau, Bill Murray, Sarah Jessica Parker.*

This is a hilarious yet touching true tale about an untalented cross-dressing dreamer and his rag-tag crew making 1950s movies so bad they're laughable. Here are some amusing lessons on how *not* to achieve artistic greatness: by setting your career goals way beyond your technical skills, collaborating with incompetent has-beens, and rushing through underfinanced projects.

Work & Prosperity	Loving Your Work
Relationships	Colleagues & Co-Workers
Transitions	Achieving Career Goals
Overcoming Obstacles	Creative Expression

Ed's Next Move
1996/81

D: *John Walsh.* **Cast:** *Matt Ross, Callie Thorne, Kevin Carroll.*

This quiet movie sneaks up on you with its wry, sometimes hilarious, tale of a jilted, 25-year-old Wisconsin man with a

After-View Feelings Key:

Feel Better/Uplift   Laughing Release   Crying Release   Violent Content

mania for planning who moves to the Big Apple. He is charmed by a folk singer who can't break off an abusive relationship and befuddled by his womanizing roommate.

Relationships	Lovers
Transitions	20s Courting

Educating Rita

1983/110

D: *Lewis Gilbert.* **Cast:** *Michael Caine, Julie Walters.*

In this retelling of the Pygmalion story, a boozy literature professor (Caine) finds an eager Cockney hairdresser student (Walters) trying to better herself. Each falls for the highest potential of what the other might be, rather than for who they actually are. She tries to improve herself and her status and wishes he would sober up and return to expressing himself as a poet. He questions whether he is changing her for the better. Both the teacher and the student end up learning from each other in an endearing way.

Work & Prosperity	Realizing Dreams
Relationships	Teacher/Student
Finding Love	28-54
Transitions	Mid-50s Passage
Overcoming Obstacles	Class Prejudice

El Norte

1983/141

D: *Gregory Nava.* **Cast:** *Zaide Silvia Gutierrez, David Villalpando.*

This tale of a brother and sister's quest for a better life in the U.S., rather than in their politically torn Guatemalan home, presents a poetic perspective on the undocumented Hispanic immigrant situation. Their long trek to El Norte (the United States) through Mexico is shown visually and musically in an arresting fashion. The harsh difference between the Latin American version of the American dream and the Los Angeles reality of it is shown in a simple, heart-wrenching way from both the brother's and sister's viewpoints.

Work & Prosperity	Realizing Dreams
Relationships	Sibling
Transitions	Moving Out/Separating Changing Careers
Overcoming Obstacles	Racial Prejudice War Adventure

Emma

1996/120

D: *Douglas McGrath.* **Cast:** *Gwyneth Paltrow, Jeremy Northam, Greta Scacchi, Toni Collette.*

Jane Austen's keen, satirical eye for the foibles of the English upper class in the Regency period, and her ear for witty, upbeat dialogue translate very well into this screen version of the tale of 21-year-old Emma Woodhouse. Emma is a girl who can't resist solving all her friends' problems while being completely blind to her own shortcomings. Her brother-in-law, the dashing Mr. Knightley, watches her antics with cynicism, then exasperation, and finally irresistible attraction. See "Clueless" for a fresh 90s spin on the same story.

Relationships	Parent/Child Friends
Finding Love	20s
Transitions	20s Courting
Overcoming Obstacles	Class Prejudice

Empire Strikes Back, The
1980/124

See *Star Wars Episodes IV, V, VI.*

Enchanted April
1992/97

D: *Mike Newell.* **Cast:** *Miranda Richardson, Joan Plowright, Josie Lawrence, Polly Walker.*

This is an upbeat tale of two depressed, lonely wives in Edwardian England who escape their cold, dreary climate and overbearing husbands by renting a villa on the Italian Riveria with two women they have never met. Free of familiar routines, all four women learn and blossom in the warmth and sun. Their quest to define themselves as independent individuals has a surprising effect on their relationships with their spouses.

Relationships	Friends Self-Esteem Married Couples
Finding Love	28-54
Overcoming Obstacles	Sexual Prejudice Entrapment Adventure

English Patient, The
1996/162

D: *Anthony Minghella.* **Cast:** *Ralph Fiennes, Kristin Scott Thomas, Julliette Binoche, Willem Dafoe.*

This powerful World War II tale of love and loss takes you on a sweeping, emotional ride full of passion, compassion and trust. The film is energized by award-winning performances and visually stunning photography.The story begins in an abandoned villa in Tuscany near the end of the war. A French-Canadian nurse cares for a dying burn patient, who spends his remaining time recalling an illicit romance with the wife of a fellow adventurer.Stragglers from the war pass through the villa for a time—an British-Indian bomb disposal expert, who has a brief affair with the nurse and a one-time thief who is looking for the man who is now burned beyond recognition.

Relationships	Lovers Colleagues & Co-Workers
Finding Love	28-54
Transitions	Courting
Overcoming Obstacles	War

Evening Star, The
1996/126

See *Terms of Endearment.*

Fame
1980/133

D: *Alan Parker.* **Cast:** *Eddie Barth, Irene Cara, Lee Curreri, Laura Dean.*

This is an inspiring examination of the four-year growth of gifted teens attending New York's High School for the Performing Arts. With talent as a common leveler, ambitious kids from every social stratum show up to learn, perform, and leave prepared to seek fame in their own way.

Work & Prosperity	Realizing Dreams Love Work
Relationships	Teacher/Student Colleagues & Co-Workers
Finding Love	Teen Years
Transitions	Teen Years Landing First Job
Overcoming Obstacles	Creative Expression

Father of the Bride (1950)

1950/93

See *Father of the Bride* (1991).

Father of the Bride (1991)

1991/105

D: *Charles Shyer.* **Cast:** *Steve Martin, Diane Keaton, Kimberly Williams, Martin Short.*

This is a funny, touching retelling of the 1950s Spencer Tracy/Elizabeth Taylor movie about a father's reluctance to accept his daughter's transformation from a dependent little daddy's girl into an independent married woman. Martin Short has a riotous character part as a tongue-twisted wedding coordinator. Watch the original 1950s version to contrast how societal attitudes change while underlying feelings remain the same.

Relationships	Parent/Child
Finding Love	20s
Transitions	Marrying Moving Out/Separating
Overcoming Obstacles	Loss

Father of the Bride II

1995/106

See *Father of the Bride* (1991).

Field of Dreams

1989/106

D: *Phil Alden Robinson.* **Cast:** *Kevin Costner, Amy Madigan, James Earl Jones, Ray Liotta, Burt Lancaster.*

When Ray Kinsella (Costner) turns 36, he has to face his worst fear: that he'll end up just like his father. This is a tale about the adventure of following your dream despite your fears and what others say. Ray has to follow a voice that says "If you build it, he will come." It's also about shifting into a new adult perspective about your childhood and making peace with your parents and their wishes for you, while still maintaining your childlike sense of innocence. If you're pursuing a seemingly impossible dream, this film holds many insights into acting on your gut feelings and keeping the faith, despite all odds.

Work & Prosperity	Realizing Dreams
Relationships	Parent/Child
Finding Love	28-54
Transitions	Mid-Life Crisis 30s & 40s Changing Careers
Overcoming Obstacles	Entrapment

Finnegan Begin Again

1984/112

D: *Joan Micklin Silver.* **Cast:** *Mary Tyler Moore, Robert Preston, Sam Waterston.*

Here's a feel-good love story between a most unlikely, mismatched couple—a widowed school teacher (Moore) in her 40s and a 65-year old crack investigative reporter (Preston) demoted to writing a lonely hearts column. While Preston's character cares for his 70-something wife, who has Alzheimer's disease, Moore breaks off an affair with a married funeral director. It starts as a platonic friendship and evolves touchingly into romance as they each let go of the past and start viewing things in the here and now. Silver directs winning performances with charm and grace.

Relationships	Elder Care Lovers Breaking Old Patterns
Finding Love	Radical Age Differences
Transitions	Changing Careers 60s & 70s
Overcoming Obstacles	Age Prejudice Entrapment

First Wives Club, The

1996/104

D: *Hugh Wilson.* **Cast:** *Goldie Hawn, Diane Keaton, Bette Midler, Sarah Jessica Parker.*

This is a hilarious tale of three rich, mid-life wives who are dumped by their husbands for younger "trophy" wives. The story arcs from their naive college days to when they display their own power. The suicide of a fourth "abandoned" college friend shakes the trio out of their complacency and they proceed to launch new lives, financed unwittingly by their ex-husbands. The very talented Hawn, Keaton, and Midler are in top comedic form. This movie's success has redefined Hollywood opportunities for 50ish actresses.

Relationships	Divorced Couples
Finding Love	28-54
Transitions	Moving Out/Separating Divorcing
Overcoming Obstacles	Loss

Five Easy Pieces

1970/98

D: *Bob Rafelson.* **Cast:** *Jack Nicholson, Karen Black, Susan Anspach.*

This is a funny, raucous, emotionally wrenching study of an immature man whose fear of success propels him into seeking the easy way out of life's challenges. He drifts as an oil rigger, slumming with a waitress who lives in a house trailer and loves bowling alleys. He returns home to try to reconnect with his dying father, a musical genius now mute from a stroke. Once again, he rejects his family's aspirations and hits the road as a self-selected failure.

Relationships	Parent/Child Lovers
Finding Love	20s
Transitions	Changing Careers 20s to 30s Passage
Overcoming Obstacles	Entrapment

Five Heartbeats, The

1991/120

D: *Robert Townsend.* **Cast:** *Robert Townsend, Michael Wright, Leon, Harry J. Lennix, Tico Wells.*

This lively musical bio-pic recounts the rags-to-riches rise of a black singing group similar to the Temptations and then examines how each member handles success over the years. The promising lead singer is most vulnerable to the trappings of fame and slips away into drug abuse. The others continue to hone their craft and renew their commitment to a long-term artistic collaboration.

Work & Prosperity	Realizing Dreams Collaborating w/ Colleagues
Relationships	Colleagues & Co-Workers
Transitions	Achieving Career Goals
Overcoming Obstacles	Racial Prejudice Creative Expression Sexual Prejudice

Flashdance

1983/96

D: *Adrian Lyne.* **Cast:** *Jennifer Beals, Michael Nouri.*

An energetic, uplifting rock & roll ballet is strung around a complicated fantasy plot. A young welder by day and go-go dancer by night falls for a rich construction owner with a Porsche. She makes her dream of becoming a ballet dancer come true. Dial down your Small Intelligence on this one. Activate your Great Intelligence with the rich sights, the engaging sounds, and the glorious movement, and enjoy every minute of this extra-long music video.

Work & Prosperity	Realizing Dreams
Relationships	Colleagues & Co-Workers Lovers
Finding Love	Radical Age Differences
Transitions	Achieving Career Goals
Overcoming Obstacles	Class Prejudice Creative Expression

Flirting with Disaster 1995/92

D: *David O. Russell.* **Cast:** *Ben Stiller, Patricia Arquette, Téa Leoni, Alan Alda, Mary Tyler Moore.*

This quirky tale of an uptight entomologist's search for his birth parents—with his dismayed adoptive parents, disoriented wife and child, ditzy adoption agency social worker, and a bisexual FBI agent in tow—firmly re-establishes the screwball comedy in the 1990s. Just sit back and enjoy a very funny satire about the meaning of family and loving relationships.

Relationships	Parent/Child Married Couples
Transitions	Becoming Parent
Overcoming Obstacles	Loss

Forever Young 1992/104

D: *Steve Miner.* **Cast:** *Mel Gibson, Jamie Lee Curtis, Elijah Wood.*

There is something irresistibly romantic and tearjerking about the notion that lost love can be regained despite an impossible lapse of 50 years' time. So have the tissue box ready for this Mel Gibson fantasy about a lovesick soldier who is experimentally frozen and forgotten in the late 1930s, until he is accidentally thawed out by two boys who take him home to mom in the 1990s.

Relationships	Lovers
Finding Love	20s
Transitions	Losing Mate
Overcoming Obstacles	Loss

Four Weddings and a Funeral 1994/117

D: *Mike Newell.* **Cast:** *Hugh Grant, Andie MacDowell.*

After *Enchanted April*, director Mike Newell has taken the funny, feel-good, uplifting afterglow to new heights with this film. This amusing tale follows a 30-something commitment-phobe (Grant) and his group of like-minded English friends to the five events of the film's title. After a one-night fling at the first wedding, Grant becomes increasingly fascinated with an American (MacDowell) and more confused about how to express about his feelings.

Relationships	Breaking Old Patterns Lovers Friends
Finding Love	28-54
Transitions	Marrying
Overcoming Obstacles	Entrapment

Frankie Starlight 1995/100

D: *Michael Lindsay-Hogg.* **Cast:** *Corban Walker, Georgina Cates, Carbria Molloy, Niall Toibin, Gabriel Byrne, Matt Dillon, Ann Parillaud.*

This is a lyrical memoir of white dwarfs—human and stellar—learning to reach out across the Milky Way of loneliness to touch the warmth of love. A beautiful, independent Frenchwoman conceives a dwarf son on an American ship after D-Day and is taken in by an Irish family. The story is told in flashbacks as the adult son interweaves his childhood experiences with his rise to fame as a novelist.

Relationships	Parent/Child Lovers
Finding Love	28-54
Transitions	Achieving Career Goals Courting Pre-Teen Years
Overcoming Obstacles	Physical Abilities

French Lieutenant's Woman, The 1981/124

D: *Karel Reisz.* **Cast:** *Meryl Streep, Jeremy Irons, Hilton McRae.*

Based on John Fowles' dense novel of Victorian love, this lush movie brilliantly updates the book's tale of sexual repression by adding the easy, adulterous, on-set romance of the modern day actors making a film of the story. Convincing and well-acted, it is a powerful visual contrast of the dramatic changes in morals over 100 years.

Relationships	Breaking Old Patterns Lovers
Finding Love	28-54
Transitions	Moving Out/Separating
Overcoming Obstacles	Sexual Prejudice Entrapment

Fried Green Tomatoes 1992/130

D: *Jon Avnet.* **Cast:** *Kathy Bates, Mary Stuart Masterson, Mary-Louise Parker, Jessica Tandy, Stan Shaw.*

This film shows how a good story can inspire a person to change their life. The listener is an oppressed, unhappily married woman (Bates) who finds a great storyteller (Tandy) in a nursing home she visits in Alabama. Tandy spins a Southern tale of sensational events that happened 50 years ago in Georgia to two women friends/lovers (Masterson and Parker). They operated a restaurant and served blacks inside, angering local rednecks, including Parker's husband. The husband disappears and is assumed murdered. Tandy's tale turns on what really happened to the drunken lout and the courage of the two women who stood up to the town's oppressive opinion. Uplifted by the tale, Bates begins to transform herself and finally wake up her sports-crazed, inattentive husband.

Work & Prosperity	Colaborating w/Colleagues
Relationships	Elder Care Self-Esteem
Finding Love	28-54
Transitions	Mid-Life Crisis 30s & 40s
Overcoming Obstacles	Racial Prejudice Entrapment

Full Monty, The 1996/90

D: *Peter Cattaneo.* **Cast:** *Robert Carlyle, Tom Wilkinson, Mark Addy, Steve Huison, William Snape.*

This delightful, belly-laughing slapstick comedy is about a group of laid-off steel-mill workers in Sheffield, England. With no job prospects, they get up the nerve to make a few bucks as male strippers. Not that they're in any great physical shape, but the saga of their eventual triumph to Donna Summer's "Hot Stuff" is guaranteed to make you feel better. The film also takes an honest look at the effect of job loss on the spouses.

Work & Prosperity	Destructuring Workplace Collaborating w/ Colleagues
Relationships	Colleagues & Co-Workers Married Couples Breaking Old Patterns
Transitions	Losing Job Surviving Downsizing
Overcoming Obstacles	Loss

Gaby, A True Story

1987/115

D: *Luis Mandoki.* **Cast:** *Rachel Levin, Liv Ullman, Norma Aleandro, Robert Loggia, Lawrence Monoson.*

Congenital cerebral palsy limits Mexican Gaby Brimmer's (Levin) physical movements to her left foot, but her sharp mind and the help of her family and devoted nurse (Aleandro) allows her to become a college graduate and well-known writer. Gaby's inspiring true story is told in a loving, compassionate way with a convincing cast.

Relationships	Parent/Child Lovers
Finding Love	Teen Years
Overcoming Obstacles	Physical Abilities

George of the Jungle

1997/90

D: *Sam Weisman.* **Cast:** *Brendan Fraser, Leslie Mann, Thomas Haden Church.*

This witty Tarzan spoof, based on a '60s cartoon series, comes to the big screen with its satirical bent in tack, making it a fun movie for the whole family. Raised by an ape family, good-hearted but awkward George (watch out for that tree!) is taken out of the jungle by a rich and beautiful San Francisco woman, over the protests of her fiance. But when his jungle family is threatened, George returns, helped by his simian brother and an elephant who acts like a dog.

Relationships	Lovers
Finding Love	20's
Transitions	Courting

Get on the Bus

1996/121

D: *Spike Lee.* **Cast:** *Charles S. Dutton, Andre Braugher, Isaiah Washington, Ossie Davis.*

This is a riveting look at a group of black men travelling by bus from Los Angeles to Washington, D.C., to participate in Louis Farrakhan's Million Man March. The movie examines a diversity of views: young vs. old, gay vs. straight, poor vs. rich. Their individual stories include a shackled father and his delinquent son finding and forgiving each other; a policeman who is a son of a policeman wanting to arrest a born-again Muslim when he confesses to childhood murders; a Jewish driver examining his racial prejudice; and a Lexus car dealer who is kicked off the bus for his blatant greed.

Relationships	Colleagues & Co-Workers Parent/Child Breaking Old Patterns
Overcoming Obstacles	Racial Prejudice

Get Shorty

1995/105

D: *Barry Sonnenfeld.* **Cast:** *John Travolta, Gene Hackman, René Russo, Danny DeVito.*

Here's an inspiring career-changing story: how to go from Miami loan shark to major Hollywood producer in just a few steps. Travolta brings his full-blown movie star charm to the role of Chili Palmer, who discovers that the show biz world can be as vicious and deadly as the mob. Russo as a movie star, DeVito as her husband, and Hackman as a B-movie producer add panache to the riotous events that unfold.

Work & Prosperity	Realizing Dreams
Relationships	Colleagues & Co-Workers Lovers
Transitions	Changing Careers
Overcoming Obstacles	Creative Expression

Godfather, Part II, The
1974/200

See *The Godfather Trilogy.*

Godfather, Part III, The
1990/161

See *The Godfather Trilogy.*

Godfather, The
1972/175

See *The Godfather Trilogy.*

Godfather Trilogy, The
1990/533

D: *Francis Ford Coppola.* **Cast:** *Marlon Brando, Al Pacino, Diane Keaton, Talia Shire, Andy Garcia.*

The masterful partnership of Mario Puzo's powerful Mafia story and Coppola's cinematic artistry has spun out three riveting Godfather movies so far—the 1972 *The Godfather* (175m), the 1974 *The Godfather Part II* (200m), and the 1990 *The Godfather Part III* (161m), with room for more. In 1981, an expanded version of the first two movies, combined and in chronological order, was released under the title *The Godfather: The Complete Epic*, 1902-1958 (386m). This three-generation saga of an Italian-American family's quest for power and redemption becomes more engrossing with each installment, with many of the original cast reprising the same roles in 1990. Watch all three back-to-back to experience the true scope of some of the best storytelling in cinema.

Work & Prosperity	Realizing Dreams Balancing Work & Family
Relationships	Multi-Generation Family
Finding Love	20s 28-54 55-81
Transitions	Achieving Career Goals
Overcoming Obstacles	Entrapment Cultural Abilities Class Prejudice

Gods Must Be Crazy, The
1980/109

D: *Jamie Uys.* **Cast:** *N!Xau, Lena Farugia, Hans Strydom, Marius Weyers, Sandra Prinsloo.*

This slapstick comedy out of South Africa tells the tale of a Kalahari Bushman's first encounter with "civilized" man. The director found N!Xau, a Bushman with no previous contact with whites, who is a natural comedian in the Buster Keaton tradition. N!Xau's honest amusement at our strange ways brings into question the lack of balance in our technological society versus the giving-and-receiving balance of "primitive" man. It is refreshing to evaluate our obsessions, idiosyncrasies, and rituals from a completely different perspective and be able to laugh at ourselves. The hilarious saga continues in the 1989 sequel *The Gods Must Be Crazy II* (97m).

Relationships	Parent/Child
Transitions	Moving Out/Separating
Overcoming Obstacles	Cultural Abilities Adventure

Gods Must Be Crazy II, The
1989/97

See *Gods Must Be Crazy, The.*

Gone with the Wind

1939/222

D: *Victor Fleming.* **Cast:** *Vivien Leigh, Clark Gable, Leslie Howard, Olivia de Havilland.*

This riveting Civil War soap opera is about the ten years it takes a brazen young woman to triumph over the horrors of war and embrace post-War prosperity, despite immature fantasies about a man she can't have and rejection of the ones she does have. Everything about this film is superb and timeless. So, get out the tissue supply, cook up some popcorn, and be gone with the emotional wind.

Work & Prosperity	Realizing Dreams
Relationships	Lovers Multi-Generation Family
Finding Love	20s
Transitions	Achieving Career Goals
Overcoming Obstacles	Sexual Prejudice Loss War

Grace of My Heart

1996/116

D: *Allison Anders.* **Cast:** *Illeana Douglas, John Turturro, Matt Dillon, Eric Stoltz, Bruce Davison.*

With an inspiring Burt Bachrach/Elvis Costello theme song, this film recounts the career ups and downs of a wealthy, successful, and dedicated woman songwriter and her professional and romantic entanglements with a series of men, mostly heartbreakers. Through it all, her commitment to her craft gives her focus, even when the balancing act of work and family obligations spins out of control.

Work & Prosperity	Loving Your Work Balancing Work & Family
Relationships	Two-Career Couples
Finding Love	28-54
Transitions	Achieving Career Goals Marrying
Overcoming Obstacles	Creative Expression

Grass Harp, The

1995/107

D: *Charles Matthau.* **Cast:** *Edward Furlong, Piper Laurie, Walter Matthau,Sissy Spacek, Mary Steenburgen, Jack Lemmon.*

This is a tender, cinematic rendition of a Truman Capote novel and features an all-star cast. In the 1930s, an orphaned boy is raised by his spinster aunts in their spacious home in a small Southern town. The boy identifies with his sweet, romantic aunt, who is cowed by her younger, domineering businesswoman sister. When the boy, the older sister, and the housekeeper bolt and set up residency in a nearby treehouse, events shift. Sudden surprises include the redefinition of both romantic and familial love.

Relationships	Lovers Multi-Generation Family Siblings
Finding Love	55-81
Transitions	Moving Out/Separating Courting
Overcoming Obstacles	Entrapment

Great Santini, The

1980/118

D: *Lewis John Carlino.* **Cast:** *Robert Duvall, Blythe Danner, Michael O' Keefe.*

Based on an autobiographical Pat Conroy novel, this wonderful character study of a dysfunctional Southern military family is both uplifting and saddening. An ace Marine fighter pilot who expects his family to conform to military standards at home faces off with his sensitive 18-year-old son, who protects three younger siblings while the muted mother suffers from the sidelines.

Work & Prosperity	Balancing Work & Family
Relationships	Breaking Old Patterns Parent/Child Friends
Transitions	Teen Years
Overcoming Obstacles	Racial Prejudice Entrapment

Green Card
1991/108

D: *Peter Weir.* **Cast:** *Gerard Depardieu, Andie MacDowell.*

This is a delicious romantic comedy of a coldhearted marriage of convenience melting into a fuzzy love affair under the hilarious scrutiny of family, friends, and the INS. To obtain a green card, a prickly French waiter marries an attractive American horticulturist, who consents so she can buy a co-op with room for her dream garden. Neither expects to see the other again, but their emotional tango begins when the INS starts asking questions.

Work & Prosperity	Realizing Dreams
Relationships	Married Couples
Finding Love	28-54
Transitions	Marrying
Overcoming Obstacles	Creative Expression

Grey Fox, The
1983/92

D: *Phillip Borsos.* **Cast:** *Richard Farnsworth, Jackie Burroughs, Wayne Robson.*

Based on a true story about Bill Miner, the Gentleman Bandit, who is released in 1901 after 33 years in San Quentin Prison. Bill faces a career crisis. He used to rob stagecoaches, but now he has to figure out a new profession. Inspired by an 11-minute movie, *The Great Train Robbery*, he finds his new calling in robbing trains. He moves to Canada and begins his new occupation with good-natured humor and patience. Along the way, he develops a romance with an independent lady photographer. Beautifully filmed in the Pacific Northwest, it's an entertaining look at adjusting to new times and technology.

Work & Prosperity	Collaborating w/ Colleagues
Relationships	Lovers
Finding Love	55-81
Transitions	Changing Careers 60s & 70s
Overcoming Obstacles	Age Prejudice Entrapment

Groundhog Day
1993/101

D: *Harold Ramis.* **Cast:** *Bill Murray, Andie MacDowell, Chris Elliot.*

This is a wry tale about an obnoxious weatherman (Murray) who is learning how to be considerate and is wooing his producer (MacDowell). He gets caught in a blizzard he didn't predict in a small town celebrating Groundhog Day. Stuck in a time warp, he keeps repeating February 2 over and over again until he gets it right. This film offers a lesson for anyone who has ever felt like their life is repeating itself, only with a different cast of characters. Murray tests the entire range of possibilities, from being more obnoxious to becoming a sweet, lovable, good citizen.

Work & Prosperity	Collaborating w/ Colleagues
Relationships	Breaking Old Patterns Lovers Colleagues & Co-Workers
Finding Love	28-54

Transitions	Courting
Overcoming Obstacles	Cultural Abilities

Grumpy Old Men
1993/104

D: *Donald Petrie.* **Cast:** *Ann-Margaret, Walter Matthau, Jack Lemmon, Burgess Meredith.*

This is an engaging, well-acted romp about two retired men who feud like little kids while vying for the attention of their sexy new widow neighbor. It points out the pitfalls of holding onto past emotions and not being able to forgive. A hilarious, salacious subtext is provided by Meredith as a 90-year-old father commenting on the act of making love.

Relationships	Friends Multi-Generation Family
Finding Love	55-81
Transitions	After Retirement
Overcoming Obstacles	Loss

Grumpier Old Men
1995/101

See *Grumpy Old Men*.

Happy Together
1990/102

D: *Mel Damski.* **Cast:** *Patrick Dempsey, Helen Slater.*

This sweet, wacky romance of an aspiring actress and would-be playwright wrongly paired as roommates in college hits just the right tenor between the elation of big dreams mixed with the deflation of underlying uncertainty. Ignore the intellectual critics' advice on this one, and take an emotional dunk back into those good old college days.

Relationships	Lovers
Finding Love	College Years
Transitions	Living Together/Moving In
Overcoming Obstacles	Creative Expression

Harvey
1950/104

D: *Henry Koster.* **Cast:** *James Stewart. Josephine Hull.*

Based on the Pulitzer-winning play, this wry fantasy explores the fuzzy line between magical illusion and demented delusion as a ditzy sister tries to commit her delightful drunk brother and his constant companion—an invisible tall white rabbit named Harvey—to a mental institution. In one of Jimmy Stewart's most engaging roles, he charms the psychiatrist with the possibility of magic amid the madness.

Relationships	Friends Siblings
Transitions	Moving Out/Separating
Overcoming Obstacles	Mental Abilities

Hear My Song
1992/104

D: *Peter Chelsom.* **Cast:** *Adrian Dunbar, Ned Beatty, William Hootkins.*

This charming, upbeat British romantic comedy is about a failing pub owner's attempt to book a famous Irish tenor on the lam from the tax authorities. It demonstrates the power of optimism over adversity. After an imposter is booed out of the small seaside town by the patrons, the proprietor-cum-promoter is forced to go to Ireland to find the real singer, who is the long-lost love of his fiancée's mother.

Work & Prosperity	Realizing Dreams
Relationships	Lovers Colleagues & Co-Workers

Finding Love	28-54
Transitions	Achieving Career Goals
Overcoming Obstacles	Creative Expression

Heart Like a Wheel

1983/113

D: *Jonathan Kaplan.* **Cast:** *Bonnie Bedelia, Beau Bridges, Bill McKinney, Hoyt Axton.*

Bonnie Bedelia's performance as Shirley Muldowney, the first woman driver in the National Hot Rod Association, rings true for anyone who has ever been the first at anything, or aspires to be. Shirley's journey to the winner's circle includes overcoming blatant sexism and making difficult choices about her marriage, her son, and her lover (Bridges) at every turn. In the end, she accomplishes her quest to win in her profession, but she never quite achieves the balance between her work and her personal relationships.

Work & Prosperity	Balancing Work & Family Realizing Dreams
Relationships	Two-Career Couples Parent/Child
Finding Love	28-54
Transitions	Achieving Career Goals
Overcoming Obstacles	Sexual Prejudice Loss

Hearts of Darkness

1992/96

D: *Bahr/Hickenlooper.* **Cast:** *Eleanor Coppola, Francis Ford Coppola.*

Subtitled "A Filmmaker's Apocalypse," this documentary tells the trials and tribulations of making the 1979 movie *Apocalypse Now* (150m) in the Phillipines. Eleanor Coppola's film diary of her husband Francis' location shoot plus after-the-fact interviews with actors and crew provide a rare glimpse inside the movie-making process. This is a first-hand, intimate look at the willingness and the courage it takes to direct and complete a film project on a day-by-day basis, through the emotional ups and downs, the uncertainty, and the synthesizing of all those seemingly unrelated variables into a coherent film.

Work & Prosperity	Loving Your Work Collaborating w/ Colleagues
Relationships	Colleagues & Co-Workers
Transitions	Achieving Career Goals
Overcoming Obstacles	Creative Expression

Holiday

1938/93

D: *George Cukor.* **Cast:** *Cary Grant, Katharine Hepburn.*

This classic screwball comedy about a rich girl who steals her sister's fiance set a new standard for witty, sophisticated movie romance. The on-screen chemistry between Hepburn and Grant is delightful, as she sympathizes with his dreams of taking a career break and her uptight sister goes into a panic.

Work & Prosperity	Realizing Dreams
Relationships	Lovers Sibling Care
Finding Love	20's
Transitions	Changing Careers
Overcoming Obstacles	Class Prejudice Entrapment

Hoop Dreams

1994/176

D: *Steve James, Frederick Marx, Peter Gilbert.* **Cast:** *Arthur Agee, William Gates.*

You don't have to like sports to enjoy this moving, life-affirming documentary. It follows the journey from age 14 to 21 of two poor black Chicago boys whose exceptional athletic talent gives them a shot at being professional basketball players. Fulfilling this type of large dream requires arduous, year-after-year effort as shown—endless practice, concentrated study, surprise victories, and stunning setbacks. The film provides a raw, inside look at the heartless manipulation of young talent and their families by high school and college sports programs.

Work & Prosperity	Realizing Dreams
Relationships	Teacher/Student Self-Esteem
Transitions	Teen Years College Years
Overcoming Obstacles	Class Prejudice

Hope and Glory

1987/118

D: *John Boorman.* **Cast:** *Sebastian Rice Edwards, Geraldine Muir, Sarah Miles, Sammi Davis.*

This is a loving, warm, upbeat look at World War II through the wide-eyed excitement of a young British boy having the greatest adventure of his life. In a meticulous period re-creation, director Boorman's autobiographical tale pits the boy's stoic mother, who distractedly raises her family by herself, against her sexually awakened teenage daughter.

Relationships	Multi-Generation Family
Finding Love	Teen Years
Transitions	Pre-Teen Years
Overcoming Obstacles	War

House Party

1990/100

D: *Reginald Hudlin.* **Cast:** *Christopher Reid, Robin Harris, Christopher Martin, Martin Lawrence.*

Set to the hip hop beat, this is a sweet, giddy tale of urban black high school students planning, attending, and recovering from a party, with a gentle lesson about how to control those raging hormones long enough to get to college. Real-life Reid and Martin are rap musicians known as Kid 'n' Play. Forget the 1991 and 1994 sequels (94m each), which fail to recapture the original's infectious spirit.

Relationships	Lovers Friends
Finding Love	Teen Years
Transitions	Teen Years
Overcoming Obstacles	Adventure

How to Make an American Quilt

1995/109

D: *Jocelyn Moorhouse.* **Cast:** *Winona Ryder, Ellen Burstyn, Anne Bancroft, Lois Smith, Jean Simmons, Maya Angelou.*

This rich, well-acted multigenerational women's film focuses on finding love and committing to marriage. The varied wise words of older women recall their own youthful choices as they prepare a wedding quilt for the bride, an indecisive, 26-year-old UC Berkeley graduate student making her third try at completing her master's thesis. She seeks refuge for the summer in her great aunt's and grandmother's house while she contemplates marrying her live-in carpenter boyfriend.

Relationships	Lovers
Finding Love	20s
Transitions	Marrying
Overcoming Obstacles	Entrapment

I've Heard the Mermaids Singing 1987/87

D: *Patricia Rozema.* **Cast:** *Sheila McCarthy, Paule Vaillargeon, Ann-Marie Macdonald.*

The film's title comes from a T.S. Eliot poem, "I've heard the mermaids singing, each to each. I do not think that they will sing to me." This is an insightful meditation on feeling left out and then realizing that everyone else does, too. An early 30s misfit, with dreams of being a photographer and no courage to display her photos, works ineptly as an office temporary. To her astonishment, she is hired by a lesbian art gallery owner who actually likes her and overlooks her flaws. The film contrasts the hapless temp learning to trust the mermaids and the sophisticate masking her loneliness behind the glitter of external success.

Work & Prosperity	Realizing Dreams
Relationships	Boss/Employee
Transitions	Achieving Career Goals 20s to 30s Passage
Overcoming Obstacles	Creative Expression

Impromptu 1991/107

D: *James Lapine.* **Cast:** *Judy Davis, Hugh Grant, Mandy Patinkin, Bernadette Peters, Julian Sands.*

This is an enjoyable satiric romp about the radical feminist novelist George Sand and her ambitious artistic friends including the composer Chopin, the painter Delacroix, and the pianist Liszt, as they spend a fortnight in the French country. As Sand bickers with ex-lovers and falls for the sickly Chopin, the group barely conceals its disdain for their overeager, social-climber hostess.

Work & Prosperity	Loving Your Work
Relationships	Lovers
Finding Love	28-54
Transitions	Achieving Career Goals
Overcoming Obstacles	Sexual Prejudice Creative Expression

In the Line of Fire 1993/128

D: *Wolfgang Petersen.* **Cast:** *Clint Eastwood, John Malkovich, Rene Russo, Dylan McDermott.*

As an aging Secret Service man, Eastwood gives a top-notch performance pitted against a menacing madman played by Malkovich in this fast-paced thriller. The memorable shot of an out-of-breath Eastwood running next to the Presidential limousine shows a man who doesn't know when it's time to move on. His surprising attraction to a much younger agent gives him yet another nudge to let go.

Work and Prosperity	Loving Your Work
Relationships	Lovers
Finding Love	Radical Age Differences
Transitions	Achieving Career Goals
Overcoming Obstacles	Age Prejudice

Indiana Jones and the Last Crusade 1989/127

See *Indiana Jones Trilogy.*

Indiana Jones and the Temple of Doom 1984/118

See *Indiana Jones Trilogy.*

After-View Feelings Key:
Feel Better/Uplift — Laughing Release — Crying Release — Violent Content

Indiana Jones Trilogy

1981/358

D: *Steven Spielberg.* **Cast:** *Harrison Ford, Karen Allen, Kate Capshaw, Sean Connery.*

This fast-paced, swashbuckling cartoon-like trilogy of the 1981 *Raiders of the Lost Ark* (115m), the 1984 *Indiana Jones and the Temple of Doom* (118m), and the 1989 *Indiana Jones and the Last Crusade* (127m) is a great way to slip back into a 10-year-old boy's sense of thrills and chills and awe that everything can turn out okay in the end. These Spielberg-Lucas films have redefined our expectations about escapist entertainment forever. Enjoy.

Work & Prosperity	Loving Your Work
Relationships	Parent/Child Teacher/Student
Transitions	Achieving Career Goals
Overcoming Obstacles	Adventure

Irreconcilable Differences

1984/112

D: *Charles Shyer.* **Cast:** *Ryan O'Neal, Shelley Long, Drew Barrymore, Sam Wanamaker.*

This film provides a wry look at the tradeoffs ambitious parents make between their careers and their children. A nine-year-old (Barrymore) sues her squabbling parents (O'Neal and Long) for a divorce so she can live with her lovingly attentive Hispanic nanny. Her parents' careers are always out of sync. First, her father becomes a successful film director, after co-writing his first screenplay while her mother stays home. Then, her father falls for a starlet (Sharon Stone), neglects Barrymore, and divorces Long. His next film with Stone bombs and his career skids to a halt. Then, he starts paying attention to Barrymore again. Meanwhile, Long becomes a best-selling novelist retelling her own potboiler tale as the scorned woman. When her career becomes all-consuming, she neglects Barrymore.

Work & Prosperity	Balancing Work & Family
Relationships	Parent/Child Two-Career Couples
Finding Love	20s 28-54
Transitions	Changing Careers Divorcing
Overcoming Obstacles	Creative Expression Loss

It Happened One Night

1934/105

D: *Frank Capra.* **Cast:** *Clark Gable, Claudette Colbert.*

With genuine 1930s atmosphere and detail, every scene in this romance between a rebellious socialite on the run and a cynical newspaper man remains fresh and funny today, including the memorable hitchhiking and Walls of Jericho confrontations. It is a charming meditation on the universal truth that wherever you go, there you are.

Relationships	Parent/Child Lovers
Finding Love	20s
Transitions	Moving Out/Separating Living Together/Moving In
Overcoming Obstacles	Class Prejudice Entrapment

It's a Wonderful Life

1946/129

D: *Frank Capra.* **Cast:** *James Stewart, Donna Reed, Lionel Barrymore.*

The classic tale of a giving man in a suicidal midlife crisis, reviewing life as if he had never been born. Only from this perspective can he begin to acknowledge his true contributions, let go of youthful dreams, and, with renewed hope, accept his life as it is. This heartbreaking but ultimately uplifting drama is an inspiration for those bleak times when you wish you had never been born.

Work & Prosperity	Realizing Dreams Balancing Work & Family
Relationships	Multi-Generation Family
Transitions	Mid-Life Crisis 30s & 40s
Overcoming Obstacles	Entrapment

Jerry Maguire

1996/135

D: *Cameron Crowe.* **Cast:** *Tom Cruise, Cuba Gooding, Jr., Renee Zellweger, Kelly Preston.*

The source of the phrase "Show me the money," this romantic parable of yuppie ambition, failed and redeemed, is set in the cutthroat world of big sports. In a momentary lapse of altruism, a top sports agent gets himself fired and is left with an equally greedy and obnoxious low-ranking football player, a moonstruck single-mom accountant, and her absolutely adorable young son. A carefully crafted script, first rate talent, and an upbeat finale make this award-winning film a real treat to enjoy over and over again.

Work & Prosperity	Balancing Work & Family
Relationships	Single Parent Colleagues & Co-Workers
Finding Love	28-54
Transitions	Courting Losing Job Achieving Career Goals
Overcoming Obstacles	Creative Expression

Joy Luck Club

1993/139

D: *Wayne Wang.* **Cast:** *Rosalind Chao, Tamlyn Tomita, Ming-Na Wen, Tsai Chin, France Nuyen.*

No other movie so movingly demonstrates how unspoken behavioral patterns are passed from one generation to the next, in an unintentional repetition of the same heartbreaking struggles to love and to survive. Based on Amy Tan's novel, this film traces four American-born Chinese daughters and their mothers in their respective tales of love, marriage, and work. The mothers' best wishes for their daughters get miscommunicated across generational and cultural lines. The daughters learn to let go of their mothers' expectations and use what works for them as adults.

Relationships	Parent/Child Multi-Generation Family
Finding Love	Teen Years 20s 28-54
Overcoming Obstacles	Cultural Abilities Entrapment

La Bamba

1987/108

D: *Luiz Valdez.* **Cast:** *Lou Diamond Phillips, Esai Morales, Danielle von Zemeck.*

Based on the true story of the '50s rock and roll star Ritchie Valens, the movie concentrates on his rise to fame, his blond girlfriend, and his relationship with his troubled half-brother. The upbeat soundtrack leaves you feeling good, despite the tragedy of his early death in the plane crash that also took the lives of Buddy Holly and the Big Bopper.

Work & Prosperity	Realizing Dreams
Relationships	Colleagues & Co-Workers

Finding Love	20's
Transitions	Achieving Career Goals Teen Years
Overcoming Obstacles	Racial Prejudice Creative Expression

Last Picture Show, The

1971/118

D: *Peter Bogdanovich.* **Cast:** *Timothy Bottoms, Jeff Bridges, Cybill Shepherd, Ben Johnson, Cloris Leachman.*

In a flawless re-creation of the sights and sounds of 1951, this meditation on small-town life uses the shut down of a movie theater in the dusty Texas panhandle as a metaphor for changing times. In a place small enough to know everything about everybody, the locals act out their entangled passions. Oscars were awarded to Johnson as Sam the Lion, the wise theater owner and Leachman, the coach's neglected wife who tries to sooth her loneliness in a hopeless affair with a high school boy. If you want to see most of the original cast in color, view the 1990 sequel *Texasville* (123m), which continues the story 30 years later in vignettes that seem incomplete by comparison.

Work & Prosperity	Destructuring Workplace
Relationships	Lovers Siblings
Finding Love	Teen Years 28-54
Transitions	Teen Years
Overcoming Obstacles	Class Prejudice Entrapment

Lawnmower Man, The

1992/108

D: *Brett Leonard.* **Cast:** *Jeff Fahey, Pierce Brosnan, Jenny Wright.*

This science fiction thriller casts the Frankenstein story with a 90s high-tech spin and an open ending for more sequels. Scientist Brosnan uses mentally retarded gardener Fahey for his experiments in mental expansion, via computer-generated virtual reality, with unpredictable results. If people learn through experience, then virtual reality opens up the possibility to explore previously unthinkable dimensions. Sensually absorbing special effects create another way, as in *2001* (see page 199), to contemplate the possibilities of man's evolutionary journey. The video restores 32 minutes of footage omitted from the theater release.

Work & Prosperity	Loving Your Work
Relationships	Boss/Employee
Overcoming Obstacles	Mental Abilities Creative Expression

Liar, Liar

1997/87

D: *Tom Shadyac.* **Cast:** *Jim Carrey, Jennifer Tilly, Maura Tierney, Cary Elwes.*

A great belly-laugher of a movie features Jim Carrey as a neglectful divorced father who'se five-year-old son is granted a wish—that his father can't tell a lie for 24 hours. It's a real and very amusing challenge for this lawyer to tell the truth and "nothing but." Between the slapstick scenes, the movie shows the touching side of a work-obsessed parent trying to bond with his son.

Work & Prosperity	Balancing Work & Family

Relationships	Divorced Couples Parent/Child Colleagues & Co-Workers
Transitions	Achieving Career Goals

Local Hero
1983/111

D: *Bill Forsyth.* **Cast:** *Burt Lancaster, Peter Riegert, Peter Capaldi.*

Like a fine wine, this movie is to be sipped, swilled, and savored for its quirky characters and gentle tale of an American oil company manager who goes to Scotland to buy up a town for a refinery from natives all too eager to sell. The man, who prides himself on his efficiency, starts to fall under the spell of the town's sheer beauty, the local innkeeper and negotiator, and an old beach bum who might not sell.

Work & Prosperity	Collaborating w/ Colleagues
Relationships	Boss/Employee Colleagues & Co-Workers
Transitions	Achieving Career Goals
Overcoming Obstacles	Entrapment

Lone Star
1995/137

D: *John Sayles.* **Cast:** *Chris Cooper, Matthew McConaughey, Kris Kristofferson, Elizabeth Peña, Joe Morton.*

This absolutely engrossing modern-day Western, set in the border town of Frontera, Texas, interweaves two generations of whites, Hispanics, blacks, and Native Americans with a sheriff's search for the truth about the bones of a corrupt sheriff—a man supposedly forced to leave town by before he was born. Breaking through his resistance to let the past be, the sheriff uncovers some surprising truths about the town, his family, and himself.

Work & Prosperity	Loving Your Work
Relationships	Parent/Child Lovers
Finding Love	28-54
Transitions	Courting
Overcoming Obstacles	Adventure

Long Walk Home, The
1991/97

D: *Richard Pearce.* **Cast:** *Sissy Spacek, Whoopi Goldberg.*

This film is a powerful emotional statement about the courage and inner strength of two ordinary women who define themselves through their families, yet become involved in the historic events surrounding the 1955 Montgomery bus boycott. One is a black maid who hides her walking to work for fear of getting fired; the other is her Junior League boss, who starts giving her a lift, despite her husband's strong objections.

Work & Prosperity	Balancing Work & Family
Relationships	Boss/Employee Married Couples
Overcoming Obstacles	Racial Prejudice Entrapment

Lorenzo's Oil
1992/135

D: *George Miller.* **Cast:** *Susan Sarandon, Nick Nolte.*

No movie better demonstrates how courage, conviction, and common sense can sweep aside seemingly invulnerable bastions of "authority" that act out of selfishness. Directed and cowritten by a medical doctor, this true, heartbreaking, yet inspiring film tells about a couple whose son contracts a rare nerve disease that attacks small boys and is always fatal. Medical research had ignored the problem because the ailing population was small and clinical trials took longer than the children lived. Untrained in medicine, the couple decides to do their own research and discovers a humble solution: olive oil. Having it accepted by the medical community became another challenge in their saga.

Relationships	Parent/Child
Overcoming Obstacles	Physical Abilities

Love Affair (1939)

1939/87

See *Sleepless in Seattle*.

Love Affair (1994)

1994/108

See *Sleepless in Seattle*.

Lucas

1985/99

D: *David Seltzer.* **Cast:** *Corey Haim, Kerri Green, Charlie Sheen, Courtney Thorne-Smith, Winona Ryder*

This is an exceptional coming-of-age movie about first love that goes beyond the cardboard characterizations and clichés and shows us the emotions of teens who genuinely care about each other, despite age and physical differences. Lucas (Haim) is a 14-year-old who is "accelerated" intellectually, but physically small and emotionally young for high school. He falls hopelessly in love for the first time with a 16-year-old girl (Green), who is a bit too mature for Lucas, but not for a football player (Sheen), who good-naturedly adopts and protects Lucas.

Relationships	Self-Esteem Lovers
Finding Love	Teen Years
Transitions	Teen Years
Overcoming Obstacles	Creative Expression Physical Abilities

Mac

1993/121

D: *John Turturro.* **Cast:** *John Turturro, Michael Badalucco.*

This is a nitty gritty autobiographical ode to Turturro's father, Mac, and his Italian immigrant dream of artistic expression practically applied to the 1950s housing boom. Mac is a difficult, critical man to live with, but his high standards push him from being a carpenter for hire to becoming a contractor who can state with pride, "I built that." Continuing the family tradition, his son John can point to this film in the same way.

Work & Prosperity	Balancing Work & Family
Relationships	Parent/Child Married Couples
Transitions	Achieving Career Goals
Overcoming Obstacles	Creative Expression

Making Mr. Right

1987/95

D: *Susan Seidelman.* **Cast:** *John Malkovich, Ann Magnuson, Glenne Headly, Ben Masters.*

A fun, upbeat, romantic spin on the Frankenstein theme, this film tells the tale of a nerdy scientist replicating himself as an almost-human android. A stylish PR whiz is hired to sell the android concept to the public. Her savvy puts her at loggerheads with the brainy geek. As he starts becoming more robotic, his android begins to acquire an all-too-human heart and falls for her.

Work & Prosperity	Loving Your Work
Relationships	Lovers Colleagues & Co-Workers

Finding Love	28-54
Overcoming Obstacles	Creative Expression

Malcolm X

1992/201

D: *Spike Lee.* **Cast:** *Denzel Washington, Angela Bassett, Albert Hall, Al Freeman, Jr.*

One of the best bio-pics ever made, this riveting, entertaining, and inspiring film explains how you can constantly transform yourself and rise above any circumstance you are confronted with. Born Malcolm Little with red hair and fair skin, this very bright boy was orphaned by the Ku Klux Klan and later became a small-time street hustler with a white girlfriend. Sent to prison in his 20s, he educated himself and converted to Islam, under the direction of black leader Elijah Mohammed. When he was released, he expanded the Nation of Islam, preached self-reliance, and expressed his incisive wit in angry sound bites for the media. Shown next to documentary footage of Malcolm X, Denzel Washington's performance is seamlessly authentic and completely engrossing.

Work & Prosperity	Realizing Dreams
Relationships	Teacher/Student Leader/Follower
Finding Love	28-54
Transitions	Achieving Career Goals
Overcoming Obstacles	Racial Prejudice Entrapment

Mambo Kings, The

1992/104

D: *Arne Glimcher.* **Cast:** *Armand Assante, Antonio Banderas, Cathy Moriarty, Desi Arnaz, Jr., Maruschka Detmers.*

Set to hot, sexy Latin tunes, this exciting film pumps up a familiar story with the passion and quick steps of a Cuban mambo. Kicked out of a Havana casino by the Mob in the 1950s, two brothers come to New York City trying to re-create their big band while working in a meat packing plant. Look for the breathtaking dance sequence with Assante and Detmers, as well as a fun bit where the brothers go on the *I Love Lucy Show.*

Work & Prosperity	Realizing Dreams
Relationships	Siblings Lovers
Finding Love	20s
Transitions	Achieving Career Goals
Overcoming Obstacles	Creative Expression

Map of the Human Heart

1993/126

D: *Vincent Ward.* **Cast:** *Jason Scott Lee, Anne Parillaud, Patrick Bergin.*

Told in flashback, this is a magical romantic adventure that sweeps you up and constantly delights you at every unexpected turn. In the 1930s, an Eskimo boy is flown out of his frozen village to a tuberculosis hospital in Toronto by Russell, a British mapmaker. There he meets the love of his life, a sickly girl of mixed race, Albertine. During World War II, he joins the RAF and reunites with Albertine in England, only to find she is engaged to Russell.

Work & Prosperity	Realizing Dreams
Relationships	Lovers
Finding Love	Teen Years 28-54
Transitions	Losing Mate

Overcoming Obstacles	Physical Abilities Racial Prejudice Loss

Marva Collins Story, The
1981/100

D: *Peter Levin.* **Cast:** *Cicely Tyson, Morgan Freeman.*

This uplifting biography of pioneer educator Marva Collins, beautifully performed by Tyson, illustrates the high rewards for taking the high risks needed to follow your heart's desire. It also demonstrates the learning advantages of the Great Intelligence versus the Small Intelligence. Frustrated by the public school system, Collins opens her own school for Chicago ghetto "slow learners" and transforms them into highly motivated geniuses.

Work & Prosperity	Loving Your Work
Relationships	Teacher/Student
Transitions	Pre-Teen Years Achieving Career Goals
Overcoming Obstacles	Mental Abilities

Marvin's Room
1996/98

D: *Jerry Zaks.* **Cast:** *Diane Keaton, Meryl Streep, Leonardo DiCaprio, Hume Cronyn.*

Make sure the tissue box is full before you watch this movie. Based on a play, it explores the emotional rewards of long-term caregiving. A middle-aged woman has been caring for her bedridden father and his looney sister for more than 20 years in Orlando. When she needs a bone marrow transplant, she asks her estranged rebellious sister and two children to help out and renew family ties.

Relationships	Multi-Generation Family Elder Care Breaking Old Patterns
Overcoming Obstacles	Physical Abilities

Michael
1996/105

D: *Nora Ephron.* **Cast:** *John Travolta, William Hurt, Andie MacDowell, Bob Hoskins.*

This quirky romance tells about a scruffy angel with a taste for wine, women and sweets being chased by two tabloid reporters in Iowa. The angel only has a few days left on earth, so he can't resist playing matchmaker to the cynical press man and the angel "expert." The Travolta dance number, set to Aretha Franklin's "Chain of Fools," is a must-see.

Relationships	Colleagues & Co-Workers Lovers
Finding Love	28-54

Mighty Aphrodite
1995/90

D: *Woody Allen.* **Cast:** *Helena Bonham Carter, Mira Sorvino, Woody Allen.*

This is another hilarious, laugh-out-loud Woody Allen film about a neurotic adoptive father tracking down his child's biological mother, who happens to be a hooker. Sorvino's outstanding performance as the mom earned her an Oscar for Best Supporting Actress. For extra grins, a Greek chorus provides a running commentary on the tragic/comic effects of the father's discovery.

Relationships	Married Couples Lovers
Transitions	Becoming Parent

Mighty Quinn, The
1989/98

D: *Carl Schenkel.* **Cast:** *Denzel Washington, James Fox, Robert Townsend, Mimi Rogers.*

Set to a reggae rhythm, this charming mystery about the relationship between a policeman and his childhood buddy who goes wrong presents an entertaining, wise look at Jamaican society. Washington offers a complex portrayal of Quinn as an easygoing local cop who has made good in his career but has made a mess of his relationships with his ex-wife and son.

Work & Prosperity	Balancing Work & Family
Relationships	Divorced Couples Friends
Transitions	Achieving Career Goals
Overcoming Obstacles	Adventure Loss

Miracle on 34th Street (1947)
1947/96

D: *George Seaton.* **Cast:** *Maureen O' Hara, Edmund Gwenn, Natalie Wood, Gene Lockhart, John Payne.*

As film critic Danny Peary notes, even the most jaded, overintellectual film buffs have a special soft spot in their hearts for this warmhearted tale of Christmas giving and believing in miracles. A Macy's parade executive (O'Hara) hires Gwenn as a last-minute Santa on Thanksgiving. While trying to persuade her young, skeptical daughter (Wood) that he is the real Santa, Gwenn is sent to a mental hospital. O'Hara's lawyer boyfriend (Payne) defends Gwenn in court. While all the adults in this drama give conditionally, with ulterior motives, the miracle happens because the child (Wood) believes the best will happen. And it does, teaching us adults a lesson about how to get what we want.

Work & Prosperity	Realizing Dreams Balancing Work & Family
Relationships	Single Parent Lovers
Finding Love	28-54
Overcoming Obstacles	Age Prejudice Loss

Mississippi Masala
1992/118

D: *Mira Nair.* **Cast:** *Denzel Washington, Sarita Choudhury, Roshan Seth, Charles S. Dutton, Sharmila Tagore.*

This is a jam-packed story of a professional Asian-Indian family forced out of Uganda by Idi Amin. They relocate to Mississippi to operate a run-down motel. The father longs for the prosperous African life that can be no more. Then their American-raised daughter falls in love with a black businessman who operates a motel rug cleaning service. This is not the life her parents had in mind for her, although in the Indian community she is considered too dark-skinned and poor to make a desirable wife. The black community also condemns the relationship after Indian motel owners boycott Washington's business. A funny, ironic commentary on racism as seen through black and Indian eyes.

Work & Prosperity	Realizing Dreams
Relationships	Parent/Child Lovers
Finding Love	20s
Transitions	Moving Out/Separating
Overcoming Obstacles	Racial Prejudice Cultural Abilities

After-View Feelings Key:
Feel Better/Uplift | Laughing Release | Crying Release | Violent Content

Month by the Lake, A

1995/91

D: *John Irvin.* **Cast:** *Vanessa Redgrave, Edward Fox, Uma Thurman.*

Set in 1937 Lake Como, Italy, in a seemingly peaceful pause before World War II, this charming romantic comedy of manners has middle-aged English lovers playing childish games of flirtation with youngsters half their age. It's fun to sit back, enjoy the scenery, and watch the characters finally break through their British reserve to express their true feelings.

Relationships	Lovers
Finding Love	28-54
Transitions	Courting
Overcoming Obstacles	Age Prejudice

Mother

1996/104

D: *Albert Brooks.* **Cast:** *Albert Brooks, Debbie Reynolds, Rob Morrow, Lisa Kudrow.*

After his second divorce, a confused middle-aged writer moves back in with his disapproving mother to try to figure out what went wrong with this first, most challenging relationship. His mother doesn't want him there and his younger, favored brother gets jealous. This movie offers an interesting perspective for adults re-evaluating their parent-child bond.

Relationships	Parent/Child
Overcoming Obstacles	Entrapment

Mr. Holland's Opus

1995/142

D: *Stephen Herek.* **Cast:** *Richard Dreyfuss, Glenne Headly, Jay Thomas, Olympia Dukakis.*

This is a moving look at an aspiring composer's thirty-year journey to acknowledge his true medium of creative expression: inspiring high school students with his infectious love of music. Mr. Holland takes a four-year teaching job at age 30 to give himself time to write his symphony and support his wife. But when his son is born deaf, he keeps his "day" job, harboring resentment toward his son about his sacrifice. For a real-life, grittier yet equally uplifting documentary version, see *Small Wonders*, a film about a Harlem elementary school violin teacher whose pupils end up playing in Carnegie Hall.

Work & Prosperity	Realizing Dreams
Relationships	Married Couples Teacher/Student
Transitions	Achieving Career Goals
Overcoming Obstacles	Creative Expression

Mr. Mom

1983/92

D: *Stan Dragoti.* **Cast:** *Michael Keaton, Teri Garr, Christopher Lloyd.*

In a hilarious fictional treatment of the *Roger & Me* scenario (see page 188), an auto executive loses his job and stays home with the kids while his wife becomes the family breadwinner. Keaton is very funny juggling the rigors of child care and housekeeping with his job search.

Work & Prosperity	Destructuring Workplace
Relationships	Two-Career Couples Parent/Child
Transitions	Losing Job
Overcoming Obstacles	Loss Entrapment

Much Ado About Nothing

1993/111

D: *Kenneth Branagh.* **Cast:** *Kenneth Branagh, Michael Keaton, Emma Thompson, Denzel Washington.*

Who says Shakespeare can't be fun and fast-paced? An all-star cast romping through a beautiful villa in Tuscany gives rise to a bawdy telling of the Bard's tale of courting. A jaded 30-something couple bicker in sarcastic rhyme while, in sharp contrast, a teenage couple succumbs to the innocent dew of love's first touch.

Relationships	Lovers
Finding Love	Teen Years 28-54
Transitions	Courting

My Cousin Vinny

1992/119

D: *Jonathon Lynn.* **Cast:** *Joe Pesci, Marisa Tomei, Fred Glynn.*

This amusing film is an inspiration for anyone considering a radical career change. If Vinny, a Bronx street tough, can become a winning trial lawyer in a Southern courtroom, there is hope for us all. The setup is a bit slow—Vinny's cousin gets wrongfully arrested driving through Dixie and calls on his novice relative to defend him. The fun begins when Vinny, to the consternation of the traditional judge, arrives in court dressed in gold chains and leather. Tomei won an Oscar for her performance as his wise-cracking, New York street-chic girlfriend.

Work & Prosperity	Realizing Dreams Collaborating w/ Colleagues
Relationships	Lovers Colleagues & Co-Workers
Finding Love	28-54
Transitions	Changing Careers
Overcoming Obstacles	Cultural Abilities

My Left Foot

1989/103

D: *Jim Sheridan.* **Cast:** *Daniel Day-Lewis, Brenda Fricker.*

Based on the gritty autobiography of cerebral-palsy victim Christy Brown, this uplifting drama shows how a boy, considered hopeless by all but his mother, teaches himself to write and paint using the only appendage he can control—his left foot. Brown overcomes his poverty to become a celebrated writer and painter, and falls in love along the way. Day-Lewis' and Fricker's performances are unforgettable.

Work & Prosperity	Realizing Dreams
Relationships	Parent/Child
Transitions	Achieving Career Goals
Overcoming Obstacles	Physical Abilities Creative Expression

Mystic Pizza

1988/101

D: *Daniel Petrie.* **Cast:** *Annabeth Gish, Julia Roberts, Lili Taylor, Vincent D'Onofrio, William R. Moses.*

A sweetly told story of three Portuguese-American high school friends who are waitresses at the local pizza restaurant, waiting out that time between high school graduation and the next stage of their lives. One (Taylor) can't decide whether to marry a local fisherman and re-create her parents' life. Another (Gish) is saving money to go to Yale while having an affair with a married architect. The third one (Roberts) is dating a preppy law school dropout with no particular ideas about what's next.

Work & Prosperity	Realizing Dreams
Relationships	Friends Lovers
Finding Love	Teen Years
Transitions	Moving Out/Separating
Overcoming Obstacles	Entrapment Creative Expression

Never Cry Wolf

1983/105

D: *Carroll Ballard.* **Cast:** *Charles Martin Smith, Brian Dennehy.*

If you enjoy furry critters and beautiful Canadian panoramas, this film—based on a real life saga—is for you. A man goes off into the Arctic tundra alone to study wolf behavior and ends up learning even more about his own personal truth. It makes you pause and question the validity of some of society's basic assumptions. For example: Wolves, instead of being vicious predators that prey on humans, actually sustain themselves primarily on a diet of mice and other small rodents.

Work & Prosperity	Loving Your Work
Relationships	Boss/Employee
Transitions	Achieving Career Goals
Overcoming Obstacles	Adventure Creative Expression

9 to 5

1980/111

D: *Colin Higgins.* **Cast:** *Jane Fonda, Lily Tomlin, Dolly Parton, Dabney Coleman.*

This lighthearted screwball comedy is a revenge fantasy about an arrogant, incompetent boss and three women who collude to even the score. Despite preposterous plot turns, this film amusingly shows the humanity of the buxom, married secretary staving off her boss' advances; the frustrated single-mother manager looking for recognition; and the frightened divorcée at her first job in the secretary pool.

Work & Prosperity	Balancing Work & Family Destructuring Workplace
Relationships	Boss/Employee Friends
Transitions	Achieving Career Goals
Overcoming Obstacles	Entrapment Creative Expression

Nothing in Common

1986/119

D: *Garry Marshall.* **Cast:** *Tom Hanks, Jackie Gleason, Eva Marie Saint, Bess Armstrong.*

This is a comedic drama about the maturing of a 30-something hotshot ad executive whose parents' divorce force him into a reluctant caretaker role. With hilarious pokes at the ad business, the movie shows the strain of achieving career goals and the loving frustration of caring for difficult, ailing parents.

Work & Prosperity	Balancing Work & Family
Relationships	Parent/Child Elder Care
Transitions	Achieving Career Goals
Overcoming Obstacles	Entrapment Loss

Now and Then

1995/97

D: *Leslie Linka Glatter.* **Cast:** *Rosie O'Donnell, Melanie Griffith, Demi Moore, Rita Wilson, Christina Ricci.*

This story flashbacks to the coming-of-age summer of four girls in their early teens then jumps ahead to their adult friendships at age 30, as they await the birth of a first child. There's enough material here for a miniseries, but it's an honest look at that point between the innocence of girlhood and the chaos of adolescence. For a darker male version of this teen transition period, see *Stand by Me*.

Relationships	Friends
Transitions	Teen Years Becoming Parent 20s to 30s Passage

One Trick Pony

1980/98

D: *Robert M. Young.* **Cast:** *Paul Simon, Blair Brown, Rip Torn, Joan Hackett.*

You don't have to be a Paul Simon fan to enjoy this underrated, complex story of a middle-aged folk singer seeking to stay true to his own definition of success. The troubadour was a big star in the 1960s, but now finds that his music is out of style. He tours smaller and smaller clubs, holding on to his old self-image and musical sound. He is torn personally and professionally. His wife, who loves him, is reluctant to follow his path and wants a divorce. He is counseled by music business hitmakers who want to change his sound to Top 40-type music.

Work & Prosperity	Loving Your Work
Relationships	Colleagues & Co-Workers Married Couples
Finding Love	28-54
Transitions	Achieving Career Goals Mid-Life Crisis 30s & 40s
Overcoming Obstacles	Creative Expression Loss

Ordinary People

1980/125

D: *Robert Redford.* **Cast:** *Donald Sutherland, Mary Tyler Moore, Judd Hirsch, Timothy Hutton.*

This film examines the deep, dark crack in the mirror of affluent, suburban, WASP family perfection. The drowning of the older teen son explodes the delicately submerged relationship issues of the parents and surviving younger son, who attempts suicide. This heart-wrenching film shows how they must adapt, learn, and grow into new circumstances. Gradually, and sadly, the well-meaning lawyer father realizes the cold-hearted truth about his pampered, cheerful, and selfish wife.

Relationships	Parent/Child Self-Esteem Married Couples
Transitions	Teen Years
Overcoming Obstacles	Loss

Parenthood

1989/124

D: *Ron Howard.* **Cast:** *Steve Martin, Mary Steenburgen, Dianne Wiest, Jason Robards,Jr., Rick Moranis.*

A wise and funny multi-generational look at the challenges of being both a child and a parent at the same time. This film shows the truth and humor in everyday situations that comprise family life. The complicated, fast-paced story focuses on married couple Martin and Steenburgen and their three children. It shows Martin's dilemma in finding balance between his work and family, which his father (Robards) never had. It's also about Martin's three siblings—bitterly divorced single mom Wiest and her two children; married sister Kozak, whose husband Moranis, insists on genius training for their only child, who is four; and ne'er-do-well

After-View Feelings Key:
Feel Better/Uplift   Laughing Release   Crying Release   Violent Content

brother Hulce, who is his father's favorite son. There is something new to be learned and laughed at with each viewing.

Work & Prosperity	Balancing Work & Family
Relationships	Working Parents
	Parent/Child
	Multi-Generation Family
	Divorced Couples
Finding Love	20s
	28-54
	55-81
Transitions	Living Together/Moving In
	After Retirement
	Achieving Career Goals
Overcoming Obstacles	Loss
	Entrapment

Paris Is Burning

1991/78

D: *Jennie Livingston.* **Cast:** *Carmen and Brooke, Andre Christian, Dorian Corey, Paris Dupree, Willi Ninja.*

This documentary on "voguing" and the drag balls of Harlem shows the hopes and dreams of gay blacks who are excluded from the straight, macho black and Hispanic avenues to success. Because the outside world rejects them as hustlers and petty thieves coping with the brutal reality of violence, the Harlem balls were organized to provide momentary escape and a place where success is redefined on their terms. The balls honor categories of their highest aspirations, such as realness (passing as women), evening wear, and executive wear (Brooks Brothers suits and brief cases), complete with Olympics-like judging. Clearly, the film demonstrates the power of imagination in creating a sense of community and support, despite society's judgments.

Work & Prosperity	Realizing Dreams
Relationships	Friends
Finding Love	Same Sex
Overcoming Obstacles	Racial Prejudice
	Sexual Prejudice
	Creative Expression

Peter's Friends

1992/100

D: *Kenneth Branagh.* **Cast:** *Emma Thompson, Kenneth Branagh, Rita Rudner.*

Due to unfair comparisons to *The Big Chill* (see page 148), this is an underrated film. But the story is a witty, sarcastic, and intelligent account of an English comedy troupe of six players who have scattered to L.A. and London, but are now reunited ten years later for a New Year's weekend in the British countryside. One member went to Hollywood, married a sitcom star, and writes for her. Another, who still falls for unavailable men, brings a not-yet-divorced man to the party. Two married each other and have a very successful music jingle business, but are emotionally frozen by the loss of a child. Still seeking "Mr. Right," a frustrated female thinks the host might just be the man for her.

Work & Prosperity	Realizing Dreams
Relationships	Friends
	Married Couples
Finding Love	28-54
Transitions	Mid-Life Crisis 30s & 40s
Overcoming Obstacles	Creative Expression
	Loss

Philadelphia

1993/119

D: *Jonathon Demme.* **Cast:** *Tom Hanks, Denzel Washington, Jason Robards, Jr.*

Another terrific, moving performance by Tom Hanks as a hotshot HIV-positive lawyer elevates this tale of the AIDS epidemic and homophobic hypocrisy to operatic proportions. Fired by his Main Line employer on trumped-up charges, the dying attorney decides to sue as his last act. Only a gay-hating ambulance chaser, played with wit and increasing tenderness by Washington, will take the case. Joanne Woodward cameos as Hanks' supportive, tear-choked but cheery-acting mother.

Work & Prosperity	Collaborating w/ Colleagues
Relationships	Boss/Employee Colleagues & Co-Workers
Transitions	Losing Job
Overcoming Obstacles	Physical Abilities Sexual Prejudice

Player, The

1992/123

D: *Robert Altman.* **Cast:** *Tim Robbins, Greta Scacchi, Fred Ward, Whoopi Goldberg, Dean Stockwell.*

Told with hilarious verve by director Altman, who was hot in the 1970s and out in the 1980s, this is an insider's sharp, satiric look at Hollywood in the 1980s as a metaphor for corporate greed and heartless actions. The story centers around a cold, calculating, temperamental, overpaid, young studio vice president whose only job is to listen to screenplay proposals and not do anything wrong politically. He has no authority to give a script a "go," but he can say "no." The intrigue begins when he starts receiving death-threatening postcards from a writer. His crime: He said he would call back the writer after a meeting and never did.

Work & Prosperity	Collaborating w/ Colleagues Destructuring Workplace
Relationships	Colleagues & Co-Workers Lovers
Finding Love	28-54
Transitions	Achieving Career Goals Surviving Downsizing
Overcoming Obstacles	Entrapment Creative Expression

Pride and Prejudice

1995/300

D: *Simon Langton.* **Cast:** *Jennifer Ehle, Colin Firth, Susannah Harker, Alison Steadman.*

This lavish Jane Austin tale of a gentile English family attempting to marry off five daughters with no dowry remains as fresh and funny today as when it was written in the early 1800's. Independent Elizabeth Bennett is reluctantly smitten with the arrogant, wealthy Mr. D'Arcy while her sister Jane falls for D'Arcy's best friend. Both sisters try to cope with their silly, ill-mannered mother and younger sisters, who shamelessly pursue local soldiers.

Relationships	Lovers
Finding Love	College Years
Transitions	Courting
Overcoming Obstacles	Class Prejudice

Private Parts

1997/108

D: *Betty Thomas.* **Cast:** *Howard Stern, Robin Quivers, Mary McCormack.*

A true tale of how a geek can rule in the world of talk radio despite years of humiliation and false starts. He succeeds by having the audacity to follow his baser instincts, much to the hilarious consternation of squeamish bosses. Shock-jock Howard Stern, as himself, of course, replays some of his more notorious radio firsts, such as his interview with a nude woman. Be sure and watch the credits all the way to the end. This film is not for those sensitive to offensive language and junior high sex jokes.

Work & Prosperity	Realizing Dreams
Relationships	Married Couples Colleagues & Co-Workers
Transitions	Achieving Career Goals
Overcoming Obstacles	Creative Expression

Queen of Hearts

1989/112

D: *Jon Amiel.* **Cast:** *Anita Zasgaria, Joseph Long, Eileen Way.*

This funny, heartfelt, and sad story tells of a Sicilian couple who defy their families and marry for love. Now middle-aged with four children, they are running a diner in England and having to face the consequences of their youthful act. Think of an English version of Moonstruck with the artistic sensibility of a great Italian movie.

Relationships	Multi-Generation Family Married Couples
Finding Love	28-54 20's 55-81
Transitions	Marrying Moving Out/Separating
Overcoming Obstacles	Entrapment

Raiders of the Lost Ark

1981/115

See *Indiana Jones Trilogy.*

Resurrection

1980/103

D: *Daniel Petrie.* **Cast:** *Ellen Burstyn, Sam Shepard, Richard Farnsworth, Eva LeGallienne.*

This is an emotionally wrenching story of the transformative power of a near-death experience. A woman has an auto accident that kills her husband and gives her the ability to heal not only herself but also the sick and disabled. This is a tale of her quest to figure out how to use this healing gift in an appropriate way. A superb cast includes Ellen Burstyn as the lead, and Eva LeGallienne as her grandmother. Both women turn in Oscar-nominated performances. Sam Shepard plays Burstyn's blue-collar boyfriend who fears she might be Christ incarnate.

Work & Prosperity	Loving Your Work
Relationships	Parent/Child Lovers
Finding Love	Radical Age Differences
Transitions	Changing Careers
Overcoming Obstacles	Physical Abilities Creative Expression

Return of the Jedi

1983/133

See *Star Wars Episodes IV, V, & VI.*

Rocky

1976/119

D: *John Avildsen.* **Cast:** *Sylvester Stallone, Talia Shire, Burt Young.*

This movie is worth watching at least once a year to reinspire you to hold onto your dreams. By now, everyone knows the story and how it turns out: A small-time thug and mediocre amateur boxer gets a shot at a fight with an Ali-type champion. It is always a pleasure to reexperience the honest sweetness between Rocky and his girlfriend and be reminded of the emotional secret to success—being flexible. Four sequels—1979 *Rocky II* (119m), 1982 *Rocky III* (99m), 1985 *Rocky IV* (91m), and 1990 *Rocky V* (104m)—continue the saga but maintain with increasing difficulty the freshness of the original.

Work & Prosperity	Realizing Dreams
Relationships	Lovers Colleagues & Co-Workers
Finding Love	28-54
Transitions	Achieving Career Goals
Overcoming Obstacles	Physical Abilities

Rocky II
1979/119

See *Rocky.*

Rocky III
1982/99

See *Rocky.*

Rocky IV
1985/104

See *Rocky.*

Rocky V
1990/104

See *Rocky.*

Roger & Me
1989/100

D: *Michael Moore.*

This inspired, funny, angry documentary examines the personal side of the decline of the auto industry in Flint, Michigan. While futilely seeking an interview with Roger Smith, head of General Motors, director Moore encounters the displaced auto workers, the sheriff who evicts families, the civic boosters promoting Flint as a tourist destination, and the aspiring entrepreneur selling rabbits as pets or for food. This film cuts through corporate insensitivity and double-speak with a work-a-day guy's and gal's vengeance.

Work & Prosperity	Destructuring Workplace
Relationships	Boss/Employee
Transitions	Losing Job
Overcoming Obstacles	Loss

Room with a View, A
1986/117

D: *James Ivory.* **Cast:** *Helena Bonham Carter, Julian Sands, Denholm Elliott, Maggie Smith, Judi Dench.*

Based on E. M. Forster's novel of manners and produced by the masterful Merchant-Ivory-Jhabvala team, this wonderfully romantic movie with a superb cast is a witty comment on the art of making emotional choices, despite societal mores. In a visual feast set to passionate Puccini tunes, an indecisive young Englishwoman and her spinster chaperone take refuge in a Florence pension to contemplate her marital options between a socially correct twit and a dashing suitor.

Work & Prosperity	Realizing Dreams
Relationships	Lovers
Finding Love	20s
Transitions	Marrying
Overcoming Obstacles	Entrapment Class Prejudice

Roots
1977/570

D: *Marvin J Chomsky.* **Cast:** *Ed Asner, LeVar Burton, Burl Ives, O. J. Simpson, Cicely Tyson, Ben Vereen, Lou Gossett, Jr.*

Based on Alex Haley's book, this exceptional television miniseries with an outstanding cast shows the epic sweep of the African-American story through the lens of a modern day black man's search for his heritage.

Work & Prosperity	Realizing Dreams
Relationships	Multi-Generation Family Boss/Employee Breaking Old Patterns
Transitions	Achieving Career Goals

Overcoming Obstacles	Racial Prejudice Entrapment War

Rosalie Goes Shopping
1990/94

D: *Percy Adlon.* **Cast:** *Marianne Sägebrecht, Brad Davis, Judge Reinhold.*

This is a wonderful sendup of mindless American consumerism told through the unquestioning eyes of a German-born homemaker in Arkansas. She provides the "best" for her American husband and family with endless credit card scams and check-kiting schemes. Despite the shady actions, her reassuring air is so convincing it propels her into a new career.

Work & Prosperity	Balancing Work & Family
Relationships	Working Parents
Transitions	Changing Careers
Overcoming Obstacles	Creative Expression

Ruby in Paradise
1993/115

D: *Victor Munez.* **Cast:** *Ashley Judd, Todd Field, Bentley Mitchum.*

Here's the female version of the coming-of-age story (after high school) sensitively acted by Ashley Judd. She's plays a girl who leaves rural Tennessee to pursue her dreams and a new sense of herself in Panama City, Florida. There, she takes a job in a tourist shop, which she eventually ends up managing, while she dates two very different types of men.

Work & Prosperity	Realizing Dreams
Relationships	Lovers Boss/Employee
Finding Love	Teen Years
Transitions	Teen Years Moving Out/Separating
Overcoming Obstacles	Entrapment

Ruthless People
1986/93

D: *Jim Abrahams, David Zucker, Jerry Zucker.* **Cast:** *Danny DeVito, Bette Midler, Judge Reinhold, Helen Slater.*

This is a funny, clever script about a nasty man whose plans to kill his obnoxious wife are interrupted when she is kidnapped. He refuses to pay ransom. The befuddled kidnappers, a sweet fashion-design couple who have been ripped off by the greedy husband's clothing firm, put the wife in the basement with an exercise bike, where to her surprise, she finally loses weight. DeVito and Midler are inspired as lovable villains.

Work & Prosperity	Realizing Dreams
Relationships	Colleagues & Co-Workers
Finding Love	28-54
Transitions	Changing Careers
Overcoming Obstacles	Loss Entrapment

Sabrina (1996)
1996/124

D: *Sydney Pollack.* **Cast:** *Harrison Ford, Julia Ormond, Greg Kinnear, Nancy Marchand.*

This update of the classic Billy Wilder fairytale, about a chauffeur's daughter who marries one of the estate's two wealthy sons offers rounder characters than the original (she's a photographer; her father chose his occupation because he loves to read; the ne'er-do-well son's fiance is a doctor; the older son and mother are workaholics), but it's difficult to top Audrey Hepburn's luminescent performance in the original. Watch them both for a good study in how relationships have changed from the '50s to the '90s.

Relationships	Lovers

Finding Love	20's
Transitions	Courting
Overcoming Obstacles	Class Prejudice

Sabrina (1954)
1954/113

See *Sabrina (1996)*.

Searching for Bobby Fisher
1993/110

D: *Steven Zaillian.* **Cast:** *Joe Mantegna, Max Pomeranc, Joan Allen, Ben Kingsley, Laurence Fishburne.*

This is an absorbing true story of a couple's discovery of their seven-year-old son's chess genius and their quest to find the best teachers for him. The child prefers the fun of a Central Park speed chess contest, but the parents force him to study with a coach who specializes in competitions. The film poignantly addresses the tricky challenges of keeping a talented child challenged and self-motivated at the same time.

Relationships	Parent/Child
Transitions	Pre-Teen Years
Overcoming Obstacles	Mental Abilities

Secret of Roan Inish, The
1994/102

D: *John Sayles.* **Cast:** *Jeni Courtney, Miele Lallay, Eileen Colgan, John Lynch.*

Beautifully photographed in Ireland, this lyrical Celtic fantasy is told through the eyes of a 10-year-old girl about mythic ancestors on an island called Roan Inish. With innocent faith, she believes her brother, who was lost at sea before she was born, is still living on the island in the care of the mythic Selkie—half man, half seal—and proceeds to reclaim him.

Relationships	Siblings Parent/Child
Transitions	Pre-Teen Years
Overcoming Obstacles	Loss

Secrets and Lies
1995/142

D: *Mike Leigh.* **Cast:** *Brenda Blethyn, Marianne Jean-Baptiste, Timothy Spall.*

This is a powerful and touching look at what shapes a person's identity. An upmarket black London optometrist goes in search of her birth mother when her adoptive mother dies. The ensuing shock of discovering her white, factory-worker mum and disgruntled half-sister draws her into the web of the newfound family's denial and disbelief.

Relationships	Parent/Child
Transitions	Mid-Life Crisis 30s & 40s
Overcoming Obstacles	Loss

Sense and Sensibility
1995/135

D: *Ang Lee.* **Cast:** *Emma Thompson, Hugh Grant, Kate Winslet, Alan Rickman, Greg Wise.*

This film delights us all with an exuberant take on the trials and tribulations of two impoverished English sisters whose only hope for happiness is marriage. The lovingly crafted script, based on a Jane Austen novel, brought Thompson an Oscar. The comedic balance between irony and warmth is maintained perfectly by a strong cast and understanding direction.

Relationships	Siblings
Finding Love	20s
Transitions	Courting
Overcoming Obstacles	Entrapment

Sex, Lies, & Videotape

1989/100

D: *Steven Soderbergh.* **Cast:** *James Spader, Andie MacDowell, Peter Gallagher, Laura San Giacomo.*

This film is an excellent meditation on the shifting nature of sexual fulfillment as we move from our 20s into our 30s. A lawyer is having a steamy affair with his frigid wife's sister when a mysterious old friend, who is impotent, shows up and moves in. The intrigue begins when the friend seduces the wife into talking about her sexual fantasies on videotape.

Relationships	Friends Married Couples
Finding Love	28-54
Transitions	20s to 30s Passage
Overcoming Obstacles	Entrapment

Shadowlands

1993/130

D: *Richard Attenborough.* **Cast:** *Anthony Hopkins, Debra Winger.*

Here's a heart-wrenching true story of a marriage of convenience that cracks open the heart of C.S. Lewis, a crusty, middle-aged Oxford don and well-known writer, just before his poet wife's early demise. Emotionally shut down since his mother's death in his childhood, Lewis channels his feelings into delightful children's stories and rigidly protects himself with his intellect and cozy academic life. His forward American wife and her son change all that and, in the end, he is left to share his sorrow with his stepson.

Work & Prosperity	Balancing Work & Family
Relationships	Parent/Child Married Couples
Finding Love	28-54
Transitions	Marrying
Overcoming Obstacles	Loss

She's the One

1996/95

D: *Edward Burns.* **Cast:** *Edward Burns, Mike McGlone, Jennifer Aniston, Cameron Diaz, Maxine Bahns, John Mahoney.*

It's a funny look at how one Irish-American family passes down relationship patterns from one generation to the next. The father gives very bad marital advice to his sons, as his own marriage in unknowingly falling apart. The slacker taxi-driving son's spur-of-the-moment marriage to one of his fares is contrasted with the disintegrating union of the yuppie son, who's two-timing his wife with his brother's former fiance.

Relationships	Multi-Generation Family Lovers Married Couples
Finding Love	20's 55-81
Transitions	20s Mid-50s Passage Courting
Overcoming Obstacles	Entrapment

Shine

1995/105

D: *Scott Hicks.* **Cast:** *Geoffrey Rush, Noah Taylor, Armin Mueller-Stahl, Lynn Redgrave.*

This true story of Australian piano prodigy David Helfgott and his triumph over mental breakdown inspires us never to give up our dreams or our hopes for happiness. In middle age, David marries a loving wife who manages his concert career. Rush received the Best Actor Oscar in 1996 for his portrayal of the adult Helfgott.

Work & Prosperity	Realizing Dreams
Relationships	Parent/Child Married Couples
Finding Love	28-54

Transitions	Teen Years College Years Achieving Career Goals
Overcoming Obstacles	Creative Expression Mental Abilities

Sister Act
1992/100

D: *Emile Ardolino.* **Cast:** *Whoopi Goldberg, Maggie Smith, Kathy Najimi.*

Here's an excellent example of a feel-good film that audiences love and critics hate, but who cares? This radical-career-change flick is so much fun, you may want to see it again and again. A Reno casino singer who squeals on her mob boyfriend must go undercover in a nunnery under the witness protection program. There she jazzes up the sisters with some heart and soul as their new choir director. The 1993 sequel, *Sister Act 2: Back in the Habit* (101m), is very slow and fails to deliver the spirit-cleansing uplift of the original. Fast forward to the rousing musical close to save yourself time.

Work & Prosperity	Collaborating w/ Colleagues
Relationships	Colleagues & Co-Workers
Transitions	Changing Careers
Overcoming Obstacles	Creative Expression Entrapment

Sister Act II: Back in the Habit
1993/106

See *Sister Act*.

Sleepless in Seattle
1993/104

D: *Nora Ephron.* **Cast:** *Tom Hanks, Meg Ryan, Ross Malinger, Rita Wilson.*

Get out the tissues for this great laugh-and-cry screwball "love at first voice" comedy, which pays tribute to the contrived tear-jerkers of the past. A Baltimore woman engaged to a boring, allergic dweeb hears a young son on a call-in radio show pleading for a new wife for his widowed Seattle father. She falls for the father when she hears his sad, tear-choked voice. Complete with goofy shots of the U.S. map with airplane routes, the rest of the film is spent creating ingenious ways to unite this bi-coastal couple. For further tissue soakings, check out this sudsy story of illicit romance and separation in three previous forms, starring Cary Grant/Deborah Kerr in the 1957 *An Affair to Remember* (115m); comedic Irene Dunne/ Charles Boyer in the superb 1939 *Love Affair* (87m); and Warren Beatty/ Annette Benning in the tired 1994 *Love Affair* (108m).

Relationships	Single Parent Lovers
Finding Love	28-54
Transitions	Courting
Overcoming Obstacles	Loss

Small Wonders
1995/77

D: *Allan Miller.*

This is an inspiring documentary about how a tireless and demanding violin teacher at three East Harlem elementary schools takes her lottery-selected students from first-grade/beginner's level to playing the national anthem at New York Knicks games and participating in a Carnegie Hall Fiddlefest with the world's best violin players. This documentary takes you into students' homes and shows involved, proud parents with their talented children. The film leaves you with an optimistic feeling about the future of arts education. See *Mr. Holland's Opus* for a fictional treatment.

Work & Prosperity	Loving Your Work
Relationships	Teacher/Student Single Parent
Transitions	Achieving Career Goals
Overcoming Obstacles	Creative Expression

Sneakers

1992/125

D: *Phil Alden Robinson.* **Cast:** *Robert Redford, Sidney Poitier, River Phoenix, Dan Aykroyd, Ben Kingsley.*

This is one of the best screen examples of team collaboration, cooperation, and co-creation in a thriller story about a motley group of five computer hackers who operate a security firm and get involved in a questionable government contract. Each member of the team contributes his own unique, offbeat skill to the firm and has a somewhat shady past. Redford, as the head of the group, is blackmailed by the government with an offer to clean up a past youthful illegal hacker episode *if* his firm will steal a code-breaking machine. But nothing is quite as it seems, and before long, everyone gets in over their heads.

Work & Prosperity	Collaborating w/ Colleagues
Relationships	Colleagues & Co-Workers
Transitions	Achieving Career Goals
Overcoming Obstacles	Adventure Creative Expression Entrapment

Soapdish

1991/92

D: *Michael Hoffman.* **Cast:** *Sally Field, Kevin Kline, Robert Downey, Jr., Cathy Moriarty, Whoopi Goldberg.*

A 1990s screwball comedy about the backstage melodrama of the cast and crew of a long-running TV soap opera. The plot is a delightful potpourri of the baser instincts of lust, jealousy, greed, and vanity, with all the characters in a state of permanent imbalance and hilarious confusion. Popular but aging star Field is being targeted for soap opera "heaven" by co-star Moriarty, who makes sexual promises to sycophant producer Downey if he'll write Field out.

Work & Prosperity	Collaborating w/ Colleagues Balancing Work & Family
Relationships	Colleagues & Co-Workers Lovers
Finding Love	28-54
Transitions	Achieving Career Goals
Overcoming Obstacles	Age Prejudice Loss

Some Like It Hot

1959/119

D: *Billy Wilder.* **Cast:** *Jack Lemmon, Tony Curtis, Marilyn Monroe, Joe E. Brown.*

Comedy doesn't get any better than this fresh, fast-paced, cross-dressing, mistaken identity tale of two musicians on the lam from the Chicago mob. The pair joins an all-girl band on its way to Miami, and both fall for the lead singer. Spectacular performances by Lemmon, Curtis, and Monroe create perennial delight.

Work & Prosperity	Collaborating w/ Colleagues
Relationships	Colleagues & Co-Workers Lovers
Finding Love	28-54

Transitions	Courting
Overcoming Obstacles	Sexual Prejudice Entrapment

Some Mother's Son

1997/111

D: *Terry George.* **Cast:** *Helen Mirren, Fionnula Flanagan.*

💧 This is a powerful story of how an apolitical teacher and mother of three is ensnared in the IRA conflict in Northern Ireland when her 19-year-old son is jailed by the English (Thatcher administration). She and another newly politicized mother are thrown into the eye of the storm when their sons take part in a prison hunger strike. Mirren's character is caught in the heartwrenching, unthinkable dilemma of honoring her son's beliefs and saving his life.

Relationships	Parent/Child Friends
Overcoming Obstacles	War

Spitfire Grill, The

1995/117

D: *Lee David Zlotoff.* **Cast:** *Alison Elliott, Ellen Burstyn, Marcia Gay Harden, Will Patton.*

💧 An audience-pleasing weeper from the Sundance Film Festival, this is a moving tale of a poor girl's struggle to establish herself in a small town after her release from prison. She works as a waitress at a diner run by a crusty old woman while her honesty about her past unnerves the residents until tragedy strikes. Then, everyone rallies around a plan to help. Keep a large supply of tissues on hand for this one.

Relationships	Boss/Employee Lovers
Finding Love	20s

Transitions	Landing First Job
Overcoming Obstacles	Class Prejudice

Star is Born, A (1937)

1937/111

See *A Star Is Born* (1954).

Star is Born, A (1954)

1954/154

D: *George Cukor.* **Cast:** *Judy Garland, James Mason.*

💧 This classic, musical rendering of a dual-career couple's conflict tells the Hollywood story of a young wife on her way up and an alcoholic husband on his way down. A terrific score by Harold Arlen and Ira Gershwin and a poignant Moss Hart script punch up the tragic mood that centers around achieving career goals at the expense of losing the person you love most. Originally 181 minutes long, a "restored" version was released at 170 minutes in 1983. Check out the outstanding original 1937 drama (111 m) with Frederic March and Janet Gaynor, directed by William Wellman and cowritten by Dorothy Parker. With less credibility, Barbra Streisand remade this in 1976 as a story about the rock music business (140m).

Work & Prosperity	Balancing Work & Family
Relationships	Two-Career Couples
Finding Love	Radical Age Differences
Transitions	Achieving Career Goals Losing Mate
Overcoming Obstacles	Creative Expression Loss

Star is Born, A (1976)

1976/140

See *A Star Is Born (1954).*

Star Trek IV: The Voyage Home 1986/119

D: *Leonard Nimoy.* **Cast:** *William Shatner, Leonard Nimoy, DeForest Kelley, Catharine Hicks.*

With a wacky plot device, the Enterprise crew must travel back from the 23rd century to current-day Earth to save the whales, so the planet won't be destroyed in the future. By far the most charming and fun of the Trek series, this really is just an excuse to play the well-known space characters off the little frustrations of modern-day life. For example: As they get kicked off a bus, they ask "What is exact change?"

Work & Prosperity	Collaborating w/ Colleagues
Relationships	Colleagues & Co-Workers
Overcoming Obstacles	Loss Adventure

Star Wars (1977) 1977/121

See *Star Wars Episodes, IV, V, & VI.*

Star Wars Episodes IV, V, & VI 1977/378

D: *George Lucas, et. al.* **Cast:** *Mark Hamill, Harrison Ford, Carrie Fisher.*

Episode IV (*Star Wars*, 1977, 121m), Episode V (*The Empire Strikes Back*, 1980, 124m), and Episode VI (*The Return of the Jedi*, 1983, 133m) paint a rich picture of a fun futuristic world populated by endearing and dangerous characters caught in mythic struggles. This spirit-cleansing saga leaves you feeling optimistic about your own ability to venture forth into the unknown. May the Force be with you.

Work & Prosperity	Realizing Dreams
Relationships	Parent/Child Colleagues & Co-Workers
Finding Love	20s
Transitions	Achieving Career Goals
Overcoming Obstacles	Physical Abilities Adventure

Starman 1984/112

D: *John Carpenter.* **Cast:** *Jeff Bridges, Karen Allen, Charles Martin Smith.*

This is a wonderfully moving, bittersweet road romance between an alien and a grieving widow. He clones her husband's body to survive on Earth. This premise is made perfectly credible by the brilliant performances of Bridges and Allen. On the run from hostile authorities, the starman adjusts to the mechanics of the human body, while the widow begins to respect the entity that only looks like her husband.

Relationships	Lovers
Finding Love	28-54
Transitions	Losing Mate
Overcoming Obstacles	Loss Entrapment

Starting Over 1979/106

D: *Alan J. Pakula.* **Cast:** *Burt Reynolds, Jill Clayburgh, Candice Bergen.*

This is a humorous look at a divorced man's confusion over falling in love again before he severs emotional cords with his ex-wife. A fresh, witty script provides an upbeat take on the heart's twists and turns as one navigates the murky road of letting go of an old relationship and moving into a new commitment unencumbered.

Relationships	Divorced Couples Lovers
Finding Love	28-54

Transitions	Divorcing Courting
Overcoming Obstacles	Loss

Strictly Ballroom

1992/94

D: *Baz Luhrmann.* **Cast:** *Paul Mercurio, Tara Morice, Bill Hunter.*

This tongue-in-cheek look at Australian ballroom dancing competition puts a couple at odds with their talented child. Scott (Mercurio) has been groomed since age 6 to win the Pan-Pacific Championship. But, he loves to dance and flouts the strict rules, shocking the judges and throwing his mother into a tizzy. The son is absorbed in his love of expressing himself through dance, while his parents seem to care only about the outcome of the competition and what others think. This is a fun look at how parents project their own unfulfilled dreams on their unsuspecting offspring. Outstanding dance numbers are performed by Sydney Ballet dancers Mercurio and Morice.

Work & Prosperity	Realizing Dreams Loving Your Work
Relationships	Parent/Child Lovers
Finding Love	20s
Transitions	Achieving Career Goals Courting
Overcoming Obstacles	Creative Expression Entrapment

Sure Thing, The

1985/94

D: *Rob Reiner.* **Cast:** *John Cusack, Daphne Zuniga, Anthony Edwards, Boyd Gaines, Tim Robbins.*

This is an engaging story about how two students in an Eastern college really fall in love—shyly and slowly. A boy develops a crush on a girl in his English class, but she rejects him. At Christmas, they are thrown together in a cross-country trip home to L.A. which is a good excuse to fight, make up, share experiences, and fall in love. They both gain a new perspective on their commitment when she visits her boring fiancé, and he half-heartedly checks out "the sure thing" his buddy has promised him.

Relationships	Lovers
Finding Love	College Years
Transitions	College Years Courting
Overcoming Obstacles	Entrapment

Terms of Endearment

1983/129

D: *James L. Brooks.* **Cast:** *Debra Winger, Shirley MacLaine, Jack Nicholson, Jeff Daniels, Danny DeVito.*

This story of the bittersweet relationship of a domineering, perfectionist mother (MacLaine) and her joyful, happy-go-lucky daughter (Winger) expresses the real-life blend of the highs of comic pleasures and the lows of sadness and hurts. The frustrated widowed mother hasn't had a date since her husband died years before and chooses a swinging bachelor astronaut (Nicholson). Her daughter marries a professor (Daniels), who has a wandering eye for coeds, and they have three children. Then something unpredictable happens to shift the tone of this tale from an upbeat comedy to a three-handkerchief ending. The mediocre sequel *The Evening Star* is not as moving.

Relationships	Parent/Child Lovers
Finding Love	20s 28-54 55-81
Transitions	Courting Marrying Losing Mate
Overcoming Obstacles	Loss Entrapment

Texasville
1990/123

See *Last Picture Show, The.*

35 Up
1992/127

See *28 Up.*

Thousand Pieces of Gold
1991/105

D: *Nancy Kelly.* **Cast:** *Rosalind Chao, Chris Cooper, Dennis Dun, Michael Paul.*

Based on a true story, this film is about a poor Mongolian woman (Chao) sold into slavery by her father and shipped to the United States to work as a prostitute in a Western mining town. Despite all odds, she refuses to accept her fate and through sheer force of will creates her own independent life in a strange land, doing other people's laundry and running a boarding house. Along the way, she finds a surprising romance with the drunken saloon owner (Cooper). This is a perfect film to inspire you to overcome any obstacles you are facing.

Work & Prosperity	Realizing Dreams
Relationships	Lovers Colleagues & Co-Workers
Finding Love	28-54
Transitions	Achieving Career Goals Courting
Overcoming Obstacles	Racial Prejudice Sexual Prejudice

Three of Hearts
1993/97

D: *Yurek Bogayevicz.* **Cast:** *William Baldwin, Kelly Lynch, Sherilyn Fenn, Joe Pantoliano.*

This is an expansive, touching 1990s spin on the romantic triangle. A scorned lesbian nurse (Lynch) wants her lover, a bisexual writing teacher (Fenn), back. So Lynch hires a male escort (Baldwin) to seduce Fenn and then abandon her. Ideally, Fenn will hate men so much she will come back to Lynch. But, things get complicated when Baldwin, who believes he can seduce any woman, any time, becomes the seductee and loses interest in his work. The presentation of the characters' sexuality is honest, nonjudgmental, and insightful.

Work & Prosperity	Radical Career Change
Relationships	Lovers
Finding Love	28-54
Transitions	Changing Careers Courting
Overcoming Obstacles	Loss

To Die For
1995/107

D: *Gus Van Sant.* **Cast:** *Nicole Kidman, Matt Dillon, Joaquin Phoenix, Casey Affleck, Alison Foland.*

This smart, dark satire of a media-obsessed world gone awry tells the story of a blindly ambitious, cable TV weather girl's obsession with fame. The only way she can figure out how to achieve fame is through a tabloid-style murder of her nice guy husband.

Work & Prosperity	Realizing Dreams
Relationships	Married Couples Colleagues & Co-Workers
Transitions	Achieving Career Goals
Overcoming Obstacles	Creative Expression

Tootsie

1982/110

D: *Sydney Pollack.* **Cast:** *Dustin Hoffman, Jessica Lange, Charles Durning, Teri Garr, Bill Murray.*

This is a fun, upbeat story about mistaken sexual identity, sexual prejudice, soap operas, and Manhattan. It never loses its feel-good freshness, even after repeated viewings and years of subtle shifts in attitudes about sexism. An unemployed but talented actor (Hoffman), desperate for work, auditions for a soap opera role as "Dorothy," a 40s female hospital administrator, and gets the part. Unfortunately and hilariously, Dorothy takes on a life of her own. Hoffman must cope with his growing love for his sweet co-worker (Lange) and her father's love for Dorothy.

Work & Prosperity	Realizing Dreams
Relationships	Breaking Old Patterns Lovers
Finding Love	28-54
Transitions	Achieving Career Goals Courting
Overcoming Obstacles	Sexual Prejudice Creative Expression

Town Like Alice, A

1985/301

D: *David Stevens.* **Cast:** *Bryan Brown, Helen Morse, Gordon Jackson.*

Based on a true story fictionalized by Nevil Shute, this wonderfully acted Australian and PBS miniseries tells the irresistibly romantic story of a genteel Englishwoman and a rough Australian man who meet briefly as Japanese prisoners of war in Malaysia. Years later, they reunite, to explore the viability of their love in the bleak center of Australia.

Work & Prosperity	Realizing Dreams
Relationships	Lovers Husband/Wife
Finding Love	20s 28-54
Transitions	Courting
Overcoming Obstacles	Class Prejudice War Loss

Toy Story

1995/84

D: *John Lasseter.* **Cast:** *Tom Hanks, Tim Allen, Annie Potts, John Ratzenberger.*

Here's the first full-length, computer animated movie that proves that toys have a life of their own when we're not around. This lively, upbeat comedy faces off a cowboy doll called Woody against a newly acquired, square-jawed spaceman named Buzz Lightyear as they vie to be their owner's favorite. The supporting cast is a delightfully wacky menagerie of colorful toy characters. This amusing and intelligent story rivals the best comedic scripts and will please all ages.

Relationships	Colleagues & Co-Workers
Transitions	Living Together/Moving In
Overcoming Obstacles	Entrapment

Truly, Madly, Deeply 1991/89

D: *Anthony Minghella.* **Cast:** *Juliet Stevenson, Alan Rickman, Bill Paterson.*

This offbeat, wry British take on the after-life death experience is a convincing, often moving, examination of healing a sense of loss. Consumed by grief over the death of her cellist boyfriend, the heroine bounces back when he returns in spirit. The fun begins when he starts showing up with pals to watch old movies in her living room. Then, a wise new lover appears and forces her to make a choice.

Relationships	Breaking Old Patterns Lovers
Finding Love	28-54
Transitions	Losing Mate
Overcoming Obstacles	Loss

Truth About Cats and Dogs, The 1996/97

D: *Michael Lehmann.* **Cast:** *Janeane Garofalo, Uma Thurman, Ben Chaplin.*

This heartwarming brains-versus-beauty tale examines a photographer's on-air attraction to a witty talk-radio veterinarian who doubts her physical allure. When he wants to meet her, she arranges for him to meet her dim-witted, but physically stunning neighbor instead. Things get complicated when both women fall for the charming Englishman.

Relationships	Lovers Friends Self-esteem
Finding Love	20's
Transitions	Courting
Overcoming Obstacles	Entrapment

Tune in Tomorrow 1990/90

D: *Jon Ameil.* **Cast:** *Barbara Hershey, Keanu Reeves, Peter Falk.*

Based on Peruvian novelist Mario Vargas Llosa's own experience, this wonderful, slapstick romance reset in early 1950s New Orleans is about a young man in his early 20s who runs off with his aunt-by-marriage, who is fifteen years his senior. They join a radio soap opera run by a wacky impresario, who stirs up real life conflict under the guise of romantic counsel to feed his story mill.

Work & Prosperity	Loving Your Work Collaborating w/ Colleagues
Relationships	Boss/Employee Married Couples
Finding Love	Radical Age Differences
Transitions	Marrying Achieving Career Goals
Overcoming Obstacles	Creative Expression

28 Up 1985/261

D: *Michael Apted.*

This is a fascinating sociological documentary series that follows a group of English children every seven years, beginning when they were 7 years old. *28 Up* was shot in 1985 (136m). The latest installment is *35 Up*, recorded in 1992 (127m). Each film intercuts pictures of the participants from previous footage at ages 7, 14, 21, 28, and 35 (for the 1992 version). Both films uncover the mystery of life's amnesia and reveals how 7-year-old hopes and dreams come into play as 28-and 35-year-old realities.

Work & Prosperity	Realizing Dreams
Relationships	Parent/Child Lovers Married Couples

Finding Love	Teen Years 20s 28-54
Transitions	Achieving Career Goals Courting Marrying
Overcoming Obstacles	Class Prejudice Creative Expression

Two for the Road

1967/112

D: *Stanley Donen.* **Cast:** *Audrey Hepburn, Albert Finney, Eleanor Bron, William Daniels.*

This is an extraordinarily honest look at the marriage of a man, Mark (Finney), and a woman, Joanna (Hepburn), who grow as individuals and as a couple over a 12-year period, from college into their early 30s. Writer Fredric Raphael wanted to create a film in which the characters "live their lives." Each person's response to this story is uniquely their own, based on the viewer's experience and ability to identify with Mark, Joanna, and/or their relationship. This film is a wonderful gauge of the evolution of your own understanding of male/female relationships. Each viewing offers a fresh perspective as you learn more about what you want and need in relationships.

Work & Prosperity	Balancing Work & Family
Relationships	Husband/Wife
Finding Love	28-54 20s College Years
Transitions	Courting Living Together/Moving In Marrying
Overcoming Obstacles	Loss Entrapment

2001: A Space Odyssey

1968/141

D: *Stanley Kubrick.* **Cast:** *Keir Dullea, Gary Lockwood, William Sylvester.*

This movie breaks all the rules and has never been surpassed in visual and musical beauty. Nor has our quest to understand our origins and evolutionary possibilities been presented in such a simple yet mind-expanding way, where every viewer takes away his or her own unique interpretation. The film opens with the "Dawn of Man" sequence, where peaceful, vegetarian apes are transformed into meat-eating ape men by a black monolith near the apes' cave. Next, in the near future, a similar monolith has been uncovered in the American sector of the Moon. Eighteen months later, a space ship is headed for Jupiter, the source of the monolith's signal, with two crewmen, three scientists in deep freeze for the trip, and the computer H.A.L., which is responsible for all the systems. Then something goes wrong. Set your logical mind aside, and enjoy the sensual pleasures of every segment of this film. *2010* (1984, 114m) continues the search for what went awry with the 2001 mission but lacks the evocative mysticism of the original.

Work & Prosperity	Collaborating w/ Colleagues
Relationships	Colleagues & Co-Workers Boss/Employee
Overcoming Obstacles	Adventure Entrapment

2010

1984/114

See *2001: A Space Odyssey.*

Ulee's Gold

1997/111

D: *Victor Nunez.* **Cast:** *Peter Fonda, Tom Wood, Vanessa Zima, Jessica Biel.*

Here's a rare and moving look at the emotional thawing of a widowed Vietnam-veteran beekeeper who is frozen in grief and loss. His focus on his premium honey business, to the neglect of his family, has produced disasterous effects on his son, who's in prison, and his daughter-in-law, who's a drug addict. Now he is reluctantly responsible for raising his granddaughters and is forced to rescue the girls' mother.

Relationships	Parent/Child Multi-Generation Family
Transitions	Mid-50s Passage
Overcoming Obstacles	Loss

Uncle Buck

1989/100

D: *John Hughes.* **Cast:** *John Candy, Amy Madigan, Jean Kelly, Macaulay Culkin.*

A great vehicle for Candy's comedic genius, this is a funny, feel-good tale of a lovable ne'er-do-well. Candy plays the family black sheep who takes care of his affluent, disapproving brother's kids for a few days and transforms them and himself. It is also an amusing look at people who live life without concern for the opinions of others.

Work & Prosperity	Balancing Work & Family
Relationships	Single Parent
Finding Love	28-54
Transitions	Mid-Life Crisis 30s & 40s Changing Careers
Overcoming Obstacles	Entrapment

Used People

1992/115

D: *Beeban Kidron.* **Cast:** *Shirley MacLaine, Kathy Bates, Jessica Tandy, Marcello Mastroianni.*

This is a fun, heart-tugging look at a Jewish family's multigenerational dysfunctionality, heightened by the unexpected courtship of a cold, 60-something widow and her Italian neighbor, who has harbored a secret 20-year crush on her. The hilarious angst of her 30-something daughters and consternation of her dottering 80-something mother provide very amusing vignettes of the emotional family dynamics that try to keep loved ones from changing.

Relationships	Lovers Multi-Generation Family Breaking Old Patterns
Finding Love	55-81
Transitions	Losing Mate Courting
Overcoming Obstacles	Loss Age Prejudice

Visions of Light

1992/95

D: *Todd McCarthy, Arnold Glassman, Stuart Samuels.*

This documentary shows the process of filmmaking from the cinematographer's point of view. The director's role of coordinating a film project and working with actors is clearly presented. Less credited, but equally important in the collaborative art of filmmaking, is the role of the director of photography (DOP), who supervises all the technical aspects, such as camera setups, lighting, and special effects. The photographic approach makes an enormous contribution to the artistry of a film. For example, Orson Welles gave DOP Gregg Toland equal directorial billing for Citizen Kane. But, interestingly, most DOPs are so absorbed in the technical challenges of their daily work that they view themselves as craftsmen, rather than artists.

Work & Prosperity	Collaborating w/ Colleagues Loving Your Work
Relationships	Colleagues & Co-Workers
Transitions	Achieving Career Goals
Overcoming Obstacles	Creative Expression

Waiting for Guffman

1996/84

D: *Christopher Guest.* **Cast:** *Christopher Guest, Eugene Levy, Catherine O'Hara, Parker Posey, Fred Willard.*

From the creator of *This Is Spinal Tap*, this film stars Guest as the emotionally overwrought, gay ex-New Yorker trying to produce a musical celebration for a small town's 150th anniversary with its no-talent unsophisticated residents. Every scene is like a hilarious Saturday Night Live sketch. The satire builds to an uproarious climax during the closing credits, so be sure to watch them to the bitter end.

Work & Prosperity	Realizing Dreams
Relationships	Colleagues & Co-Workers
Transitions	Achieving Career Goals
Overcoming Obstacles	Creative Expression

Walking and Talking

1996/86

D: *Nicole Holofcener.* **Cast:** *Catherine Keener, Anne Heche, Todd Field, Liev Schreiber, Kevin Corrigan.*

This is the 1990s version of the thirtysomethings ups and downs of romance, therapists and all. Issues covered include getting engaged, getting married, breaking up and staying friends, bad dates with geeks, long-distance phone sex, and jealousy. When one couple, Laura and Frank, becomes engaged, it changes their relationship and sex becomes routine. Laura's best friend Amelia, after successfully breaking up with her boyfriend and remaining friends with him, surprises herself by falling for a geeky video store clerk.

Relationships	Lovers Friends
Finding Love	28-54
Transitions	Courting Marrying
Overcoming Obstacles	Entrapment

Wedding Banquet, The

1993/111

D: *Ang Lee.* **Cast:** *Winston Chao, May Chin, Mitchell Lichtenstein.*

This is a hilarious comedy of errors about Chinese tradition conflicting with a family's sexual orientation secrets. A wealthy, naturalized Taiwanese man is living happily in New York with his gay Jewish lover when his parents pressure him to marry. Wedding a woman in need of a green card, he watches his deception unravel as his lover protests, his parents keep silent, and his wife starts to desire him sexually.

Relationships	Lovers Parent/Child
Finding Love	28-54 Same Sex
Transitions	Courting
Overcoming Obstacles	Sexual Prejudice Entrapment

After-View Feelings Key:

Feel Better/Uplift — Laughing Release — Crying Release — Violent Content

Welcome Home, Roxy Carmichael 1990/98

D: *Jim Abrahams.* **Cast:** *Winona Ryder, Jeff Daniels, Laila Robins, Dinah Manoff.*

This is an insightful, underrated satire of love, adoption, and celebrity, starring Ryder as a quirky teen who obsesses about the return of a local girl made famous on the West Coast. The re-creation of the stifling 1960s small town Ohio atmosphere bolsters the plausibility of the teen's fantasy of famous parentage, fueled by her mother's and father's reluctance to tell the whole truth.

Relationships	Parent/Child
Transitions	Teen Years
Overcoming Obstacles	Loss

When Harry Met Sally 1989/96

D: *Rob Reiner.* **Cast:** *Billy Crystal, Meg Ryan, Carrie Fisher.*

This beloved, feel-good romance about loyalty and fear of commitment strikes a deep chord for many. It details the long, bickering, platonic friendship of a man and woman and what happens when it takes a sexual turn after 20 years. The clever script is aided by the inspired improvised acting of Crystal and Ryan.

Relationships	Lovers Friends
Finding Love	28-54 College Years
Transitions	Courting
Overcoming Obstacles	Loss

Widow's Peak 1994/101

D: *John Irvin.* **Cast:** *Joan Plowright, Mia Farrow, Natasha Richardson.*

This is an amusing look at the silliness of social mores in a 1920s Irish resort town, which is ruled by widow Plowright. The perfect order of conformity is upset by the entrance of newly widowed Richardson, who attracts Plowright's dimwit son. Strongly cast, the film swings between a satire on snobbishness and the truth about what power an outcast can hold over conformists.

Relationships	Multi-Generation Family Friends
Finding Love	28-54
Transitions	Losing Mate
Overcoming Obstacles	Loss

Wonderful, Horrible Life of Leni Riefenstahl, The 1993/182

D: *Ray Müller.*

A riveting examination of an artist who directed Nazi propaganda films but was so focused on the creative act that she never accepted responsibility for the social impact of her visual images. Still physically active in her 90s, Leni is inspiring for her continued good health, beauty, intelligence, and high energy. Told in a combination of current interviews and documentary clips, Leni horrifies us with her blind denial about the consequences of her artistic expression.

Work & Prosperity	Loving Your Work
Relationships	Colleagues & Co-Workers
Transitions	After Retirement
Overcoming Obstacles	Creative Expression

Working Girl

1988/115

D: *Mike Nichols.* **Cast:** *Harrison Ford, Melanie Griffith, Sigourney Weaver, Alec Baldwin, Joan Cusack.*

A well-told, 1980s corporate Cinderella tale about a Staten Island secretary's (Griffith) quest to be respected for her business acumen and to find a way into management. Her obstacles would be formidable for anyone with less drive and stamina. She must transform her lower-class accent and personal appearance (a self-admitted "head for business" and "bod" for sin), give up her fisherman fiancé (Baldwin), scheme behind her boss' (Weaver) back, and enlist an expert's (Ford) help in putting together a clever merger that could make or break her. Carly Simon's music rounds out this inspirational and uplifting film.

Work & Prosperity	Realizing Dreams
Relationships	Boss/Employee Lovers
Finding Love	28-54
Transitions	Late 20s to 30s Passage 20s to 30s Passage Changing Careers
Overcoming Obstacles	Class Prejudice Entrapment

Wuthering Heights (1939)

1939/103

D: *William Wyler.* **Cast:** *Laurence Olivier, Merle Oberon, David Niven.*

This classic Victorian tragic tale of smoldering soul-mate passion is brought to life by an all-star cast under the deft direction of Wyler. Forget the last scene: it was tacked on without Wyler's okay.

Relationships	Lovers
Finding Love	Teen Years
Transitions	Moving Out/Separating
Overcoming Obstacles	Class Prejudice

Year of Living Dangerously, The

1983/114

D: *Peter Weir.* **Cast:** *Mel Gibson, Linda Hunt, Sigourney Weaver.*

Never has a little-known time and place been so well re-created as in this political adventure about the uncertainty of Indonesia in 1965, just before President Sukarno's fall. The film's exotic sights and explosive sounds evoke the sour taste, the clammy touch, and the sweaty smell of Europeans caught in a place they do not belong. The lyrical commentary of narrator Billy Kwan (Hunt), a Eurasian photographer who knows everything and everybody, sets the pace as he befriends an ambitious, thrill-seeking Australian journalist (Gibson), shows him the ropes, and introduces him to a beautiful British attaché (Weaver) two weeks before she's due to return home.

Work & Prosperity	Loving Your Work
Relationships	Lovers Colleagues & Co-Workers
Finding Love	28-54
Transitions	Achieving Career Goals
Overcoming Obstacles	War Entrapment

Bibliography

Conners, Martin, ed. *VideoHound's Golden Movie Retriever.* Detroit: Visible Ink, 1998.

Cousins, Norman. *Anatomy of an Illness as Perceived by the Patient.* New York: Norton, 1979.

Friedan, Betty. *Fountain of Age.* New York: Simon & Schuster, 1993.

Gardner, Howard. *Creating Minds: An Anatomy of Creativity Seen Through the Lives of Freud, Einstein, Picasso, Stravinsky, Eliot, Graham, and Gandhi.* New York: BasicBooks, 1993.
— *Leading Minds: An Anatomy of Leadership.* New York: BasicBooks, 1996.

Glassner, Barry. *Career Crash: The New Crisis—and Who Survives.* New York: Simon & Schuster, 1994.

Goleman, Daniel. *Emotional Intelligence.* New York: Bantam Books, 1995.

King, Viki. *How to Write a Movie in 21 Days.* New York: HarperPerennial, 1988.

Klein, Alan. *The Healing Power of Humor.* New York: Tarcher/Putnam, 1988.

Kosko, Bart. *Fuzzy Thinking: The New Science of Fuzzy Logic.* New York: Hyperion, 1993.

Machado de Andrade, Luiz. *The Brain of the Brain.* Rio de Janeiro: State University of Rio De Janeiro, 1992.
— *Principios de Emotologia e Emotopedia.* Rio de Janeiro: State University of Rio De Janeiro, 1984.

Martin, Mick, ed: *Video Movie Guide 1998.* New York: Ballantine Books,1997.

Sheehy, Gail. *New Passages: Mapping Your Life Across Time.* New York: Ballantine Books, 1995.

Sher, Barbara. *I Could Do Anything if I Only Knew What It Was.* New York: Delacorte, 1994.

Viscott, David. *The Language of Feelings.* New York: Pocket Books, 1976.

Video Information

Internet Movie Database. www.imdb.com (Imdb) is the largest source of movie knowledge in any medium.

LightSpheres Publishing. www.laughcry.com offers additional information about each movie in this book. New Laugh & Cry Movies are added as they are released. You can generate a personalized list of movies based on your life challenge and age.

Movies Unlimited. 1-800-523-0823. 6738 Castor Avenue, Philadelphia, PA 19149. Their 700-page catalog is an excellent reference source for more than 20,000 titles on video.

Suggested Reading

Great Intelligence Applications to Creativity

Armstrong, Thomas. *7 Kinds of Smart: Identifying Your Many Intelligences.* New York: Plume Book/Penguin, 1993.

Arrien, Angeles. *The Four-Fold Way: Walking the Paths of the Warrior, Teacher, Healer and Visionary.* San Francisco: HarperSan Francisco, 1993.

Campbell, Don. *The Mozart Effect™: Tapping the Power of Music to Heal the Body, Strengthen the Mind, and Unlock the Creative Spirit.* New York: Avon Books, 1997.

Cameron, Julie. *The Artist's Way: A Spiritual Path to Higher Creativity.* New York: Tarcher/Putnam, 1993.
— *The Vein of Gold: A Journey to Your Creative Heart.* New York: Tarcher/Putnam, 1996.

Chopra, Deepak. *Ageless Body, Timeless Mind.* New York: Harmony Books, 1993.

Edwards, Betty. *Drawing on the Right Side of the Brain.* Los Angeles: Tarcher, 1989.

Goldberg, Natalie. *Wild Mind: Living the Writer's Life.* New York: Bantam New Age, 1990.
— *Writing Down the Bones.* Boston: Shambhala Publications, 1986.

Jeffers, Susan. *Feel the Fear and Do It Anyway.* New York: Fawcett Columbine, 1989.
—*End the Struggle and Dance with Life*: New York, St. Martin's Press, 1997.

Kline, Peter. *The Everyday Genius: Restoring Children's Natural Joy of Learning—and Yours Too.* Arlington, VA: Great Ocean Publishers, 1997.
— *Ten Steps to a Learning Organization.* Arlington, VA: Great Ocean Publishers, 1997.

Sternberg, Robert J. *Successful Intelligence: How Practical and Creative Intelligence Determine Success in Life.* New York: Simon & Schuster, 1996.

New Science Perspective on Change

Briggs, John. *Fractals, The Patterns of Chaos: A New Aesthetic of Art, Science, and Nature.* New York: Touchstone/Simon & Schuster, 1992
— *Turbulent Mirror: An Illustrated Guide to Chaos Theory.* New York: HarperPerennial, 1989.

Schneider, Michael S. *A Beginner's Guide to Constructing the Universe: The Mathematical Archetypes of Nature, Art and Science.* New York: HarperPerennial, 1994.

Schlain, Leonard. *Art & Physics: Parallel Visions in Space, Time, and Light.* New York: Quill, 1993

Talbot, Michael. *The Holographic Universe.* New York: HarperCollins, 1991.

Wheatley, Margaret. *Leadership and the New Sciences.* San Francisco: Berrett-Koehler, 1992.

Using Movies for Counseling

Hesley, John W. *Rent Two Films and Let's Talk in the Morning: Using Popular Movies in Psychotherapy.* New York: John Wiley & Sons, 1998.

Horenstein, Mary Ann. *Reel Life/Real Life: A Video Guide for Personal Discovery.* Burlington, VT: Fourth Write Press, 1994.

LightSpheres Publishing. www.laughcry.com offers a customized movie report service for counselors to provide clients. A personalized list of movies is given, based on the client's specific life challenge and age.

Sinetar, Marsh. *Reel Power: Spiritual Growth through Film.* Ligouri, MO: Triumph Books, 1993.

Solomon, Gary. *The Motion Picture Prescription: Watch This Movie and Call Me in the Morning.* Santa Rosa, CA: Aslan Press, 1995.

Index

About the Author

Cathie Glenn Sturdevant is an executive coach and consultant who advises individuals and organizations undergoing change. She has developed a proven approach to career management, project management, and achieving goals by synthesizing principles of the new sciences, creative arts, and accelerated learning.

A lifelong movie buff, Cathie teaches seminars using movies as an educational tool to demonstrate the true nature of constant change and the secrets to achieving goals. She is available for speaking engagements, conferences, and lectures throughout the country.

For more information, visit the LightSpheres web site at **www.lightspheres.com** or contact:

Cathie Glenn Sturdevant
LightSpheres Consulting
P.O. Box 884
Larkspur, CA 94977
TEL: 415-925-1540
FAX: 415-461-7845
e-mail: cathie@lightspheres.com

Suggestion Box

If you have movie suggestions for the book or web site, please fill out the form below and send your thoughts to:

Laugh & Cry Movie Suggestions
P.O. Box 884
Larkspur, CA 94977
e-mail: suggestions@laughcry.com

Movies I'd like to see added to the book and web site:

1. ______________________________

2. ______________________________

3. ______________________________

4. ______________________________

5. ______________________________

If you'd like to be on our mailing list, please provide:

Name: ______________________________

Address: ______________________________

City/State/Zip: ______________________________

Phone: ______________________________

e-mail: ______________________________

Other comments about the book or web site:

Visit our web site at **www.laughcry.com**.
New Laugh & Cry Movies are added as they are released. You also can generate a customized list of movies based on your own life challenge and age. If you are a counselor, a movie report service is available to provide you with a customized list of movies for each of your clients.

Order Form

Use this form to order additional copies of *The Laugh & Cry Movie Guide*™.

Call toll-free: 888-LAUGHCRY (528-4427)
Have your credit card ready.

Fax your order: 415-461-7845

Mail to: LightSpheres Publishing
P.O. Box 884
Larkspur, CA 94977

The Laugh & Cry Movie Guide™
Please send me ___ copies of at $17.95 each. Price **$**

Shipping & Handling *Please add $3 for first book or software package, and US$1 for each additional item.* **$**

8.5% Sales Tax (CA only) **$**

Total (US$) **$**

☐ I enclose check or money order in US Dollars.
☐ Please charge my credit card. ☐ Visa ☐ MasterCard

Card No. ____________________ Exp. Date ____________

Signature ____________________

Name ____________________

Company ____________________

Address ____________________

____

City ____________________ State ____________________

Country ____________________ Zip/Postal Code ____________________

Telephone ____________________

Call toll-free and order today!

Suggestion Box

If you have movie suggestions for the book or web site, please fill out the form below and send your thoughts to:

Laugh & Cry Movie Suggestions
P.O. Box 884
Larkspur, CA 94977
e-mail: suggestions@laughcry.com

Movies I'd like to see added to the book and web site:

1. ________________________
2. ________________________
3. ________________________
4. ________________________
5. ________________________

If you'd like to be on our mailing list, please provide:

Name: ________________________

Address: ________________________

City/State/Zip: ________________________

Phone: ________________________

e-mail: ________________________

Other comments about the book or web site:

Visit our web site at **www.laughcry.com**.

New Laugh & Cry Movies are added as they are released. You also can generate a customized list of movies based on your own life challenge and age. If you are a counselor, a movie report service is available to provide you with a customized list of movies for each of your clients.

Order Form

Use this form to order additional copies of *The Laugh & Cry Movie Guide*™.

Call toll-free: 888-LAUGHCRY (528-4427)
Have your credit card ready.

Fax your order: 415-461-7845

Mail to: LightSpheres Publishing
P.O. Box 884
Larkspur, CA 94977

The Laugh & Cry Movie Guide™
Please send me ___ copies of at $17.95 each. Price $

Shipping & Handling *Please add $3 for first book or software package, and US$1 for each additional item.* $

8.5% Sales Tax (CA only) $

Total (US$) $

☐ I enclose check or money order in US Dollars.
☐ Please charge my credit card. ☐ Visa ☐ MasterCard

Card No. ________ Exp. Date ________

Signature ________

Name ________

Company ________

Address ________

____

City ________ State ________

Country ________ Zip/Postal Code ________

Telephone ________

Call toll-free and order today!

Suggestion Box

If you have movie suggestions for the book or web site, please fill out the form below and send your thoughts to:

Laugh & Cry Movie Suggestions
P.O. Box 884
Larkspur, CA 94977
e-mail: suggestions@laughcry.com

Movies I'd like to see added to the book and web site:

1. ______________________

2. ______________________

3. ______________________

4. ______________________

5. ______________________

If you'd like to be on our mailing list, please provide:

Name: ______________________

Address: ______________________

City/State/Zip: ______________________

Phone: ______________________

e-mail: ______________________

Other comments about the book or web site:

Visit our web site at **www.laughcry.com**.
New Laugh & Cry Movies are added as they are released. You also can generate a customized list of movies based on your own life challenge and age. If you are a counselor, a movie report service is available to provide you with a customized list of movies for each of your clients.

Order Form

Use this form to order additional copies of *The Laugh & Cry Movie Guide*™.

Call toll-free: 888-LAUGHCRY (528-4427)
Have your credit card ready.

Fax your order: 415-461-7845

Mail to: LightSpheres Publishing
P.O. Box 884
Larkspur, CA 94977

The Laugh & Cry Movie Guide™ Please send me ___ copies of at $17.95 each.	Price	$
Shipping & Handling *Please add $3 for first book or software package, and US$1 for each additional item.*		$
8.5% Sales Tax (CA only)		$
Total (US$)		$

☐ I enclose check or money order in US Dollars.

☐ Please charge my credit card. ☐ Visa ☐ MasterCard

Card No. ______________________ Exp. Date ____________

Signature ______________________

Name ______________________

Company ______________________

Address ______________________

____

City ______________ State ______________

Country ______________ Zip/Postal Code ______________

Telephone ______________________

Call toll-free and order today!